CW00740626

BREAKING CHAINS

Breaking Chains

The Evolution of the Black Madonna

Nic Phillips

PUBLISHED BY AVALONIA
WWW.AVALONIABOOKS.COM

PUBLISHED BY AVALONIA

BM AVALONIA
LONDON
WC1N 3XX
ENGLAND, UK

WWW.AVALONIABOOKS.COM

BREAKING CHAINS

THE EVOLUTION OF THE BLACK MADONNA

COPYRIGHT © NIC PHILLIPS, 2020

ISBN: 978-1-905297-83-2

FIRST EDITION, FEBRUARY 2021

DESIGN BY SATORI

COVER ART: OUR LADY, BREAKER OF CHAINS BY NIC PHILLIPS

ALL IMAGES IN THIS VOLUME ©NIC PHILLIPS

BRITISH LIBRARY CATALOGUING IN PUBLICATION DATA. A CATALOGUE RECORD FOR THIS
BOOK IS AVAILABLE FROM THE BRITISH LIBRARY.

EVERY EFFORT HAS BEEN MADE TO CREDIT MATERIAL, AND TO OBTAIN PERMISSION FROM
COPYRIGHT HOLDERS FOR THE USE OF THEIR WORK. IF YOU NOTICE ANY ERROR OR OMISSION
PLEASE NOTIFY THE PUBLISHER SO THAT CORRECTIONS CAN BE INCORPORATED INTO FUTURE
EDITIONS OF THIS WORK.

THE INFORMATION PROVIDED IN THIS BOOK HOPES TO INSPIRE AND INFORM. THE AUTHOR
AND PUBLISHER ASSUME NO RESPONSIBILITY FOR THE EFFECTS, OR LACK THEREOF, OBTAINED
FROM THE PRACTICES DESCRIBED IN THIS BOOK. EVERY EFFORT HAS BEEN MADE TO BE
CULTURALLY AND RACIALLY SENSITIVE WHEN USING AND DISCUSSING TERMS OF RACE AND
COLOUR, USING THE MOST CURRENT AND WIDELY ACCEPTED WORDS AND CAPITALISATIONS.
THE USE OF ANY TERMINOLOGY THAT MAY CAUSE OFFENSE, EITHER AT THE TIME OF WRITING
OR IN THE FUTURE, WHEN THE ACCEPTED TERMS MAY CHANGE, IS ENTIRELY UNINTENTIONAL.
EDUCATING AND CHECKING OURSELVES SHOULD BE AN ONGOING PROCESS FOR LIFE.

ALL RIGHTS RESERVED. NO PART OF THIS PUBLICATION MAY BE REPRODUCED OR UTILIZED IN
ANY FORM OR BY ANY MEANS, ELECTRONIC OR MECHANICAL, INCLUDING PHOTOCOPYING,
MICROFILM, RECORDING, OR BY ANY INFORMATION STORAGE AND RETRIEVAL SYSTEM, OR USED
IN ANOTHER BOOK, WITHOUT WRITTEN PERMISSION FROM THE AUTHOR, WITH THE EXCEPTION
OF BRIEF QUOTATIONS IN REVIEWS OR ARTICLES WHERE APPROPRIATE CREDIT IS GIVEN TO THE
COPYRIGHT HOLDER.

ACKNOWLEDGEMENTS

This book represents a journey over several years of complicated and sometimes maddening research. I would not have been able to see it through to conclusion without the support of certain people.

I would like to thank my parents Paul and Margaret Phillips for always believing in me and taking an interest in my work, reading chapters, and offering comment.

To Matt Arathoon for supporting my interests and accompanying me on quests to find Black Madonnas and remote churches!

Katie Player for helping me dream this research into being, and Yeshe Matthews for her words of wisdom.

To Kim, Sarah and Craig and the whole Vodou family whose input has been invaluable. I would also like to thank Sorita d'Este, Anna Dear, and all the friends who have taken an interest in this project's development. This book is for you!

Table of Contents

Author Biography

Nic Phillips is an English artist and writer living in Somerset, UK, where he works in the heritage industry. Spare time is spent painting aspects of divinity, including the illustrations in this book. Previous published works include *Celtic Saints of Western Britain* (Avalonia 2015), and two tarot decks – *Sol Invictus: The God Tarot* (Schiffer 2007) and *Pistis Sophia: The Goddess Tarot* (Schiffer 2020), both with Kim Huggens.

After completing his book on the saints, Nic began researching the Black Madonna, a journey which took him across France and Spain, and to encountering Black Madonna usage in ceremony as well as in diverse traditions from around the world.

Nic has a keen interest in history, heritage, mythology and world religion, and enjoys travel, the countryside, animals, and tea!

For more information visit www.nicphillipssacredart.com or search 'Nic Phillips Sacred Art' on Facebook, Instagram and Etsy, where more of his artwork can be found.

Foreword

30 May 2020 – I am writing this at a strange time in our history. As I approach the last few paragraphs of the book, I am witnessing people in the United States rising up. One death too far. A tipping point. As the protests grow and spread around the country and indeed the world, I am optimistic that this time there will be a change.

07 June 2020 – On the day I finish the book I see protestors in Bristol, UK, toppling the statue of a 17th-century slave-trader and I feel hope. I see newscasts of strong, proud, black women holding their own and speaking with such power as to inspire a nation. Not just city mayors but everyday people, moved to go out in a time of crisis and protest against the injustices that Black people face every single day. I see the Black Madonna in those women's faces. She is the strength to stand up and spea k up. I think of all the cultures I have researched over the course of my writing and the times and places that she has been present – the Haitian Revolution, Cuba, Brazil. She is the most potent, and most needed symbol of our times, and she always prevails.

Introduction

What is a Black Madonna? This seems like a pertinent question with which to begin our exploration. 'Black Madonna' most frequently refers to a class of statues from Europe, and predominantly France, which depict the Virgin Mary. They vary in material, from wood to metal to stone, but share the characteristic that their hands and faces are black or brown. In his book *L'Enigme des Vierges Noires* (1972), French scholar Jacques Huynen categorised what he called the 'authentic' Black Virgins of Western Europe by 13 shared characteristics. Fewer than 50 of the 500+ worldwide Black Madonnas share these traits, which includes being of the 12th century, of similar proportions, and seated 'in majesty' facing forwards. These statues are certainly 'of a class', bearing striking similarities, but many authors, myself included, also count the many other Black Madonnas of the world under this title, including those who stand, who are two dimensional painted icons, or who hail from outside of Europe.

Besides being objects of devotion within Catholic communities, Black Madonnas have proven to be the subject of much speculation in literature, particularly through the second half of the 20th century. Authors have theorised for decades about the reason that some Madonnas are black, and what this signifies.

Before I began this work I, like so many others, was enamoured by the modern discourse that states that the Black Madonna is significant because of some great 'secret' surrounding her existence, or that she is evidence of an unbroken line of Goddess worship from the time of Egyptian and near-Eastern prototypes. Authors on this esoteric angle search for ancient traces, proofs of her significance being something greater or other than 'just another Virgin Mary statue'. Having read some of these kinds of books, this is the standpoint I began from myself, a desire to delve into

Above: "Our Lady, Breaker of Chains". This modern rendition of the Black Madonna as an African-American woman was partly inspired by the Orisha Oshún and partly by the novel The Secret Life of Bees *by Sue Monk Kidd which features a Black Madonna, Our Lady of Chains. I wanted to depict a powerful, active Madonna breaking the chains of slavery, prejudice, and injustice in the modern world.*

11

mystery, to uncover hidden knowledge encoded by medieval minds or carried through the centuries by faithful acolytes.

When talking about the European statues of the Middle Ages that bear the name Black Madonna, the evidence points to any grand mystery being unlikely. Much of the significance of the Black Madonna seems based on the later accretion of both myths and smoke that has darkened the statues into something outside of the standard dogma of the Church. However, during the Middle Ages, there seems little evidence that her colour was even notable. Many of these statues were just 'a dark statue of the Virgin Mary' as opposed to 'a statue of a dark Virgin Mary', and it seems the colour was more of an indicator of antiquity and Eastern origin rather than race. The miraculous origin stories are founded in later medieval propaganda pieces used to promote a holy site rather than based on the annals of its history.

Upon discovering this, it appeared that the Black Madonna phenomenon might be one entirely of modern/early-modern creation. There was a temptation to abandon the research there: mystery solved, or rather, no mystery to solve in the first place. This is why the Black Madonna has not gained as much interest outside of esoteric circles; art critics and most theologians do not find the phenomenon particularly remarkable or worthy of comment, as they do not believe the pieces to hold a wider significance. Yet I would argue that the Black Madonna at large is just that, a phenomenon, that is bigger than a subset of medieval Marian images.

Throughout this work I will look at manifestations that contribute to the 'persona' or which are facets of the whole construct that we today call 'The Black Madonna'. Chapter 1 deals with the Chartres Black Madonna(s). This was my first experience visiting a Black Madonna in person and one that made a remarkable impression, since on arrival I discovered that the famous 'Lady of the Pillar', whose dark visage could be seen on statues and cards in shops leading to the Cathedral had been recently whitened. This raised a lot of questions and began my thinking on how the Black Madonna has been interpreted ethnically; today and in the past. Chapter 2 addresses this further, when looking at the history of Our Lady of Le Puy, another French

Black Virgin of considerable fame. We will look into when exactly it was that descriptors which label the Madonna as racially Black were first used and how the passage from the well-known biblical canticle *The Song of Songs* (or *Song of Solomon*) became attached to the personage of Mary. The famous line, "I am Black but Beautiful", became associated with the Black Virgin, affecting how not only the Black Madonna, but Black people were viewed.

Chapter 3 deals with Our Lady of Montserrat, a Catalonian Black Madonna whose image has been reproduced in numerous different ways through the centuries. After the Spanish began conquering the Americas, we see a potential reverse influence in how the Virgin was viewed racially arriving in dark depictions of the Virgin from the New World. From there we cross over to Mexico in Chapter 4 and see the full effects of syncretism in a frontier population. The Nahua people of what is now Mexico whole-heartedly embraced a new apparition of the Virgin Mary – Our Lady of Guadalupe – possibly too whole-heartedly for the Catholic Church's liking since elements of worship to their native Tonantzin appeared to be bound up in their devotion. We will see Guadalupe's importance to Mexican women and her relation to the cultural figures in her shadow, including La Malinche, La Llorona, and Santa Muerte.

Guadalupe is only the first of many Madonnas we will encounter where syncretism has played a major part in the development of their cults. We move to the African diasporic communities of Haiti, Cuba and Brazil in Chapters 5 and 6 where people from many parts of Africa were brought as slaves over the course of centuries. Wrenched from their cultures and forced to recreate traditions, Africans blended their native beliefs and practices with the Catholic iconography around them. In Haiti, the Black Madonna arrived amidst the country's greatest time of upheaval, the revolution that would overturn slavery. The Black Madonna of Częstochowa, brought in the bags of Polish legionaries, became inextricably connected with the Lwa (Vodou spirit) that was at the forefront of the revolution, Ezili Danto. Similarly, in Cuba, the Virgin of Caridad del Cobre became syncretised with the Orisha (Yoruban/Lucumí spirit) Oshún, and Our Lady of Regla with the Orisha Yemayá. In Brazil they became known under other names, Nossa Senhora Aparecida and the Virgin of the Immaculate Conception. We will look at the migration of the Vodou and Orisha religions into the USA and address the question of the value of syncretism versus the call for de-syncretisation of the Orisha from Catholic saints.

Chapter 7 takes us to Trinidad where the Indian Diaspora worship Kali in the form of a Black Madonna, La Divina Pastora. We will examine Caribbean attitudes to Kali compared to her native Indian devotions. From India, we travel back to France in the company of the Romani, coming full circle to witness the annual pilgrimage made to a Black Madonna who is not a Mary – the Romani patron saint Sara la Kali, and look at her links to the cult of Mary Magdalene. Modern theories on the identity of the Black Madonna take us into Chapter 9, where we look at some of the published literature on the Black Madonna in the popular realm, and unravel its allure.

The most significant departure in this book from others on the subject is that I am not suggesting any of the similarities, correspondences or patterns in some way 'prove' any inheritance of tradition, symbology, esoteric knowledge, or conscious intent. The subtle difference is that we have the privilege in our multimedia modern world to have access to a degree of knowledge of these elements of the past, and the sophistication to weave disparate threads into one formidable image that serves so many around the world. Some may baulk at this presumption that the Black Madonna is a man-made construct, but I would argue that it is the *image* of her that is man-made, just as it is with depictions of any gods. It is far more presumptuous to assume that how we have chosen to depict a deity is accurate. How many of us have met one in person?

CHAPTER 1

Chartres
A Black Virgin No Longer

INTRODUCTION

Chartres, in northwestern France, like Glastonbury in Somerset, UK, is a place with a long religious history and one that has become so intertwined with myths that for the casual visitor it becomes difficult to tell the fact and the fiction apart, especially when certain myths have been treated as facts over the centuries. Like the abbey at Glastonbury, Chartres Cathedral endured fires and periods of rebuilding; and like the claims that developed in the medieval period about Glastonbury's very early foundation, so too did a legend develop during the Middle Ages about the origins of Chartres. However, in this case, Chartrian clerics claimed the Virgin Mary was worshipped there even *before* the birth of Christ. The legend states that Chartres was an important gathering place for the druid priests of the Gauls, and that they worshipped a statue of a *Virgo Paritura,* a Virgin About to Give Birth. This statue is said to be a miraculous portent of the Virgin Mary and also the progenitor of the statue that now sits in the crypt of Chartres, named *Notre Dame Sous Terre,* Our Lady Under the Earth. This statue is designated by enthusiasts as a Black Madonna, as was a second statue in the main church, titled *Notre Dame du Pilier,* (Our Lady of the Pillar). Today, these two Madonnas, the druid legend, and the famous and iconic labyrinth on the floor of the cathedral intrigue and draw in thousands of Christian and non-Christian visitors alike.

A STARTLING ENCOUNTER

In April 2017, I took my first trip to France to see some real Black Madonnas face to face as part of my research. Our first stop was the Cathedral of Chartres, an auspicious site, since I had heard it contained not one but two Black Madonnas, not counting any of those venerated in the stained glass of the cathedral which have sometimes been described as such. The Renaissance statue, *Notre Dame du Pilier* (Our Lady of the Pillar) stands in the upper church, whilst *Notre Dame Sous Terre* (Our Lady Under the Earth), a copy of a much earlier statue resides in the crypt. I had read much on the legends surrounding the Cathedral and the mound it was built on, but was not prepared for what I was actually presented with, at what would be my first encounter with a 'real' Black Madonna.

After an hour and half train journey from Paris with my partner, we located the Cathedral. The approach via the west end is impressive, and teases the grandeur hidden within. A tour leader had gathered his group outside, using a pocket mirror like a laser pointer as he narrated the ornate carving of Christ in Majesty amongst others above the Royal Portal, all in fabulous condition. Rather than going in immediately, we skirted around to inspect the rest of the exterior. The north side gave a preview of Chartres' famous labyrinth, rendered in grass, and the southwest corner, a sundial-bearing angel, the original of which I later saw in the crypt where it had been placed for its preservation. I was prepared for the fact that most days now, the huge labyrinth design on the floor is obscured by rows of chairs, but knew that many pilgrims would be disappointed by not being able to walk it.

My prime mission was to find the Black Madonna, the 'official' one on the ground floor. On locating the Lady Chapel my first thought was, "this can't be it, it must be further on", but it was. The statue called Our Lady of the Pillar was virtually unrecognisable from the pictures I'd seen of her online and as miniature statues already in the souvenir shop windows when we first arrived in Chartres. Here she was, without gowns, in full polychrome glory... with a white face.

The effect was frankly rather ghastly. The nearby sign explained the 'restoration' that had taken place in recent years, not back to the wood of the original 16th-century carving however, but to the paint that had been applied in the 19th century and subsequently later covered in an unspecified 'dark greyish coating' which the curator in charge of the restoration, Brigitte Estèves, regarded as 'unsightly'. I was not overly surprised that the statue had at one point been painted white, I had heard of this happening in other places. Such trends seemed to occur in phases – the Church paints them white, then at the protests of the parishioners, they are repainted dark to match the original dark wood, or the covering of soot to which people had become accustomed. I was quite surprised, however, to see this 'white-washing' happening again in the modern age, although I probably shouldn't have been.

The bias of the curator and her superiors, is apparent in the information panel, explaining that their choice has 'considerably enhanced' the piece, which tellingly they do not refer to anywhere as a Black Madonna in the literature or signage of the Cathedral. This attitude is somewhat surprising when she was one of the main draws to the cathedral (and they knew it, judging from all the statues, cards and candles of her - still black-skinned – that I saw in the shop). This backed up by the other Marian attractions of the (thankfully untouched) wooden Madonna in the crypt, the 'Blue Virgin' of the stained glass, and the relic of the Virgin's Veil.

So rather than coming face to face with my first real Black Madonna I found myself faced with the slightly waxy and eerie face of what? Racism? Denial? Ignorance? A genuine case of doing the wrong thing with good intentions? A prayer box stood in front of her chapel, with slips to write on and deposit. Rather than asking something for myself or loved ones, I wrote of my desire to see the reversal of such a desecration, in prayer and perhaps in hope that someone from the Cathedral would see it. Were there other voices of disapproval like mine amongst the prayers?

I found out later by searching online that there had indeed been some reaction to the questionable curatorial choices. In December 2014, American architecture critic Martin Filler published in the New York Review of Books a general criticism of the recent 'clean-up' of the cathedral, which specifically mentioned the whitening of

Our Lady of the Pillar.[1] It was here I learned that the cathedral is in fact the property of the State, not the Church, and it was they who commissioned the $18.5 million makeover to return the cathedral to some form of medieval majesty. Filler was aghast at the use of colour, coupled with electric lighting that makes the painted walls far brighter than they would have been. He reported that the polychrome paint job on the Black Virgin had alarmed observant Catholics, accustomed to her dark appearance, and compared the restoration to repainting Greek statues in garish colour. We know that at one point such masterpieces were decorated this way, but to try to recreate that now would be unthinkable.

A few days later, the Guardian news site reported the response of Patrice Calvel, the architect-in-chief from French Ministry of Culture's Historical Monuments division.[2] Utterly dismissive of Filler's opinion, he said he would not respond to the writer as he "has no competence in this matter". His dismissive attitude extended to the local community, when asking if the parishioners had been consulted. Calvel said "I'm very democratic, but the public is not competent to judge".

The Guardian also quoted British historic interiors conservator Helen Hughes on the imposition of the changes by the State, which contrasted with the more consultation-based procedures of the UK. On French historic interiors, Hughes commented that she "noticed that conservators talked about the state rather than the involvement of taxpayers and stakeholders".

Discussing with a friend, an ex-conservator, in the week following my visit, she was appalled, not only from a spiritual point of view but also from a conservation angle. She could not imagine the justification for introducing new foreign material and such intrusive procedures to an already fragile artefact. We could not shake the worrying feeling that the imposition was not from a well-intentioned desire to preserve. We had both noted the rise in visibility of hate crimes and open racism in the wake of the UK's Brexit referendum and the USA's presidential election the previous

---

[1] www.nybooks.com/daily/2014/12/14/scandalous-makeover-chartres/
[2] www.theguardian.com/artanddesign/2014/dec/19/us-architect-sparks-row-chartres-cathedral-restoration-paul-calvel

year, and couldn't help fearing that it was a global trend. Was this some State agenda to erase diverse appearances of race from one of its major tourist sites? Or perhaps to deter the alternative pilgrims who came to see the statue; pilgrims who might once have walked the labyrinth before its covering of chairs? It must be known by the cathedral that for many visitors, the Black Madonna represents a force outside the control of the Catholic Church. If this was some act of deterrence, then it is contradictory to the fact that they rely on these same mysteries as the draw for a large proportion of the groups and individuals who visit.

I wondered whether the cathedral would continue to trade off the images of the Black Madonna in their shop or whether these would gradually be replaced with postcards of the sickly Virgin of the Pillar. An updated news story in 2017 citing similar dismay to Filler's article confirmed that since my visit, the shop stock had changed over to portray the painted Virgin.[3] In the same article, the damaging effect of the 'removal of darkness' on people's appreciation of the stained glass was noted. The increase in ambient light, was thought to diminish the impact of the stained glass, like "watching a film in a cinema where they haven't switched off the lights." said art critic Adrien Goetz.[4] Long-standing tour guides at the Cathedral have defended the restoration. In a 2015 article in the Independent, 81-year-old English guide Malcolm Miller insisted the interior was meant to be light and blamed the 'dirty' look on smoke accretions – "There was nothing natural about its darkness. It was nothing to do with the ageing of the stone."[5] It seemed that 'darkness' had become a dirty word. No mention of the virtues of darkness for meditative contemplation, or for practical uses like viewing treasured stained glass.

Fortunately, the tour of the crypt offered a much closer experience to what I was expecting, and the darkness lacking from the ground level. I did not ask the tour guide about the restorations in the main church, as the effect of the painted Virgin was still

---

[3] www.nytimes.com/2017/09/01/arts/design/chartres-cathedral-restoration-controversial.html
[4] Ibid.
[5] www.independent.co.uk/arts-entertainment/architecture/chartres-cathedral-clean-up-row-experts-dvided-over-whether-dirt-should-be-left-in-place-to-keep-a6706627.html

sinking in. The guide led a group of us below ground, visiting the chapels and ambulatory that were only reopened to the public in the 20th century.

The crypt itself is in fact not an addition to the later Norman cathedral, but was all that survived of the Carolingian cathedral on top of which the later one was built. 12th century friezes adorn the passages in impeccable condition. The darkness of the crypt of *Notre Dame Sous Terre* extended away, tempting exploration, like the catacombs we had visited in Paris. Before the chapel, we reached the Well of the Saints Forts, an ancient spring where two early Christians were said to have been martyred, falling to their deaths. Despite the rather gaudy tapestry behind her, the aesthetics of the simple wooden Virgin were restorative after witnessing the eerie Lady of the Pillar. The carving is reportedly a copy of an earlier statue destroyed in the French Revolution. She sits in majesty on a throne staring straight ahead, like many of her 12th-century counterparts, with her son on her lap. In this form, she was understood to represent the seat of Wisdom, as represented by Christ. Her throne was linked to that of Solomon, whilst she also represents the throne itself. After what seemed like barely any time with her, we were whisked back off to the ground level, the tour our only opportunity to interact with the Lady Under the Earth.

Following my research into the cathedral restoration, I couldn't help but wonder if the Black Madonna would have remained unscathed if Chartres had remained in the hands of the Church rather than State. Although statues and icons such as these have been known to cause embarrassment and been an awkward talking point for some clergy, the Church does seem to acknowledge, however ambivalently, the significance of Black Madonnas. However, from what I could tell, they had not objected to the statue's repainting. It seems clear that the Black Virgin had been swept up in the general opinion of the curators that the cathedral was dirty and needed to be cleaned. They had not taken the time to consider that, whether this was candle soot or black paint, the darkness of the statue had a significance that they were erasing from its history in not only their actions but also their attitudes.

HISTORIOGRAPHY OF CHARTRES

Many of the 'alternative' pilgrims to Chartres have no doubt been influenced by 20th century authors who have written popular books on the esoteric meanings of the Cathedral. We find another parallel with Glastonbury in the work of Louis Charpentier, whose *Les Mystères de la Cathédrale de Chartres* (1966) has influenced many other mystery hunters. The jacket of the English translation compares the work to that of Frederick Bligh Bond at Glastonbury, who in the early 20th century published theories on the use of sacred geometry in the abbey's design, and in fact appears to have shared benefactors with Charpentier in members of the Research Into Lost Knowledge Association. Besides Charpentier, another influential scholar on Chartres is Jean Markale, whose *Cathedral of the Black Madonna* (1988) discusses some of the same theories as Charpentier on energy lines and druidic foundations, but focuses much more on the Black Madonna. His theories on the Celtic significance of the site are romantic and intriguing though his sourcing is questionable. Unhelpfully, both authors quote very few sources and assert several theories as fact in their quests to uncover Chartres' hidden meaning. Theories are great, and encourage our minds to open and enquire further, but they should always be labelled as only theories. As enticing as ideas of 'spiritual truths' are, we must be careful to separate the possibility of a pre-Christian goddess cult on this site and other esoteric theories from the historical evidence of the cathedral in our discussions. Charpentier's starting point is the druidic legend, which he presents as fact,[6] without mention of its probable medieval origin. This allows him to assert that the location of the church was chosen for its powerful telluric energy, of which he alleges the druids were aware, and which consequently influenced the later builders of the cathedral.

Rather than using the legends as our starting point, but without discarding their influence altogether, it is more useful to look at the features of the cathedral and the actual history of the statues, patchy though the evidence is, and then see how the legends fit into giving these Madonnas the legendary status they enjoy today.

---

[6] Charpentier 1972: 18

THE FORM OF THE CATHEDRAL
AND THE FEMININE

As with many churches of medieval importance, its foundation myth dates it to the early centuries of the Common Era. This is based on legends about the origins of the well and the statue in the crypt that did not in fact fully form until the later Middle Ages. The earliest church is thought to have been built in the 4th century, surviving until 858 when the Vikings laid siege to Chartres and destroyed every trace. Immediate rebuilding began, but the cathedral was again to be destroyed by fire in 1020 and 1194. The western portal, one of the bell towers and crypt are the only parts of the Romanesque cathedral that survived the particularly destructive fire of 1194. The New Bell Tower on the northwest side does not match the Old. Jean Markale, whose extensive book weaves the features of the cathedral with its legends, comments on the disparate and unequal elements visible in the cathedral's external appearance, added over time, "a synthesis of rather odd elements that without the genius of architects, could have been a graceless and heteroclite jumble".[7] In this way, the cathedral shows, through its appearance, a refusal to be static at one point in time. This could be likened to an entity breathing, or to the 'Virgo Paritura' of legend, the Virgin about to give birth beneath its floors. More on that legend further on. Markale compares the cathedral to the crown of mountain mother Cybele, referencing the possibility of a goddess cult on this site before the coming of Christianity. "The cathedral crowns the mound of Chartres... Our Lady of Chartres, the Virgin crowned with towers – as once Cybele, mother of the gods, was crowned – in her perpetual labour giving birth: The cathedral is truly the exaltation of this image, both divine and maternal, a sublime arch that holds the world in gestation".[8] It should, however, be noted that the site itself is not linked to any cults of Cybele.

Markale makes some interesting comments on the position of the Lady Chapel, which contains Our Lady of the Pillar, on the north side of the cathedral. He picks out various connotations here,

---

[7] Markale 2004: 39
[8] Markale 2004: 37-8

not all of which are positive. When facing east, as one generally does during a Christian church service, the north side is on the left, the *sinister* side. The north is also the coldest and darkest side of a building by nature. Therefore, carvings on this side were normally more of the hellish variety. Women were traditionally seated on the left in church, closer to this 'evil', therefore becoming subtly associated with it.[9] Although this points to the subjugation of women, Markale surmises that Mary's chapel was often positioned on this side, as at Chartres, to represent her triumph over Satan or perhaps hinted at the darker secrets that the Feminine had to offer. The external North Portal of Chartres is certainly suggestive of it, featuring various figures associated with wisdom, including Solomon and Sheba, and the Sibyl.[10]

Another draw to the cathedral is the multitude of stained glass. Chartres' iconic flying buttresses, which bear the weight of the walls, allow for more windows, and therefore more opportunities for depictions in glass. Foremost amongst these, already briefly mentioned, is the 'Blue Virgin' or *Notre-Dame-de-la-Belle-Verrièr*, another artefact that, against the odds, escaped the fire of 1194. The blue of her cloak is of the famed 'Chartres blue', particular to this region. Although not a dark-skinned Madonna, she has been the subject of much speculation, as to whether she represents the likeness of one of the earlier statues of the cathedral, now destroyed.

Mary is also at the centre of a very large rose window, seated as the throne of wisdom receiving the gifts of the Holy Spirit and sits as a girl on the lap of a dark-skinned Saint Anne in the middle of the windows beneath it. Devotion to Saint Anne was popular in the region centuries before the dogma of the Immaculate Conception was made official in the 19th century. The cathedral even held the head of St Anne as a relic, donated by the Countess of Chartres in 1205, a product of the Fourth Crusade.[11]

Inside the cathedral, the 13th century floor is unbroken by grave markers, making Chartres almost unique in this aspect, and significant in itself in making the entire cathedral an explicit

---

[9] Markale 2004: 43-4
[10] Markale 2004: 45-6
[11] Bugslag 2005: 168

representation of Mary: "There are no tombs in the cathedral itself; it is dedicated to the Majestic Virgin and has therefore triumphed over death".[12] A pronouncement by the Parlement of Paris in 1475 explicitly states that so many miracles take place at Chartres through the virginity of Mary, and because the body of the church is not polluted by the burials of private donors.[13] Despite this disassociation with death and burial, a large, and popular, chthonic focus lay beneath the floors in the crypt.

THE CRYPT, WELL, AND THE VIRGO PARITURA

The current crypt is named after Saint Fulbert, the bishop of Chartres who oversaw its construction as part of the rebuilding of the 1020s, following the destruction by fire of the Carolingian cathedral. Fulbert's crypt wraps around the footprint of the Carolingian cathedral in a horseshoe, indicating that the floor level was the same.[14] The only vestige of the Carolingian building that remained was its crypt of Saint Lubin, on a level lower still than the later crypt. James Bugslag asserts that it was Fulbert's intention that rather than being a cathedral with a crypt, the building functioned as an 'upper and lower church', the lower being the focus of pilgrimage activity, with its associated antiquity: "it would appear that the pre-1020 structures not only formed the starting point for laying out Fulbert's church, but were, in a sense, enshrined by it, almost as relics".[15]

Within the crypt is the *Puits des Saints-Forts* (Well of the Strong Saints), thought to be of ancient origin and located outside what would have been the Carolingian church. The story surrounding the name is that the bodies of two Christian martyrs, Altin and Eodald, were thrown into it by the Norse who besieged Chartres in 858. An alternate account has earlier Christian missionaries Savinian and Potentian being sent to Gaul and finding a church already founded at Chartres, which they consecrated before their death and disposal in the well at the hands of the Roman

---

[12] Markale 2004: 38
[13] Bugslag 2005: 162
[14] Markale 2004: 66
[15] Bugslag 2005: 138-9

governor.[16] Though they more likely date from the fourth-century foundation, later chroniclers pushed the lives of Savinian and Potentian back even further, making them disciples of Saint Peter. Such tales of apostolic foundation were a popular trope of the medieval Church, asserting their authenticity and authority.

In close proximity to the well is the statue of *Notre Dame Sous Terre*, an echo of a statue that is supposed to have stood in this place since before the birth of Christ. The statue I witnessed only dates from 1976, according to Ella Rozett,[17] and is one in a line of reproductions following destruction by fire and revolution. Despite the later copies bearing less resemblance to the various drawings made of the earlier statue, it bears the Latin *Virgini Pariturae* – the 'Virgin about to give birth', which indicates to the modern observer the legend with which the crypt statue was associated.

The legend in its basic form states that druids were active in the area BCE and worshipped a statue of the *Virgo Paritura*, a pre-Christian idol that was interpreted as a miraculous portent of the coming of Christ. The earliest Chartres chronicle to mention the legend, the *Vieille Chronique* of 1389, does not use the word 'druids' but does suggest pre-Christian usage, which was interpreted as druidic in the following century. The *Vieille Chronique* tells that Chartres was founded before the life of Christ by people who worshipped a Virgin about to give birth. A local prince then donated a statue of a Virgin holding a child on her lap and the priests cherished it amongst their other idols.[18] The anonymous chronicler, a cleric of Chartres, supposedly heard the story from elderly parishioners, but I wonder whether details were shaped to match the statue that was present in the crypt at the time of writing. Why would the prince donate a statue of a Virgin and child that was then venerated by the inhabitants of Chartres if their deity was a pregnant Virgin?

Whereas the myth became an accepted and much-repeated origin story by the late Middle Ages, it is unmentioned before the 14th century. There is no evidence of a statue in the crypt before

---

[16] Markale 2004:66-7
[17] Interfaithmary.net/blog/chartres
[18] Markale 2004: 246

the 12th century, and as earlier mentioned, it matches the 'in majesty' form of several other French Black Madonnas of this era. The original statue is estimated to date from between 1010 and 1029 at the earliest, based on documentary evidence.[19] This suggests it only became a feature after the modelling of Fulbert's crypt, not a concern around which the building work was centred.

Little pilgrimage evidence remains, so we can only guess at the types of devotion carried out by the ordinary visitor to the crypt. However, the statue's placement in close proximity to the well no doubt leant it some chthonic presence. This, coupled with the druidic legend, once it had taken hold in the later Middle Ages, caused unrest amongst the Chartres clergy, possibly drawing a little too close to pagan worship, so in the 1640s the well was blocked and covered.

That the myth only appeared after Chartres was well established as a Marian cult site is telling. Proof of longevity was a preoccupation of the medieval Church, and in order to solidify legitimacy, cathedrals and abbeys would often utilise legends to push back their foundation as close to apostolic times as possible. What is interesting is that Chartres went one better in claiming veneration of the Virgin had been unbroken since a time even *before* the birth of Christ. Malcolm Miller, the same no-nonsense tour guide who refuted that the darkness of the cathedral was natural, has rejected the common belief that the site was one of pre-Christian importance and ceremony. This does not stop popular modern literature about the cathedral stating as fact that Chartres was a place of druidic worship. Although the druidic legend only became popular in the 15th century, is there any likelihood that Chartres was a site of Gallic importance?

LEGENDARY FOUNDATION

The name of Chartres is widely believed to derive from the name of the Gallic tribe, the Carnutes, who inhabited the area. Belief in Chartres being the centre of druid activity in the region

---

[19] Ilene Forsyth states that Bernard of Angers, who had been a pupil of Chartres, wrote disparagingly of cult statue worship in a visit to southern France in 1013, suggesting no such Madonna was already being venerated at the cathedral (Bugslag 2005: 144).

stems from the writings of Julius Caesar who mentions in his commentary on Gaul that druids "assemble at a fixed period of the year in a consecrated place in the territories of the Carnutes, which is reckoned the central region of the whole of Gaul".[20] This has been later assumed to be Chartres, due to its later importance, topographical prominence, and roughly central geographic location. Caesar would have known the town by its Roman name, Autricum. Another possible location of the Carnutes' capital was Cenabum, modern-day Orléans, but Caesar mentions neither explicitly by name. Markale advocates for the site being Chartres based on various place-name etymologies, including the area of Beauce, Belsa in Latin, which he believes to mean clearing. We know from various accounts of the druids that their meetings were conducted in *nemetons*, or sacred clearings, so if this area was a large nemeton within the vast Gaulish forest, it would be a likely location.[21] However, this is all still conjecture. Charpentier and Markale trace Belsa back to the name of a Gallic goddess Belisima, consort of sun god Bel,[22] but again, material evidence of worship at Chartres is lacking.

We have no archaeological evidence to support the druid theory, nor does there appear to be a correlation between known druidic sites in France and other churches with Black Madonnas. Historic record suggests that the druids had no religious buildings, and that all their ceremonies were conducted out in nature, so to search for any sort of temple building beneath the crypt of Chartres would likely be in vain. Hypothetically speaking, this doesn't preclude the possibility that a cave, accompanied by the spring of the later *Saints Forts*, might have existed and been attractive to them, if they had indeed worshipped a pregnant mother goddess carving. In theory, a subterranean space might enhance the feeling of gestation within the earth for the purpose of ritual, although perhaps this is only our modern lens that is making this supposition. Anna Fedele found that the kinds of experience shared by less-orthodox modern pilgrims indicate a feeling of 'tuning in' with the currents of earth energy, and healing wounds, particularly associated with femininity and sexuality by making a

[20] Caesar (McDevitte & Bohn, Trans. 1869): Book 6, ch. 13
[21] Markale 2004: 75
[22] Charpentier 1972: 22, Markale 2004: 75

connection between these traits and the Underworld.[23] Jungians would argue that this link between the psyche and the chthonic realm is a trait of humans throughout the ages, but without being able to put ourselves into the minds of people thousands of years ago we are unable to assert that this would have been the case. Assuming the beliefs of ancient people can be misleading and at worst, hazardous.

In the question of whether there were druids worshipping here or not, we should take care to note that the absence of evidence does not favour either possibility. Although we are left with the chance of there being a Celtic foundation we must remember that the drive for this claim came from the romanticisms of a later age and the medieval PR of the clergy, keen to push back the antiquity, and thus the spiritual potency, of Chartres to the earliest possible date.

THE UPPER CHURCH AND OUR LADY OF THE PILLAR

Returning from Fulbert's 'Lower Church', we find as much of interest for pilgrims within the main cathedral. The nave is home to a 40-foot wide labyrinth design, massive both in its size and its renown. Like the appearance of the cathedral's Madonna swinging between black and white, the labyrinth has alternated between periods of being more accessible and being covered. Daniel K. Connolly reported that in the early 2000s, chairs were removed and the labyrinth was exposed due to increasing tourist requests and the popularity of copies in churches elsewhere.[24] This was not the case when I visited in 2017, being only partially visible beneath rows of chairs. The labyrinth is apparently now cleared for walking only on Fridays, from Lent until November.

One austere explanation of the labyrinth noted by Markale is that "paradise lies at the end of a difficult road full of snares".[25] This description at first seems inadequate, being more suggestive of a maze with multiple dead ends, like the most famous labyrinth

---

[23] Fedele 2013a: 110
[24] Connolly 2005: 285
[25] Markale 2004: 50

of Crete, which was in fact a maze. The terms were used interchangeably in the Middle Ages, but even the single path labyrinth was interpreted by early medieval minds as a twisting, turning road through the material world of mundane temptations distracting one from the straight and narrow path to God.[26]

However, this labyrinth, one of several constructed in France in the late 12th to early 13th century, is widely thought to have been created to provide a micro-pilgrimage to Jerusalem; their creation being seen as a direct response to the loss of Jerusalem to Muslim forces in 1187.[27] In medieval maps, Jerusalem was commonly regarded as the centre of the world, and so walking a route to a representation of Jerusalem at its centre was a substitute in miniature for actual pilgrimage to the city. Being the homeland of Christ, Jerusalem was of utmost importance to medieval Christians, which is why it was the alleged place of provenance of so many relics, including many of the European Black Madonnas. A bronze plaque once sat at the centre of the labyrinth, which may have depicted the holy city, but by the time of its removal in the late 17th century, had been too worn away to identify.[28] One alternative account from that century suggested a scene of Theseus and the Minotaur could be discerned,[29] linking it directly to the ancient goddess-worshipping culture of Crete, with its famous myth of the labyrinth.[30] Like so many features of the cathedral, the labyrinth can be ascribed esoteric as well as exoteric meaning. Markale mistakenly relates that one of the remaining nubs of the plaque's nails is an addition by Canon Estienne to create a meridian with a

---

[26] Connolly 2005: 302

[27] Connolly 2005: 287

[28] It was a recognised tradition that the church symbolised a microcosm of the wholeness of creation, and within this, the labyrinth represented the world. Whereas the east end of the Church symbolised heaven, the Nave, where the Chartres labyrinth is located, was the earthly domain. This was reflected in its function as an increasingly mundane space where trade and social gatherings took place. Not long before the removal of the labyrinth's plaque, a 1696 engraving shows the nave as a busy social space, and an earlier 17th century account tells of how visitors would noisily walk or run around the labyrinth, even during services, suggesting its earlier reverent meaning had been largely forgotten.

[29] Connolly 2005: 288

[30] In brief, King Minos had the labyrinth of Crete constructed as a prison to house the Minotaur - the abominable offspring of his wife, Queen Pasiphae and a bull, which she had been made to lust after by the gods as a punishment for Minos' pride. Children were regularly sacrificed to the Minotaur until the hero Theseus slays it and escapes the labyrinth with the help of Ariadne.

ray of sunlight on St John's Day.[31] The much-talked-about nail is actually in the south transept and aligns with the sunlight on the Summer Solstice three days earlier, according to Charpentier.[32]

It is recorded that our no-longer-Black Madonna, the surviving 16th century wooden Lady of the Pillar was in fact the last in a line of several Marian statues to grace the main church. The most important was a silver gilt figure donated in 1220 by the archdeacon of Vendôme that stood above the altar. Most expensive was a bejewelled gold statue known as *Notre Dame Bleue,* given by the Duke of Berry in 1404; its reliquary base holding hairs of the Virgin. Another silver statue was given to the cathedral by the English in 1432, which was known as *Notre Dame Blanche* due to the whiteness of the silver. It is not known where this statue stood, but a reliquary base was added in 1559 containing milk of the Virgin and also referred to as *Notre Dame de Lacte*.[33]

The current polychrome Lady of the Pillar was commissioned around 1508, possibly modelled after the first silver statue on the altar.[34] The late 19th/early 20th-century hypothesis of Black Madonnas being black because of the oxidation of silver[35] has been somewhat disregarded as limiting because of the variety of statues and their circumstance. However, it occurred to me that, perhaps in this case, after 300 years in the cathedral, the silver statue had in fact turned dark, and the 16th-century wooden copy been created dark to match her. There seems to be some uncertainty around the nature of the original statue. The French governmental record says that it was a wooden statue and only layered with silver and gold,[36] whereas Delaporte, writing in the 1960s, said that the statue was silver, and survived until 1769 when it was melted down to pay for redecoration of the choir.[37] Perhaps there has been some confusion between this and *Notre Dame Blanche?*

Whether a replacement of or in addition to the earlier statue, it

---

[31] Markale 2004: 226

[32] Charpentier 1972: 9

[33] Bugslag 2005: 146-7

[34] Bugslag 2005: 148

[35] Claimed by Charles Rohault de Fleury in 1878 and furthered by Stephen Beissel in 1909. See Scheer 2002: 1418

[36] www2.culture.gouv.fr/public/mistral/palsri_fr?ACTION=CHERCHER&FIELD_1=REF&VALUE-1=PM28000094

[37] Delaporte 1965: 58

would seem the 1508 statue was installed to become a new focus for pilgrim activity. She was set on the left of the rood screen, supposedly because Marian devotion around the High Altar had become too popular and the queues of pilgrims had become distracting for the canons carrying out their services. In 1763, when the rood was demolished, she was moved to the northwest pillar of the transept. Then for a short time, she switched places with the Lady of the Underground, brought out from the then inaccessible crypt in 1791. The re-veneration of *Notre Dame Sous Terre* only lasted two years before she fell to the torches of revolutionaries in 1793.[38] Two years later, worship in the cathedral was reauthorized and Our Lady of the Pillar was brought back out from the crypt and reinstalled in the transept, before being moved one final time in 1806 to her current position on the north aisle. Use of the name 'Our Lady of the Pillar' itself is first recorded in 1825, and she was later crowned in 1855. Her status as a Black Madonna, according to the official French government web page regarding the statue, comes only from confusion of this statue with *Notre Dame Sous Terre* caused by the period they switched places, and by the will of a late 19th/early 20th century restorer who painted her as dark to match earlier discolouration.[39] It seems clear that the government officials who commissioned the 2013 whitening of the statue categorically do not regard her as a Black Madonna, or do not ascribe any value to her darkened appearance.

Our Lady of the Pillar sits with her son on her left knee, who holds an orb whilst she holds a pear. The pillar itself is a remnant of the rood screen to which the statue used to be affixed. Sometimes the statue is bare and at other times adorned in the rich, vaguely triangular garb we find common on Black Virgins. Markale comments that it is fitting she be cloaked, as the Cathedral's most important relic was a piece of the Virgin's tunic, the *Sancta Camisa*,[40] given to Charlemagne by the Emperor of Byzantium and donated to Chartres by his grandson Charles the Bald in 876.[41] However,

---

[38] Markale 2004: 54

[39] www2.culture.gouv.fr/public/mistral/palsri_fr?ACTION=CHERCHER&FIELD_1=REF&VALUE-1=PM28000094

[40] Markale 2004: 52

[41] The authenticity of this relic is dubious, as Charlemagne's crusade during which he was meant to have acquired the tunic was fictitious. However, it was convincing

the donation is not mentioned in records before the 12th-century. As we have seen, Marian devotion used to dominate the altar area, where the various statues and reliquaries stood, including that of the tunic. It narrowly escaped destruction by fire in 1194, being taken beneath trapdoors by fleeing priests. In 1712, it was decided that the reliquary would be opened, and rather than a tunic, a length of silk was found, which was thereafter referred to as the Virgin's veil instead.[42] Like the Marian statues, the chest containing the *Sancta Camisa* was eventually exiled to the ambulatory, as the focus was projected away from the main altar.

CONCLUSIONS

For all Chartres' claims of being a pure and triumphant symbol of the Virgin, with its lack of burials, and wealth of Marian relics, it appears that at some point it was regarded as *too* successful as a Marian shrine, and these items were no longer deemed appropriate for the main altar. In the same way, the pilgrim activity of the crypt must have become so intense that the clergy felt the need to curtail it by blocking up the well. Nevertheless, Chartres Cathedral as a whole continued to embody that well-spring, and still does, centuries later, welcoming pilgrims from a variety of backgrounds.

It is ironic that the druidic foundation legend eagerly disseminated by the clerics of Chartres in the 15th century has drawn so many non-Christians or non-traditional Christians to find particular significance in the place. The legend was meant to prove the triumph of the Virgin and of Christ; that it was so powerful that they were somehow worshipped even before his birth, essentially 'pre-converting' these Gallic pagans. The placement of a subterranean Madonna, alongside a well – a potent symbol of the Feminine, beneath a labyrinth – a relic of pre-Christian antiquity, provides an irresistible draw to the modern pilgrim who is searching for esoteric meaning beneath the medieval façade.

This is without mentioning the more prominent no-longer-Black Madonna, Our Lady of the Pillar. Time will tell if it continues

---

enough that French queens would be given a shirt touched by the reliquary holding the veil when they were pregnant as a charm (Markale 2004:56).
[42] Bugslag in Blick and Tekippe eds. 2005: 165

to draw as many visitors, or whether at some point its appearance will once again be changed to suit the contemporary socio-political climate. Besides my material concerns for the statue's preservation, it is the decision of the authorities to choose a particular era of the statue's life to present as being the only 'authentic' one that I found most troubling. I daresay they could argue that wanting to present the statue as black is just as subjective, but their interpretive notices and their public statements indicate that they see no value in blackness and only see dirtiness. In the next chapter, we discover that the very concept of a Virgin Mary statue being labelled as a 'Black Madonna' appears to be an early-modern invention, rather than the will of the original craftsmen or their patrons, but this should not equate to the conclusion that her blackness has never held, nor currently holds any significance. As a layer of meaning ascribed to a historical artefact, the phenomenon of it being venerated as a Black Madonna and holding special qualities because of this is not one that should be hastily swept away as ignorant or delusional. Why are the devotional practices and beliefs of modern pilgrims any less authentic than those of medieval ones? Furthermore, asserting that the Virgin being black had no significance to earlier audiences just because there is no record of her being titled as so is assuming the beliefs of a society far removed from us based only on the official recordings of the Church. Gradual darkening over time may have been unintentional, but it was at the very least accepted, if not protected and even replicated, rather than regularly cleaned away. Assuming the insignificance of the dark-skinned appearance of the Madonna and trying to erase this period of its history is disrespectful to whole generations of her followers.

CHAPTER 2

The Virgin of Le Puy
Racially Black?

HISTORY OF THE BLACK MADONNA OF LE PUY

As with so many Black Madonna sites, the origins of Le Puy in the Auvergne region of southern central France are shrouded in mythical early Christian foundation, fertile soil for a Black Madonna legend to take root. The 10th-century legend places the origin of the cathedral of Le-Puy-en-Velay in the hands of saints Front and George, reportedly sent by Saint Peter to proselytize Gaul. The saints supposedly founded their church at Vellavorum, an area of the Gaulish Vellavi (from which Velay stems). From here on, the story grows increasingly fantastic. The cathedral was said to have been built around an ancient dolmen, the only survivor of a pagan temple on Mont Anis. The dolmen was integrated into the cathedral under the virtue of a story, telling how a very ill woman prayed to the Virgin Mary upon the stone that she would be healed. She received an apparition of Mary on that spot - the Virgin claiming the place as her own, along with instruction to lie on the stone to be cured of her illness, which she did. Due to the miraculous healing, the dolmen became known as the Fever Stone, and one of the first bishops,[1] on hearing of the apparition, went to investigate for himself. Although it was the middle of July, the hill was covered in snow. The bishop saw a stag, whose footprints had traced out the layout of what would become the sanctuary, and he marked them out with dry thorny bushes. On later returning, the dead branches were all blooming.[2] Differing accounts say that Mary

---

[1] The cathedral's website claims it was St Vosy with the help of St Scutaire, though other sources name various other legendary bishops such as George. See www.cathedraldupuy.org

[2] Interfaithmary.net/blog/black-madonna-le-puy-one-and-two

would have to wait between ten years and two centuries for her Cathedral,[3] and it was only after another miraculous healing on the Fever Stone that the Pope granted permission for such a 'completely exceptional thing' as a church built around a former pagan site.[4] This was of course not an exceptional case, and neither are the other features of the story, which are tropes repeated in saints' *vitae* around Western Europe.

The dolmen was at first treated with reverence, and was said to have been kept near the main altar of the original church, the throne for a statue known as Our Lady of the Rock. However, the dolmen was broken up and thrown out of the church at some point by the 8th century for its all-too-pagan appearance, though the capstone was saved for use as a paving slab. It was eventually brought back inside in 1998 and housed in a side chapel.

The early statue did not survive either. A later statue, the one which enjoyed legendary status in medieval times, was traditionally said to have been gifted by King Louis IX who had retrieved it from the East. By the 15th and 16th centuries, Le Puy had become a major French bishopric and one starting point for the Santiago de Compostela pilgrim route. As at Chartres, the histories of the Cathedral written at this time delve back into a pre-Christian origin for the statue, to really cement its position as a premier pilgrimage site in the country. The stories claimed that the statue had been carved by the prophet Jeremiah, despite him having lived 500 years before Christ. This is based upon a 12th-century French biblical commentary in which Jeremiah was said to have fled Jerusalem to Egypt where, hidden in a cave, he carved a Virgin and Child which was venerated by the Egyptians.[5] The Le Puy chroniclers claimed this statue to be theirs, brought back from one of the Crusades. In this context, 'Egypt' was connoted with the vague 'East' of the Holy Land and the backdrop of the Bible rather than with Black Africans or the people of ancient Egypt although as we will see, this connotation was drawn in later centuries.

---

[3] The local Diocese's website places the apparition at 420AD, with the first church completed by 430AD. www.catholique-lepuy.fr/histoire/aux-origines-de-leglise-du-puy-racines-paiennes-et-racines-chretiennes-pere-michel-cubizolles-archiviste-diocesain/

[4] Interfaithmary.net/blog/black-madonna-le-puy-one-and-two

[5] Foster 2016b: 7

In 1794, the statue burned at the hands of the French Revolutionaries. One legend reported that as it ignited, a hidden compartment popped open and a parchment from within rolled to the floor.[6] Apparently, no one stopped it from burning to learn what was written there. Although unverifiable, it is entirely possible that such a niche in the statue existed, as many Marian statues doubled as reliquaries.

In 1856 another Black Madonna statue was inaugurated in the cathedral, and Notre Dame du Puy resumed her place.[7] Whilst the appearance of the statue was not based on drawings of the earlier one, it needed only to inherit the name to also take on the miraculous aura of the original. To this day, there is an awareness of the fact that this statue is not the 11th-century Virgin, but Foster comments that "those who come to venerate her image are often complicit in this deception".[8] To them it is the name and history and that which she represents, rather than the vessel that inhabits the space, which is important. Whilst a superstitious element surely persists around physical Black Madonna statues, particularly those that can be touched by the public, this shows that there is a subtle difference in the treatment of them when compared to a miraculous relic. A pilgrim may visit a saint's bones and know that their authenticity is uncertain, but in the case of a Black Madonna it is usually made clear when the statue is not original. They are nevertheless treated with no less respect. It is the symbol, ultimately, that is important, which is why pilgrims and congregations accept replacement statues.

A QUESTION OF ETHNICITY?

Much of what can be described as the 'enigma of the Black Madonna' in general comes from the fact that she is spoken about in terms of being racially Black. To some people this is confusing, as they would expect her to be a woman of Middle Eastern origin, or because they are used to the many Eurocentric depictions of Mary as a blonde, fair-skinned woman. To our modern eyes, the

---

[6] Markale 2004: 184

[7] Although a 1990 copy based on drawings of the pre-Revolution statue exists in the cathedral, it does not take centre stage as 'Notre Dame du Puy'.

[8] Foster 2016b: 1

Black Madonna also suggests something subversive, alluring in its break from the institutionally accepted version of the Virgin. Because of our growing awareness of the struggles of Black women around the globe, and the barriers that both women and Black people have started to overcome in the last century, we see her as a symbol of strength and defiance. However, this is a strictly modern view. This is not to say that such connotations of the Black Madonna are 'wrong', just that they are of their time, and in later chapters I will argue the validity of these modern meanings being no less than those of any time period. What they are *not*, however, is founded in the statues' historical meanings. Through reading the works of Monique Scheer, Agnes Bernard, Sylvie Vilatte, Elisa A. Foster and others, I discovered that our modern concept of race and ethnicity is far removed from a medieval perspective on colour, and in fact the colour of these statues is likely to have held a completely different significance.

Foster and Scheer found that before the 16th century, the dark appearance of these statues was connoted with the East and antiquity, particularly the time of Jesus, "so that blackness in this context signalled both old age and Eastern provenance within Christian biblical history. A Black Madonna was therefore an 'old' sculpture, one that was closer in age to the Virgin Mary herself. As in the case of a sacred relic, the older the image could claim to be, the more authoritative it became."[9] Besides indicating an aged piece, as Scheer points out, the darkness of the wood may also indicate a valuable type found in the Eastern Mediterranean such as ebony or cedar, thus linking it even more definitively with the Holy Land.[10] Scheer argues convincingly that in the early Middle Ages the colour had significance, *but* that it was not to do with race. This symbolism was reflected in a particular statue's origin stories. Most often, it was proclaimed that: the piece was very old, it came from Jerusalem, and was made by the hands of St Luke, giving it extra gravitas. Gradually over time as society changed, although the stories remained, this association with her appearance was forgotten. When asked why she is black, theories and explanations came into being such as the typical 'blackened by the candles of the faithful', whilst others began to seek alternative rationalisations in Scripture.

'I AM BLACK BUT BEAUTIFUL'

In the 17th century, the Jesuit Order began to explicitly link the image of the Black Madonna, particularly the one at Le Puy, to the description of the Bride of the biblical *Song of Songs* in their publications. The famous line *"Nigra sum sed Formosa"* (I am Black but Beautiful) became firmly associated with the image, and its first recorded use in this context is thought to be in a play from circa 1518 by Claude Doleson, *Le mistere et historie miraculeuse de Nostre-Dame du Puy d'Anis.*[11] Bernard of Clairvaux had previously written about the verse in the 12th century, stating what he thought the line signified.[12] He believed the Bride's skin to be dark, not from sin, but from being burned by the hot sun of the region.

The later Jesuits seized upon Bernard's writings and the 'Black but Beautiful' formulation to help explain away any contemporary or previous misgivings about the colour black, such as the association in medieval art with Satan or sinners. Obviously, the Jesuits could not allow the Virgin to be associated with those things, nor with the 'infidels' that her complexion mirrored. The 17th-century Jesuit leader Odo de Gissey rationalised that the Le Puy Virgin was the same colour as Muslims to appeal to them and prompt them to convert.[13] However, this equating of colour with religion was a later convention, and 'Moors', as they were typically named, were depicted and described as a variety of shades and skin tones in earlier history. As Foster notes, in Spanish art especially, representations of Muslims were diverse.[14]

The effect of the Jesuits' connection of the statues with the verse was long-lasting. Scheer quotes an 18th-century sermon from Teising, Germany, home of a Black Madonna, which begins with the 'Black but Beautiful' line and asks "Who can believe that?...

---

[11] Foster 2016b: 7
[12] Although Bernard of Clairvaux compared the Bride to Mary and was writing around the time many of the Black Madonnas were being created, it is thought unlikely that his writing influenced the statues' appearances.
[13] Vilatte 1996: 752
[14] Foster 2016a: 22

Who does not know that the colour black has always been considered a metaphor and sign of sadness, grief, and hideousness?"[15] Having already been successfully linked with the Bride, (and also being representative of *Ecclesia,* the church), Mary is explained as being darkened by grief at the Crucifixion, and also the power of her love which is like the sun which darkens the Bride. Parallels are also drawn between the Bride's humility in the *Song of Songs* and Mary's at the Annunciation, which then is applied to the Black Madonna of Teising as one of her best qualities.[16]

Although it can be clearly demonstrated that classification by race was a later, early-modern invention, this does not mean that earlier people were not capable of racism – discriminating on the basis of skin colour and assigning stereotypes to them. Bartlett writes that this idea that skin colour was determined by (and could be changed by) geography was prevalent in the Middle Ages. Bernard of Clairvaux and his 12th and 13th-century contemporaries believed not only that climate controlled a person's skin colour but also their characteristics. The Dominican Friar Albertus Magnus typified Indians as clever, saying that a little heat aided mental ability, whilst Africans were not, because too much heat impaired it.[17] Such assumptions were almost always culturally biased, favouring the writer's own race. Chroniclers typically described foreigners, particularly their enemies in detrimental terms. Discrimination was always there; medieval people just tended to identify groups in terms of religion rather than race.

Kate Lowe provides a fascinating investigation into the far-reaching consequences of the mistranslation of one tiny word, the 'but' in the *Song of Songs'* "I am Black but Beautiful". Lowe argues that the translation from Hebrew to Latin should have read "Nigra sum *et* Formosa" – I am Black *and* Beautiful, and that the adoption of this mistake caused an entire detrimental view of Africans in Renaissance Europe.[18] When first translated into Greek around 100BCE, the Hebrew ן (*vav*) was rendered καὶ, which both largely mean 'and', but by the time the first full Latin translation, the Vulgate, had been finished by St. Jerome in 405CE, the word had

---

[15] Scheer 2002: 1431
[16] Scheer 2002: 1431
[17] Bartlett 2001: 47
[18] Lowe 2012

changed to 'but'. Lowe states:

> *"For his translation of the Old Testament, he went back to the original Hebrew and Aramaic, and his proclaimed purpose was to render the sense of a passage rather than to provide a literal rendition of the words. Assuming that Jerome's knowledge of Hebrew was sufficiently good for him not to have mistaken the range of the word ?, for him there must have been an opposition between 'Black' and 'Beautiful', so he rendered the phrase: 'I am Black but Beautiful', and the 'Black but …' formulation entered the Western European repertoire".[19]*

In a translation of the *Song of Songs* that Jerome made earlier in life from the Greek, he rendered the passage "I am dark and beautiful", so he made a conscious decision to change it in his later work on the Vulgate.[20] This became the only translation of the Bible used in medieval Europe, and the first book to be printed there, so belief in the canonical truth of its every word became enshrined, and with it the idea that 'Black' and 'Beautiful' were adversarial terms. So too when it came to be translated into English, where the translators of the 1611 King James Version chose the words "I am black but comely", and in the summary points of the page wrote: "she confesseth her deformity", belying their attitudes to the Bride's colour.[21]

The 'Black but' formula also continued to appear in vernacular discourse, such as in the record of the Congolese ambassador to Pope Paul V, who was described as Black *but* possessing positive qualities such as piousness – "The 'Black but...' formulation worked by insisting that it was noteworthy or exceptional, although not impossible, for a Black African to be in possession of these character traits."[22] In Portugal, which had the highest proportion of Africans in Europe in the 15th and 16th centuries, the formulation was common to express a degree of surprise that a Black person could possess civil and stereotypically 'White' qualities. The attitude seems to have been that being Black was an impediment to be overcome, such as in the writings on the life of the first Black

---

[19] Lowe 2012: 546
[20] Which is consistent with his equating of the black skin of Ethiopians with the darkness of sin in his homilies.
[21] Lowe 2012: 547
[22] Lowe 2012: 548

person to be made a saint in Europe, Benedetto il Moro, who overcame hardships that were seen as inherent to his race.[23]

The advent of the printing press and dissemination of the Vulgate in the mid-15th century coincided with the rise of the slave trade, and although the original mistranslation may not be wholly responsible for the atrocities that this brought to African people, Lowe argues that it brought into commonplace discourse the rationalisation that Black people were inferior, though not beyond possessing positive attributes.[24] Thus, by the time of the attribution of this quotation to the Black Madonna of Le Puy, this inherent adversarial thinking was ingrained in the European mind.

THE BLACK MADONNA IN PRINT

So when do we start to see explicit references to the Madonnas as racially Black? Up to the 17th century, descriptions made of the statues at cult sites tend not to mention anything about the colour but instead focus on the miracles wrought by them. Illustrations of statues later named Black Madonnas from that time often do not show the Madonna with a darkened complexion, but due to various other inaccuracies, appear to often have been drawn from a secondhand description rather than by eye. If so, the person relating the image gave no instruction that the Madonna should appear Black.[25]

The Le Puy Madonna, however, is one of the first to be described and depicted in such a way, in a French book of hours produced between 1462 and 1481, with brown skin and arguably African features, (yet white hands, like the later replica).[26] Analysis showed a pink layer of paint beneath, but Foster believes this to be an artistic layering convention rather than a likelihood of later recolouring. The book is thought to come from the court of René d'Anjou, who was devoted to Notre Dame du Puy and was a collector of Eastern relics and fashions. Foster surmises that in combining the appearance of the traders at his court with the Eastern/Egyptian origin story of the statue: "If his court

---

[23] Lowe 2012: 550
[24] Lowe 2012: 552
[25] Scheer 2002: 1422
[26] Foster 2016b: 10-11

illuminators saw Moors, or black Muslims from North Africa, at René's court, it is possible that the artist conflated iconographical features of Egyptians and Black Africans when composing the Le Puy image",[27] which would explain the racially Black appearance.

However, the Le Puy Virgin was not consistently shown as dark from this point and appears as fair-skinned and blonde in 16th-century woodcuts. Following the Jesuit influx into Puy, she appears as dark, adorning the cover of Odo de Gissey's history of Notre Dame. She appears again as dark in a 1657 compendium of Marian pilgrimage sites. Scheer finds that it was another century until such depictions actually became commonplace in the votive plaques of the supplicants at Black Madonna shrines.[28] Before 1739, the plaques at Teising and Altötting show a White Virgin. By 1750 they are always depicted as Black. It being unlikely that both statues (which are of different ages) turned black over ten years, Scheer pinpoints this as the time when perception of the Madonnas changed and her blackness became popularly construed as a racial marker.

The last etching of the Le Puy Madonna made from direct observation was by Veyrenc, the illustrator of Barthèlemy Faujas de St-Fond in 1777, sixteen years before the statue was destroyed at the hands of revolutionaries. Faujas St-Fond was a geologist working in the area rather than an art historian or affiliated with the Church, and recorded the statue's appearance in his memoirs. In his analysis, Faujas St-Fond compares her skin to that of 'Ethiopians or Moors', and despite his insistence that he would only provide a scientific description of the statue, he appears influenced by the Egyptian origin legend, comparing her enthroned pose to that of Egyptian statues.[29] On further examination he found that the wooden statue had been covered in a thin gauze, which we know today indicates a method of marouflage for repainting the statue, yet he likened it to the bandages of an Egyptian mummy, therefore finding this proof enough of the statue's Ancient Egyptian origins!

An 18th-century redrawing of Odo de Gissey's frontispiece

---

[27] Foster 2016b: 12

[28] Scheer 2002: 1422

[29] Foster 2016b: 8

notably changed the colour of the Virgin's skin and removed the *Nigra sum sed Formosa* line, in a deliberate reimagining that moves away from the Jesuit's emphasis. By the 19th century, race seemed to be the only interpretation of the Black Madonnas' colour in secular circles, and usually not in a positive light. The *Song of Songs* exception was all but forgotten and Scheer quotes Karl Marx amongst others, talking about the ugliness of Black Madonnas: "Bad as your portrait is, it serves me to the best purposes, and now I understand how even the 'black Madonnas', the most offensive of the portraits of the divine mother, could find indestructible veneration, and even more venerators than the good portraits"[30] She also finds the first explicit description of a Black Madonna as African – not counting the implied ethnicity of the Ethiopian Bride of the *Song of Songs* – in a quote from Johann Wolfgang von Goethe in 1816:

> *"How the most unhappy of all appearances could have crept in – that probably for Egyptian or Abyssinian reasons, the Mother of God is portrayed as brown, and the face of Our Savior printed on Veronica's veil was also given a moorish colour – may be clarified when that part of art history is more closely examined".*[31]

As, over the centuries, the significance of the statues' colour being a mark of its age and authenticity became lost, communities struggled to rationalise why they would appear to be black-skinned. Thus the 'candle smoke' explanation took hold. Scheer comments that this notion that 'Mary wasn't originally black' fits the narrative of the late 19th and early 20th century, where European apparitions of the Virgin such as at Lourdes emphasised her appearance as a White European woman.[32]

MODERN REINTERPRETATION

So we come to the 20th-century reinterpretation of the statues' significance. Chances are, that if you have read a book about the Black Madonna written in the 20th century, it will claim the Black Madonna is the continuation of the worship of a goddess cult from ancient times, symbolizing the blackness of the fertile earth, and

---

[30] Scheer 2002: 1438
[31] Scheer 2002: 1438
[32] Scheer 2002: 1439

sometimes that the statues are literally recycled images of Demeter, Isis, and others, redressed as the Virgin Mary. According to Scheer, this idea goes back at least as far as 1835 to Jakob Grimm, who in his *Deutsche Mythologie* makes this connection:

> *"the ancients also depicted the wrathful earth goddess Demeter as black... indeed from time to time, even her daughter Persephone, the fair maiden... Pausanius mentions the black Aphrodite (Melanis)... [T]he Ephesian black Diana is well known, as is the fact that in the Middle Ages, black images of Mary were carved and painted; the Holy Virgin appears then as a mourning goddess of the earth or the night: images such as this at Loretto, Naples, Einsiedeln, Würzburg... Ottingen... Puy... Marseilles and elsewhere".*[33]

This connection was expanded upon by French scholars Marie Durand Lefebvre in 1937 and Emile Saillens in 1945; and was presented to an English-speaking audience for the first time mid-20th century, by anthropologist Leonard Moss at a conference of the American Association for the Advancement of Science in 1952 during which priests and nuns allegedly walked out in disgust.

The very idea that there is a great mystery surrounding the Black Madonnas, described in works such as Ean Begg's *The Cult of the Black Virgin,* as being about the secret goddess in Christianity and a survival of pagan traditions has fueled enthusiasts for the last few decades. Stephen Benko's *The Virgin Goddess* cites examples of Black Madonna churches being built over former temples dedicated to goddesses as proof of this. Despite the fact that the intention behind building upon pagan sites was more probably about erasure than integration, it is easy to see how it is tempting to believe when we actively look for this kind of evidence to support our own theories. For example, an 11th-century legend of St George says that the city of Puy was called 'Vetula' when he founded the church there. Vetula means 'old woman' in Latin, and a word linked in another medieval saint (Eligius)'s hagiography in a list of condemned pagan practices that were still occurring. The making of 'vetulas' is mentioned implying the creation of images such as corn dollies to represent the goddess. We could therefore surmise that the Black Madonna of Le Puy is a descendent of a Gaulish deity of this name and state it as true because it 'feels' right.

---

[33] Grimm 1835: 195 in Scheer 2002: 1418

To take another example, Jean Markale instead invokes the name of the mountain, Anis, to also provide a link to the Celtic past, suggesting the Black Madonna of Le Puy is a relation of the goddess Ana and the hag Black Annis.[34] When we look for patterns in the etymology of names, we can mislead ourselves that there is a connection there, especially if it reinforces our own beliefs. When pagan artefacts survive the coming of the Church, such as the Fever Stone at Le Puy, they are cited as proof of continued practices not just as a physical survivor of a pre-Christian age. Yet it should be considered that their survival alone is not proof of this.

Scheer was one of the first to criticise the continuation school of thought as lacking in evidence, particularly around Black Madonnas taking on not only the likeness of pre-Christian statues but their cultic meanings. She states that such writers find multiple symbolic significances in her colour, yet ignore cases where the same meanings have been applied to White Madonnas. She equally criticises those who deny that the figures have any particular significance, and argues that in the preoccupation with *why* she is Black, which veers between the power and mystery cited by the continuation theorists at one end, to the accidental candle soot theories at the other, both sides fail to pick up on the actual historical significance of the colour which has changed over time since the statues' creation.[35] As the meaning of ancient and Eastern origin were forgotten, replaced with the early-modern idea that the colour could only be about race, discussions on the Black Madonnas have been fogged ever since. As avidly as the voice of the Church has tried to rationalise why medieval people would portray Mary as racially Black, there are those of pagan and goddess communities who project modern beliefs about ancient origins onto them. If you start from your conclusion and try to find evidence, you can usually find something that will support that particular belief. In attempting to prove an unbroken line of goddess worship, it is possible to 'reverse engineer' it, using Black Madonna images as evidence, whilst not fully examining their medieval context. Although the theories are not all about skin colour but include symbolism of the fertile soil, and the blackness

---

[34] Markale 2004: 176
[35] Scheer 2002: 1419-20

of Jungian archetypes, the starting point nevertheless always seems to be the early-modern idea of the colour being about race. Historicizing the meaning of the colour is the only way to get past this idea and as Scheer says, demystify it.[36]

MARY THE EGYPTIAN

We return again finally to the Black Virgin of Le Puy, 'the Egyptian', and examine it in light of these conclusions about colour. Modern audiences have, ever since the analysis of St-Fond, speculated about the possibility that this statue was based on or indeed was a surviving representation of Isis with the infant Horus. This is due in part to the repeated mentions of Egypt throughout it, and Le Puy's legendary history.[37] However, as we have seen, the connotation of the word Egyptian in the medieval era was with the biblical 'East' rather than ancient Egypt. The story of the carving by Jeremiah inspired this Egyptian connection, and Odo de Gissey's writings cemented it, steering St-Fond's analysis, at a time when interest in ancient Egypt was in vogue at the end of the 18th century. However, if this were a statue of Isis, as he hypothesised, why did it have features more associated with medieval Marian statues, such as the reliquary?

Agnes Bernard gathered a 21st-century perspective on the Le Puy Madonna and why she is black from the clergy and congregation of the church, which show the power of the repetition of some of the aforementioned theories. The Rector of Notre-Dame-du-Puy gives a rather rambling explanation that includes that she absorbs our sins like candle smoke, is symbolically more relatable to all than a White Virgin, is a reference to the *Song of Songs*, and even throws in for consideration that Mary says in the Gospel "He covered me in his shadow".[38] Others working at or involved with Le Puy claim that the colour of the statue is unimportant, rather it is what it points to that is important and to which they pray. Yet in the same breath they state that the colour is important in attracting pilgrims because it looks 'different' and is

---

[36] Scheer 2002: 1440
[37] Such as the founding saint Front becoming conflated with Fronto of Nitria, giving him Egyptian origin.
[38] Bernard 2011: 5-6

a talking point to open up discussion. Whereas historically Black Madonnas may have been used to appeal to Muslims and others as being more relatable, today the attraction is certainly more about her 'otherness', a perception of her subversive nature within the Church. Bernard finds that such images are indeed a propaganda tool to this day, though her interviewees disagreed, not liking the connotations of the word propaganda, preferring to think of the Black Virgin as a 'communication medium'. However, this is essentially the same thing. Just like how the medieval connotations with the blackness of the Black Virgin statues were forgotten, modern audiences have become unfamiliar with the origin of the word propaganda, which was only turned from a neutral term to one meaning biased (and usually political) messaging in the 20th century. The word came into use in 1622 when the Catholic Church formed a new body, the *Congregation de Propaganda Fide* as a means of propagating their faith during the Counter-Reformation. The role of the Le Puy Madonna as a communication tool which Bernard's interviewees speak about, in that she speaks to people of different backgrounds in different ways, is more akin to the original meaning of the word propaganda, yet this is a word with which they all heavily resist association.[39] This goes to show that the changing of a concept over time can create far-reaching change in how we think about and interpret the past. From our standpoint in the 21st century we attempt to make sense of hundreds of years of shifting meaning, but without careful historiography we can confuse ourselves and others, through the repetition of popular stories.

CONCLUSION

When we examine Black Madonnas in this way, which some might call 'debunking' their mystery, are we rejecting them and saying that they should hold no particular significance to a modern audience (as some authors have suggested)? I would argue that this is not the case and that gaining a greater awareness of fact, fiction, historiography and reinterpretation does not preclude a spiritual connection with the Black Madonna or recognition of the power

---

[39] Bernard 2011: 11

her image holds today. The fact of the matter is that a phenomenon has developed, through a weaving of history and legend over centuries, which influences believers today and supports many in a pastoral sense. This connection with divinity through the use of symbolism is no less real than it has ever been, and in later sections we will examine what the Black Madonna means to people today.

CHAPTER 3

Mountain Mother
Our Lady of Montserrat

We move from France over the border into Catalonia, an autonomous region in northeastern Spain. Not far from the large city of Barcelona is the mountain abode of another of Europe's most famous Black Madonnas, Our Lady of Montserrat. For all that this statue conforms to Salliens' list of 'authentic' Black Madonnas that we mostly find in France, this region has a different ethnic dynamic, moulded by Muslim rule and consequent Christian reconquest. I had heard that this was one of the most impressive examples of a Black Madonna and in a fantastic setting, so I arranged a trip to see her for myself.

A VISIT TO MONTSERRAT

On a chilly November morning I took the rack railway up to Montserrat – literally 'serrated mountain' in Catalan. The distinctive fragmentary rock formations stand out from the other rolling peaks surrounding Barcelona, and are surely why the mountain has attracted attention for centuries. Interest in the mountain dates back to Roman times, when it is said a temple of Venus stood there, and probably even farther back than that.

My fellow passengers and I passed through a ring of cloud ascending the mountain on the Cremallera, the railway line that has served Monserrat since 1892, and once through it we were suddenly in another place, Her domain, the Lady of the Mountain. Passing the cable car – the other way up the mountain, the train alighted opposite the monastery plaza. The monastery has perched on a small shelf at 700m above sea level and some 500m below the ultimate peak of the mountain since the 11th century. Several chapels are also dotted around the dips and summits, the most famous being the 'grotto' chapel, said to be the spot where the statue of Our Lady of Montserrat was first found.

My first destination was the monastery's basilica. The queue had already formed along the right-hand cloister. There is no escaping tourists on a trip to Montserrat. The draw of one of the most famous Black Madonnas in Europe, coupled with the impressive scenery brings tourists in their droves even in winter. Entering the ornate basilica, already crowded with visitors, the first glimpse of Our Lady is in the archway above the altar, shining in the baroque darkness of the surrounding church. Unlike at Chartres, where the Madonna has since been relegated to a side chapel, here she is the star of the show. High up and behind the altar, she sits in a niche which is entered by a side passage. The silhouettes of the faithful (and the touristic) can be made out, having mere seconds to pray in front of Our Lady, or in many cases take a photograph with her, before being moved along. Saving the close-up experience for later, I next visited the Museum of Montserrat.

Besides featuring art of the local area and archaeological finds, the Museum has a section devoted entirely to the Black Madonna. Her image has been reproduced scores of times over the last few centuries. Later in the chapter, I will explore the topic of her presentation as racially Black in some of these paintings and sculptures. On exiting the Museum, I found that the warm winter sun had burnt away the clouds, affording wonderful views down the mountain.

I next undertook the 30-minute walk down to Santa Cova, the chapel marking the place where legend states that the statue was found. After the heavily crowded parts of the monastery, the walk felt decidedly more spiritual; the route gently winding around the natural curves of the mountain. It occurred to me that despite the name being 'serrated mountain', the outcrops are far softer, and reminiscent of the soft pads of fingers. Looking back up at the monastery and the peaks beyond I imagined them as the giant hand of the Mountain Mother gently cradling her worshippers, which inspired a painting of her that I produced on my return.

Above: "Montserrat – Mountain Mother". Our Lady of Montserrat, is patron saint of Catalonia and sits in a monastery high up in the clouds. Rather than sharp serrated rocks, which its name implies, the mountain reminded me of the smooth pads of fingers. I decided to draw the mountain as a great hand of the earth mother, cradling the Black Madonna image, who herself holds the globe of the earth in her hand.

This walk to Santa Cova, a mini-pilgrimage within a pilgrimage is marked out with sculptures, mosaics and reliefs depicting the Stations of the Cross. For the Christian pilgrim familiar with these images, they provide a rhythm and an anticipation of the end destination. For the non-Christian, the views across the valley are inspiring enough to keep anyone pressing on. At this time of year, dark brown acorns litter the path, reminiscent of the shape and colour of the face of Our Lady, who is nicknamed 'La Moreneta' – 'little dark one'.

The Chapel, small and cruciform, appears to have been squeezed under a bulge of rock that looks ready to absorb it. Inside, one wall is open to the bare rock, and there on a shelf above the main altar is a replica of the statue that sits up in the monastery. Although much less crowded than the main church, there were still plenty of visitors who were undeterred by the fact this was not the 'real' statue. Here it is much more possible to take a personal moment with the Black Madonna, to light a candle, sit quietly for as long as one likes, or go up to touch the foot of the statue, as I witnessed many people doing.

Back at the basilica I joined the queue, which had not dwindled all day, and made my way up the gilded passageway to the niche of Our Lady of Montserrat. The statue itself was bigger than I had anticipated, standing at almost a metre in height, with the handsome dark face and hands of mother and child contrasting beautifully against her gilded clothing and opulent surroundings. She is almost entirely encased, with only the globe and her hand being available for pilgrims to touch. Touch is a powerful and underrated sense in terms of pilgrimage. Being able to lay a hand on a holy object, to then touch it to one's head or heart creates a lasting connection. Although brief, being able to not only see but touch something so precious and ancient provides a surely satisfying moment for most pilgrims.

Once past the niche of the Black Madonna, we discover the Lady Chapel, set behind her, with a view of the statue's back as its main focus! A statue of St Jordi (St George), patron of Catalonia, also inhabits the elliptical chapel. Once outside, a walkway filled with visitor candles stands testament to the devotion of thousands.

The mountain itself seems inextricable from the Virgin. It

features prominently in almost every painting of her in the Museum and around the site. The hymn *Virolai* that is sung daily to her in the basilica echoes this; its first lines being: "Rose of April, Dark Lady of the Mountains, Star of Montserrat". As with many Black Madonnas, she is deeply entwined with the history and geography of her locality. This inevitably prompts theories about her existence as a pre-Christian mountain goddess here, though you won't find mention of such in any of the books for sale at Montserrat. For Catalans, her significance is in her protection of the locality. This particular form of Mary belongs to them and they to Her.

I think in order to experience Montserrat as a pilgrim one must accept that the tourist aspect of the site is inescapable. The popularity of the sanctuary is unlikely to wane and the crowds must simply be accepted. Making a return visit having seen all the sights and tourist distractions, browsed the gift shops and ridden the funiculars, it may become easier to make a more personal pilgrimage, to spend time in the basilica or chapel without worrying about the time of the last train back to Barcelona. This is of course not to say that many visitors here are not simultaneously tourists and pilgrims. In today's world of relatively easy travel, holidays that combine sightseeing with a yearning for spiritual experience are becoming more popular and possible.

HISTORY OF THE MOTHER OF MONTSERRAT

The iconic mountain location has been attractive to the monastic lifestyle for centuries, with evidence suggesting hermitages on Montserrat since the 7th century. The first documented mention of churches on the mountain comes from 888 when their lands were donated by the Count of Barcelona to the Monastery of Ripoll. However, it was not until 1025 that monks from Ripoll established a Benedictine community on the mountain and built the Monastery of Santa Maria.[1] Despite the legend suggesting a very early date for the Black Madonna, it is unlikely that a statue was present in the monastery church in its early years, as the statue has been dated to the end of the 12th century. This dating is based on a number of factors: the statue conforms to the

---

[1] Pérez 2018: 24-5

Romanesque 'seated in Wisdom' pose popular at the time, the basilica was modified at the end of the 12th century, possibly to accommodate more pilgrims, and ecclesiastical records start to show an abundance of donations for votive lamps at the altar, suggesting the introduction of a cult statue at this time. A book from the latter 12th century records miracles at Montserrat, but there is no mention of a statue; the first direct reference being in the late 13th-century songbook *Las Cantigas de Santa María*. This text refers to the specific local variant of the Virgin of Montserrat and that her miraculous reputation was widespread,[2] suggesting that it must have originated during that century.

The legend, as with most Black Madonna origin stories, gives ancient provenance to the statue, and is also typical in its explanation of the statue's remote location. The story states that the figure was carved by St Luke, and brought to Catalonia from Jerusalem by St Peter following Muslim occupation of the city. In apparent response to the Muslim occupation of Catalonia in the 9th century, the statue was hidden in a cave (Santa Cova) until in 880. Shepherds saw a glowing light and heard angelic singing emanating from the cave, and on investigation accompanied by the local bishop they discovered the statue. They decided to take the statue to the more accessible neighbouring town of Manresa, but in typical Black Madonna fashion, she obstinately refused to move and grew heavy, thus explaining why she stayed in Montserrat.[3]

The statue itself faces directly forward with the Child Jesus sat squarely on her lap, unaided by her touch. He holds a pineapple, supposedly a later addition from when the hands of both Mother and Child were replaced after damage done in the war of 1811-12. Before this he held an orb, as does his mother, which is said to symbolise the Universe.[4] Tests in 2001 found the original statue to be polychrome, turned dark by either a chemical reaction of the silver in the varnish used or the age-old explanation of smoke accretion. It was proven that she had been painted black at some point to recreate this characteristic, probably during the 19th

---

[2] Foster 2016a: 31

[3] Pérez 2018: 42

[4] Pérez 2018: 39-40

century when it was hidden away due to war and heavily restored in secret whilst a copy stood in its place.[5]

RACIALLY BLACK?

The legend of the statue's origins was first introduced in the early 16th century by Abbot Burgos of Montserrat and was also the first to make mention of her *morena* (brown) tone.[6] The story emphasises the threat to Our Lady from Muslims twice-over – in Jerusalem and again in 9th-century Catalonia. It would appear her colour first became a notable factor at this time because of contemporary feelings about the racial complexion of Catalonia.

Foster argues that although it is likely that the colour of the Black Madonnas originally had nothing to do with race, in the case of Our Lady of Montserrat, we should factor in how "devotion to *La Moreneta* must be viewed in its Iberian context, where the historical presence and continued memory of a non-Christian 'other' that was often conceived of as non-white may have altered the understanding of the sculpture's dark colour".[7] Following dissemination of the legend, descriptions and depictions of her as Black in terms of race continue from the 16th century. By this time, Spain was firmly a Christian kingdom once again, but with echoes of Islamic culture that it could not escape. The 16th and 17th-century miracles of the Virgin of Montserrat seem to become increasingly focused on anxieties about Muslims in their midst, often depicting them as violent savages to be converted.[8] Foster shows that, because of this, the Virgin came to be seen as a response to this Muslim presence – a protector and a conversion tool[9] – rationalising her dark skin. As we will see in later chapters, this was also given as a reason for the dark complexion of some of the Madonnas in the New World around the same time – that having a similar skin tone made them appealing to the native people that the Spanish wished to convert.

One of the most oft-repeated legends about the Lady of

---

[5] Foster 2016a: 44
[6] Foster 2016a: 39
[7] Foster 2016a: 22
[8] Foster 2016a: 40-1
[9] Foster 2016a: 23

Montserrat tells how a painter began to retouch the statue but as soon as his brush touched it, he fell blind. After three months of praying to the Virgin his sight was restored and he vowed her appearance should never again be altered because it is a sacred work not of human hands. Foster suggests a sort of chicken-and-egg scenario for the origin of this story. Whilst some may think it proves the importance of her blackness, it could be an explanation for a recent repainting of the statue: "a cautionary tale to those who not only might wanted to lighten the image, but also to those who suspected her blackness was perhaps not as miraculous as her legend purported".[10]

IMAGERY OF THE MOUNTAIN MOTHER

Visual renderings of the statue certainly did not depict its dark colour from its inception. The late 13th-century *Cantigas de Santa María* contain four miracles in which the Virgin of Montserrat is illustrated but her colour is not mentioned. She is fair-skinned in the pictures, though Foster deduced that this did not necessarily mean that the statue was white. The images of the Virgin are generic and in line with other Marian depictions in the book, so it is quite possible that the artist had never seen or had no visual reference for the Montserrat statue,[11] whether it was polychrome or dark by this time. As present in the images as the Virgin herself are the mountains of Montserrat, and it is this attachment which Foster says was the most important identifying characteristic of the Virgin at the time rather than her colour or appearance.[12]

The later *Llibre Vermell* (late 14th/early 15th-century) mentions her dark colour in two miracle tales including the story of the blinded painter, but still does not depict her as so in its drawings, another probable case of the artist either not having seen the statue or not seeing it as important that they give a faithful rendering of the statue. It was, after all, just another artistic representation in itself. It does however once again show the mountain as a visual marker of 'who she is' and the locale to which she belongs.[13] In

---

[10] Foster 2016a: 43
[11] Foster 2016a: 32
[12] Foster 2016a: 34
[13] Ibid.

these, the mountain almost becomes her throne, a stylistic choice repeated in later imagery. Followers of the theory that Black Madonnas inherited the thrones of pre-Christian goddesses might see this as an indicator of an antecedent such as Cybele, the Mountain Mother, who is associated with other Black Virgin sites such as Tindari in Sicily, though there is not enough supporting evidence to suggest continuation of any cultic goddess worship on Montserrat.

She continues to be depicted as light-skinned throughout the 15th and 16th centuries. As mentioned in the previous chapter, renderings in print of Black Madonnas as dark – and therefore perception of these statues in terms of skin colour – did not widely occur until the Jesuit promotion of the *Nigra sum sed Formosa* connection became widespread in the 17th century. As with the Black Madonna of Le Puy, early modern ideas about race and ethnicity have muddled what we today think the dark colour signified in the Middle Ages, allowing for the myths about pagan origins to flourish and the colour to take precedence.

CONCLUSION

Which is more significant? That the statue was not originally dark or that it spent the majority of its existence as brown or black? To the majority of modern respondents, it is likely to be the latter. Foster predicts a similar outcry to that at Chartres if the black paint of Our Lady of Montserrat were ever to be removed, despite it not being original. To modern audiences, it is an integral part of her identity – a sign of her power and exceptionality, not the antiquity and association with the Holy Land of medieval audiences.[14] However, besides the argument of historical accuracy versus spiritual authenticity, erasure of images that are perceived by many as racially Black in our modern age opens up a whole raft of suspicions as to the intentions of those in charge of these public images.

The portraits of Our Lady to be found in the Museum of Montserrat which are from the 17th to 20th century unfailingly depict her as dark-skinned. The connection with the mountain is

---

[14] Foster 2016a: 46

not lost, being present in almost every image. The Virgin is usually depicted as towering over the region, as in a 19th-century piece where her throne hovers in the cloud cover above the monastery.

Interestingly, a variant design appears with an ornate golden crown on the Virgin's head. The painting, *The Mother of God of Montserrat on a Throne of Red Velvet,* is an anonymous work brought from Mexico in 1627 and the crown is in fact akin to that of the original Lady of Guadalupe in Extremadura, the namesake of the Mexican Virgin of Guadalupe. This form of Our Lady of Montserrat, sometimes called *La Mexicana,* is copied in further images produced in the 17th century which feature increasingly ornate crowns. Foster presents a fascinating theory that works of art from the New World may have provided a reverse influence on how the Black Madonna of Montserrat was viewed ethnically. Whilst images such as our Lady of Guadalupe in Mexico were based on Spanish designs, it is thought that they were made purposely dark to appeal to the Indigenes. Images sent back to Spain that also presented Mary in this way may have strengthened the racial interpretation of her skin, which was already being considered at this time because of the Muslim presence in the region.[15] In the next chapter we will look in depth at the Lady of Guadalupe and its native and Spanish influences.

---

[15] Foster 2016a: 49-50

CHAPTER 4

Standing in the Shadow of Guadalupe

INTRODUCTION

In this chapter, we will visit Mexico to examine the cult of the most popular manifestation of Mary in the Americas and its most famous Black (or Brown) Madonna – Our Lady of Guadalupe. We have already encountered discussion of the European images of Mary being possibly influenced by the imagery and traits of pre-Christian goddesses, but here we see it happening in a more immediate way, as the deities and living traditions of Indigenous people were woven into this apparition. In the post-conquest era of the history of the Americas, the people's deities were suddenly replaced by an alien god of whom they had to make sense. The translation of fundamental religious ideas such as the son/sun as the saviour and the mother as a maternal, fertile force helped the Nahua (the people of what became Mexico) accept these new beings into their lives and core beliefs.

The Virgin of Guadalupe is the likeness of an apparition to native new Christian convert Juan Diego in 1531. It is the only 'truly supernatural' appearance of Mary in the Americas, the other Marian cults arising around discovered statues.[1] The legend states that Mary was said to have appeared to the man on a mountainside and conversed with him in his own language, giving him the task of convincing the Bishop to have a chapel erected to her on the site of their meeting. Diego had difficulty in his task, not only from the Bishop's doubt about his claims, but from his own self-doubt about his worth. Eventually, a miracle occurred involving the

---

[1] Gebara and Bingemar 1989: 144

Opposite: 'Guadalupe-Tonantzin'. Like much of the folk art of Mexico and the USA featuring Our Lady of Guadalupe, this painting displaces her from her usual setting. Here she stands amongst the carvings of her predecessors. Looming above her is the statuesque body of Coatlicue, two headed snake goddess and mother of all. On the right is the maiden Xochiquetzal, a deity of fertility, butterflies and flowers. On the left is the grandmother, Toci, sometimes conflated with Tlazolteotl, the sin eater. She rides a broomstick and grasps a serpent in her hands. And beneath the feet of Guadalupe, replacing the cherub who holds up the lunar crescent, is the dark moon goddess, the forgotten daughter Coyolxauhqui. Her body is torn and dismembered by the male sun god in an act of war and domination. All of these elements can be seen as contributing to the personage of Guadalupe as understood by the Nahua when she was adopted as their new precious mother 'Tonantzin', the epithet they had previously given to their goddesses.

image of Mary being revealed on the *tilma* (cloak) of Juan Diego; convincing the Bishop of his story's validity.

The significance of the image, which has become one of the most iconic features of Mexican culture, is in the cultural blending of influences, present not only in the image, but also in the story of its origin, and its timing at the inception of a new people, born of the mixing of the Spanish conquerors and the native Nahua. Guadalupe can be classified as a Black Madonna because of her brown-skinned, Indigenous appearance. She is often affectionately called 'La Morenita' (Little Dark Lady). The icon bears the hallmarks of both European and Aztec art, just as her likeness resembles the newly emerging *mestizo*[1] people. She is ostensibly an apparition of Mary from the future, taking the form of the Mexican people to come.

The phenomenon of the Virgin of Guadalupe can be examined in several parts; the visitations and the telling of them, the iconic image itself, and the miracles it is said to have wrought, not to mention its very survival and origin, which inspires wondrous claims about its supernatural properties. We will look at what her perceived ethnicity means to her devotees, and also look at what could be called her 'shadow aspects' – the figures of La Malinche, La Llorona and Santa Muerte, who are, to an extent, reflections of her, and are as intrinsic to Mexican culture and identity as the Virgin herself.

We will also look at the social significance of the Virgin to the Mexican and Mexican-American people, women in particular, and the thread that draws them all together. As much as possible, I have sought the writings of Mexican authors and those who have interviewed mestiza women, to gain authentic insight and give as much vocality to the people to whom this heritage belongs.

THE WRITTEN SOURCES

The fullest and most significant account of the apparitions is the *Nican Mopohua* ('Here It Is Told'), a short manuscript that has been dated to the mid-16th-century and due to its linguistic style, is

---

[1] People of mixed Spanish and Indian heritage.

widely attributed to native Nahua scholar Antonio Valeriano. The *Nican Mopohua* was first published much later, in 1649, within a compilation known as the *Huei Tlamahuiçoltica* (The Great Event), by Luis Lasso de la Vega, chaplain of the shrine of Guadalupe, who is thought to have used Valeriano's text. Valeriano had worked closely with Bernadino de Sahagún, a Franciscan friar who had come to New Spain (as Mexico was then called) as a missionary, devoting many years to the study of the Aztec culture and language. Arguably, this was a conversion tool, allowing Sahagún to convey the Christian message to the people in their own language. One might expect the writings of a religious man of a conquering culture to include only bias and portrayal of the natives as savages, but he was meticulous in his recording of pre-Conquest Mexican culture. His works are regarded as faithful, even pro-Nahua, and he commended his student Valeriano highly.

The events of the *Nican Mopohua* are corroborated by a Nahuatl translation of an account by the interpreter to Archbishop Zumárraga, Juan Gonzalez, who would have been present to translate the conversations with Juan Diego.[2] Curiously, however, Zumárraga, a prolific writer, left no account of his own; a fact often highlighted by sceptics. The Franciscan archbishop was succeeded by a Dominican, Alonso de Montúfar, who promoted the Guadalupan cult. The Franciscan leader Francisco de Bustamante countered by accusing the devotees of the chapel of superstitious idolatry and worship of the Nahua goddess under the guise of Mary; suggesting that the image was not miraculous but a mere painting by a native (thought to be Marcos Cipac de Aquino, an artist of the time). Archbishop Montúfar responded by later removing the chapel from Franciscan hands.

Another piece of evidence surfaced in the 1990s, reportedly the earliest account of the apparitions of 1531. It is a single parchment known as the Codex Escalada, named after the man who brought it to light in 1995. This piece depicts the event in pictorial form and bears both the dates 1531, and 1548, which it records as the year of the death of Juan Diego. Significantly it also shows a figure drawn in the two-dimensional native style labelled 'Judge Antonio

---

[2] Rodriguez 1994: 18

Valeriano' and a signature taken to be that of Bernadino de Sahagún. Assessments of the piece have deemed the signature to be real and the parchment to date to the mid-16th century. However, it is suggested that it is later than 1565 when Valeriano first became a Judge-Governor. Detractors have been suspicious of the codex's authenticity, particularly when its publication in 1997 came midway between Diego's beatification in 1990 and canonization in 2002, and only served to record his death rather than add anything further to the tale. It appeared to be convenient proof at a time when certain Catholic schools of thought were doubting that Juan Diego ever existed.

The inclusion of Sahagún's signature was another cause for suspicion, due to the strong reservations he held about the cult in later life. Like his fellow Franciscan, Bustamante, Sahagún wrote that the cult's popularity was likely nothing more than lip service to the new religion who used the same name, Tonantzin ('Our Mother'), for Mary and for their own Mother Goddess.[3] He writes: "[O]n Tepeyacac… they had a temple consecrated to the mother of the gods, called Tonantzin, which means 'our mother'…and people came from afar… and they brought many offerings" (*Historia General* [1956] 3: 352).[4] Tepeyac was the site of the apparition and later church site, and he suggests the motivation for their continued visits being allegiance to the goddess. However, supporters of the Codex's authenticity could point to the fact that Sahagún's work had previously been sympathetic to the Nahua, and it was only in later years that he was forced to issue pro-Spain revisions and translations, for fear of association with any potential native uprising.

The Church appears to have been well aware of the significance of the site, and as at so many other sites in Europe, the new religion was overlaid on sites of the old, in an attempt to eradicate it. The Council of Lima in 1552 ordered "that all the cult idols and edifices found in the villages where Christian Indians reside be burned and destroyed, and if the site is suitable, a church or at least a cross

---

[3] Sahagún observed the same attention paid to Saint Anne, as Toci, 'Our Grandmother', far more adoration than her personage would normally attract, suggesting a continued worship of Toci under a new name. Sahagún p.90
[4] Oleszkiewicz-Peralba 2007: 52

should be planted there."[5] However, the Church unintentionally facilitated the synthesizing of the old Goddess with the new, rather than eradicating her. Temples might be destroyed but she would always reside in the ground beneath them. F. Gonzalez-Crussi imagines Tonantzin buried beneath the foundations of the new temple to the Mother, her chthonic power influencing the shaping of the Virgin's cult.[6] This brings to mind the proverb: *"They tried to bury us; they didn't know we were seeds"*, which has become popular within the Chicano[7] movement in recent years. Although frequently mislabelled as an old Mexican saying, and in fact a paraphrase of Greek poet Dino Christianopoulos from the 1970s, its reappropriation neatly describes the struggles of Indigenous people and their histories, as well as the enduring underground current of the Black Madonna worldwide.

THE GUADALUPE MYTH

I will briefly relate the story as it appears in the English translation of the *Nican Mopohua*, a narration of the apparition in Nahuatl, the Indigenous language.

In the year 1531, Juan Diego, a native convert and man of Cuauhtitlán, was travelling near the hill of Tepeyac at dawn, when he heard delightful singing, sweeter than birdsong. Wondering if he had stepped into a heavenly realm, he looked to the peak of the hill from where the music originated, in the direction of the rising sun. The singing stopped and a voice called his name. Juan Diego approached, a feeling of calm and peace washing over him. At the top of the hill stood a maiden radiant as the sun, who made her surroundings also shine, like jewels beyond earthly beauty.

The lady asked Juan Diego where he was going, to which he answered that he was going to church in Mexico-Tlatilolco to worship God. "Know, be sure, my dearest-and-youngest son" she addressed him, "that I am the Perfect Ever-Virgin Holy Mary, mother of the one great God of truth who gives us life"[8]. She told

---

[5] Oleszkiewicz-Peralba 2007: 53
[6] Gonzalez-Crussi in Castillo 1996: 5-7
[7] *Chicano* normally refers to Mexican-Americans or Mexicans in the US. Whilst sometimes being a slur, it is also a title reclaimed by the pro-Indigenous movement.
[8] *Nican Mopohua*: 26

him that she desired her place of worship to be built where they stood, and asked him to go to the Bishop of Mexico City as her emissary, to deliver her request, and tell the Bishop all that he had seen and heard.

Juan Diego took leave of the Virgin and went directly to Mexico City and the palace of the Bishop, a Franciscan named Juan de Zumárraga. On finally obtaining an audience with the Bishop, Juan Diego related his story, though in response the Bishop was quite unmoved. Juan Diego returned to Tepeyac where Our Lady awaited him. He explained that he did not think the Bishop believed him, being just a poor Indian, and begged that she send someone of greater esteem to carry her word. The Virgin assured him that she had no lack of other servants to whom she could assign the duty, but was quite sure that it was he alone that she wished to perform this task, so begged and ordered him to return to the Bishop.

On the following day, Juan Diego attended Mass, and then sought out the Bishop once more. Again, he struggled to be seen, but eventually was able to recount everything he had witnessed. Although the Bishop listened, he told Juan Diego that his word was not enough, and to return with proof that his request really came from the Queen of Heaven. On dismissing Juan Diego, he had his servants follow the man, but on approaching Tepeyac they lost sight of him. Angered by this, the servants returned to the Bishop and told him not to believe Juan Diego, vowing to prevent him from seeing the Bishop again. Meanwhile, the Virgin happily agreed to provide Juan Diego with a sign and asked him to return the next day.

However, Juan Diego was unable to return the next day, as his uncle Juan Bernardino was taken gravely ill. Thinking he was nearing the end, Juan Bernardino sent his nephew to fetch a priest to administer the last rites. Juan Diego decided to avoid Tepeyac, lest he be diverted from his urgent mission. Taking a different path, Juan Diego was met by the Virgin nonetheless, who had descended the hill to meet him. Ashamed at having avoided her, Juan Diego told her of his uncle. He vowed to come back the following day to complete his task. The Virgin allayed his worries, and told him not to fear for his uncle, who at that moment would be made well.

Comforted, Juan Diego agreed to go to the Bishop with a sign. Our Lady directed him to the top of the hill to gather the flowers he found there and return to her. At the summit he was amazed to find an abundance of flowers blooming out of season on the normally barren earth. He cut them and carried them in his tilma back to the Virgin, who took up the flowers in her hands and placed them back in his tilma. She sent Juan Diego back to the city and bade him only open his tilma once alone with the Bishop.

On reaching the palace of the Bishop, Juan Diego was kept waiting by the house staff, who tried to take his precious offering away from him. Juan Diego resisted, and eventually was granted audience with the Bishop. He related his most recent meeting with the Virgin to Zumárraga, and then let the flowers tumble from his tilma to the floor. There, imprinted on the fabric was the image of Our Lady. The Bishop wept in awe and sadness, begging Juan Diego to forgive him for not believing him.

Following the encounter, Juan Diego showed the Bishop where the Virgin wanted her chapel to be built. He then took his leave to check on his uncle, who had made a full recovery as the Virgin promised. Juan Bernardino told his nephew, and the church officials who had accompanied him, of the visitation he had also received at the moment he was healed; describing the Virgin in exactly the same way as Juan Diego. She had told him to go to the Bishop to tell of how he had been healed and to name her image the Perfect Virgin, Holy Mary of Guadalupe.

The church was then built on Tepeyac and the image of Our Lady of Guadalupe moved there, becoming the focus for the adoration of the whole of Mexico City.

WHAT'S IN A NAME?

In assessing the story, we must consider differences in language. The account was first written in Nahuatl before translation into Spanish. There are subtle conventions in the text that would have spoken to the native people in their own symbolic language, which often uses a union of two complementary words to convey one meaning.[9] Although the image on the tilma became the main focus of the story, the flowers are significant in being symbols of authenticity. According to Rodriguez, the flowers Juan Diego brings are symbols of his truth, and to the Nahuatl, truth brought in the form of flowers would symbolise the god Quetzalcoatl. Guadalupe says she comes from 'the true God for whom one lives', a Nahuatl expression associated with their god, giving a clear indication of the correlations that underlie the text.[10]

The description of the apparition is reminiscent of biblical theophany. The forces of nature appear to shift into a different reality, which denotes the importance of the message to be delivered. What is also important is that Guadalupe delivers this message to Juan Diego in his own language, indicating that she is allying herself with him rather than the conquering culture.[11] This serves to bolster the Indian's confidence in her love for him, and is what helped lead to the acceptance of this foreign deity by the Nahua as their Mother. If we consider this in a cynical light, we might see Juan Diego, and the Nahuatl language that the *Nican Mopohua* was written in, as a proselytizing tool. Juan Diego's original Indian name was Cuauhtlatoatzin, meaning 'he who speaks like an eagle', and it has been posited that the name somewhat reflects a position of respect amongst his people, a village spokesperson or elder.[12] As a village elder, Diego would have been a prime candidate for conveying the message of Christianity to the Nahua. Or, less cynically, if the figure who appeared to Juan Diego was a native goddess, she recognised that the only way her worship could survive was through transformation and integration. It gave the Indigenous people something to have confidence in again, after the religious vacuum produced by the 'defeat' of their gods at the hands of the god of the Spanish. This was a deity who had come to live amongst them and protect them, not subjugate them.[13] In this way, Tonantzin was returned to life.

In the Spanish version, the use of diminutives by both Mary and Juan Diego gives the impression of a close, almost familial

[9] Rodriguez 1994: 37
[10] Rodriguez 1994: 38
[11] Gebara and Bingemar 1989: 147-9
[12] Rodriguez 1994: 52
[13] Gebara and Bingemar 1989: 153

relationship. It is common in Spanish-speaking cultures when talking to a younger family member to add –*ito* to names, eg. Juanito, Diegito, as Mary does in the Spanish translation. It is odd to our modern English-speaking minds to see Juan Diego also refer to the Virgin in these terms, and see him call her 'my child'. However, if we look at the Nahuatl text, the diminutive suffix used is –*tzin*, which is more commonly used in a more reverential way, such as Juan Diego's Nahuatl name suggests: Cuauhtlatoa-*tzin*. As mentioned, the epithet used for the Nahua goddess was Tonan-*tzin*, meaning 'Our Mother', so this way of addressing each other denotes a higher level of mutual respect than the Spanish translation might suggest.

The name given by Juan Diego's uncle had significance to both the Spanish and Nahua. Whereas the Spanish may have approximated and rationalised it to be 'Guadalupe' in honour of the Virgin of their homeland,[14] it has been suggested that the name spoken was 'Tlecuauhtlacupeuh', meaning 'She who comes flying from the region of light like an eagle of fire'.[15] This connection with eagles in both this name and Juan Diego's Indian name, is a direct association with the realm of the sun god. Other hints in the story suggest correlation with the sun god, including the time of day in which the initial apparition takes place (Dawn) and the direction Juan Diego is facing (East). The date of the final apparition, 12 December, is significant as this supposedly coincided with the winter solstice in 1531, a time when Tonantzin was also celebrated.

So, to what extent does the image of the Mexican Black Madonna reflect its namesake, the original Spanish Virgin of Guadalupe? Whilst it has been suggested that the image was painted by a native Nahua artist, who portrayed the Virgin in such a way that she reflected his own race, elements of the composition may owe their inspiration to various other Marian depictions. On such source is the banner carried by Hernán Cortés, the famous conquistador who led the first Spanish colonization of what is now Mexico in 1519-21. Cortés was born in Extremadura in Spain, the

---

[14] Guadalupe was originally the name of a river in Spain before a Marian apparition happened nearby; said to have its basis in the Arabic word *wadi*, meaning riverbed. The second half of the name has variously been interpreted as deriving from the Arabic for 'hidden', the Latin for 'wolf', and even 'river of love and light'.
[15] Rodriguez 1994: 46

location of the original Virgin of Guadalupe, to whom Cortés was a devotee. One might expect that he brought her likeness to the New World but, curiously, neither his banner nor the Mexican Virgin bear a similar visual appearance to the original Guadalupe – a Black Virgin on a pillar in a triangular cape. It is in fact another relief in the same church that sat opposite the Virgin that has the most resemblance to the painting. Although the Mary of the relief holds a child and the Mexican Virgin does not, the other details such as her star covered cloak, the cherub beneath her, and the shape of the sunrays bursting out from behind her are virtually identical. Meanwhile, Cortés' banner featured the same crown, inclination of the head, and position of the hands that all reappeared in the Mexican Mary. The combination of the two sources appear to give us her artistic reference point.[16]

With such a clear visual link to Guadalupe in Spain, if not the Black Madonna of Extremadura herself, it seems unlikely that the naming of the Mexican Virgin was simply a misinterpretation of a significant Nahuatl title. Those in power consciously chose this name for her, in order to replicate European devotion in this newly converted land. If the name sounded like an important epithet in Nahuatl, all the better for ensuring the devotion of the Indigenous people.

A MIRACULOUS IMAGE

Whilst not a Black Madonna in the same sense as the statues of Europe, or even the Byzantine-styled icons of Częstochowa. et al., the image of the Virgin of Guadalupe is one that inspires the same kind of adoration, arguably even greater than any other, in its continent-wide matronage. The mystique of the piece is in the image that was said to have appeared on the tilma (cloak) of the native Juan Diego fully rendered. The tilma has been examined many times over the centuries. Royal physicians in 1666

---

[16] There have been other suggested sources of inspiration including an early 16th-century Italian Madonna del Soccorso by Latanzio da Foligno and Francesco Melanzio (Oleszkiewicz-Peralba 2007: 55). This particular Madonna del Soccorso has the same cloak, dress and similar mandorla (almond shaped halo around the body reserved for only the holiest figures) to the Mexican Virgin. The main difference is her club or flail which are not carried by Guadalupe and the fact that she is not black or brown. Another Italian Madonna del Soccorso, however, is black, notably with a white baby Jesus.

proclaimed it 'inexplicable' in its makeup. For believers, this is no mere painting, but something more akin to the Turin Shroud than to other sculptures or paintings of Mary. The likeness of the subject is inherent in the piece, some even claiming the image itself is 'living'. On top of the Catholic reverence for miraculous relics, is the Aztec principle of the *ixiptla*, the idea that every religious icon, priest, and even the human sacrifice were imbued with the cosmic essence of the divine like an avatar, rather than being purely representative of the 'greater beyond'.[17] With this doubling up of belief in the sanctity of certain objects, it is unsurprising that the image gained such fame and status amongst both the Spanish and their converts.

The painting underwent an infra-red study in 1979 by biophysicist Philip Callahan and Prof. Jody Brant Smith. Features of the familiar image were allegedly added at later date, in the 16th/17th century, including the moon, mandorla, cherub, and stars of her cloak, according to the study published in 1981.[18] They thought that the artist who made the additions was probably the Marcos Cipac de Aquino mentioned in the old records.

The study by Callahan has been warped by questionable internet news sites that claim 'the NASA analysis' of the image (a tenuous link – Callahan was once a consultant to NASA) 'proves the image is alive'. Apparently, the pupils of the Virgin expand and contract in response to light, and the temperature of the painting is always the same as the human body. It is even alleged that a stethoscope on the belly of the image revealed the typical heart rate of a child in utero. Needless to say, these claims spiral away from the context of the study. What Callahan actually reported was the difficulty in seeing how the image was painted or how it had retained its quality.

Another oft-repeated legend regards the eyes of the Virgin, which are said to reflect a scene containing various figures, presumably those present when Juan Diego revealed the tilma image to the Bishop and his attendants. This claim comes from photographic images of the eyes taken in the 20th century in which certain shapes give the appearance of the features of an old White

---

[17] Oleszkiewicz-Peralba 2007: 71
[18] Callahan 1981: 6-13

man and possibly other figures. I could not find evidence of more recent studies undertaken since the further advancement of digital technology but the claims continue to be repeated on Catholic-based blogs and websites.

Other such claims from Catholic internet sites include miracles at the shrine such as the tilma repairing itself after an acidic cleaning solvent was spilled onto it in 1785, and the image escaping damage from a terrorist bomb planted on the altar amongst flowers in 1921. The bomb is alleged to have destroyed the nearby marble rail and bent a brass crucifix yet left the tilma untouched. No doubt these calamities happened, but they have been repeated so many times without source that the truth of the extent of the damage is questionable. Other imaginative findings include the topography of Mexico and the constellations on the date of the apparition recognised on the Virgin's clothing. The amount of interpretation that the image has been subject to is virtually unparalleled.

Scientific truth aside, the fervour with which such stories are shared shows the need of the faithful for this to be more than just another painting, however sacred the subject matter. Rodriguez comments that the truth of the apparition is inconsequential. For believers, no explanation is necessary. For non-believers, no explanation will suffice.[19]

To me, the most intriguing part of Callahan's study is the fact that he discovered that variations in the weave of the cloth were used to accentuate and provide depth to the image.[20] When examined over a light source, it can be seen that denser patches of the cloth give the impression of shadow. What if the original image was no painting at all but a miraculous imprint, similar to the Turin Shroud or an instance of Pareidolia (recognising images such as Jesus in a cloud or piece of toast)? What if, on witnessing the flowers tumbling from Juan Diego's tilma, the Bishop saw an image behind them in the weave of the cloth? Maybe the original paint was applied to make the image clearer, gradually being added to over time, until the story changed to assert that the image appeared fully formed as we see it today. We will probably never know, unless future analysis of the cloth reveals any further secrets.

---

[19] Rodriguez 1994: 127
[20] Callahan 1981: 14-15

However, this curious feature might suggest that it truly is a 'sacred thread'.

ICONOGRAPHY AND ITS USES

As already mentioned, it is thought that various additions and modifications were made to the Guadalupe image. Much has been written about the significance of certain symbols used, which draw, at least in part, from Aztec religion.

The face is obviously one of the most important features in any religious portrait, and the fact that she appears in a form more alike to the native people than the Europeans who introduced her to them is significant. At some point the fingers were shortened, allegedly to make them look more Indian, so even if appearing like a *mestiza* was not initially important, it may have been later, as her cult swelled among the native people.

Scholars have found a plethora of Aztec symbolism in the image, much of which is thought to be later addition. The *cinta,* a cord worn high around the waist by pregnant women in Mexican culture, is thought to have been added later to signify Mary is with child. This is compounded by the flower on her cloak, positioned over her womb. This has been interpreted as the nagvioli flower, a symbol of the sun god. As mentioned earlier, flowers are significant in the story and to the Nahua represented a symbol of truth. The flowers that Juan Diego brings are symbolic of the authenticity of his account, as well as being a sign from the one true god.[21] It seems, as in other cultures, that Jesus was equated with the Nahua's own solar deity.

Some believe the shades of turquoise blue and deep red to have significance in their associations with certain Aztec deities. Whether true or not, colour variation has played a subtle part in the evolution of the image's use. In the myriad reproductions of Guadalupe found on bumper stickers, candles, and more, the colour of her clothing has shifted towards a brighter red and a greener cloak, possibly to identify her with the colours of the Mexican flag. Throughout the last few centuries, her image has

---

[21] Rodriguez 1994: 37

been used in revolution, war, and protest, and become inextricably linked with national identity.

Nahua significance behind the sun, moon and stars in the image has also been claimed, although practically every culture has myths surrounding the celestial bodies, so this is perhaps a less specific correspondence. A much wider school of thought considers that the symbolism signifies that she is the woman of the Apocalypse from the Book of Revelation, "a woman clothed with the sun, with the moon under her feet and a crown of 12 stars on her head" (12:1, NIV). As this unnamed biblical woman came to be identified with Mary, so depictions of her in the Middle Ages began to portray her in this way. This was also true in Mexico, the parallel of Guadalupe with the Apocalyptic Woman being explicitly stated in the writings of Miguel Sánchez in 1648, the year before the *Huei Tlamahuiçoltica* was published.[22] Guadalupe was in fact originally crowned, a feature that was removed in 1888 for an unknown reason, with the frame being shortened to mask the erasure.

The symbolism of the passage from Revelation would certainly have had significance to the Nahua. After the serpent is cast down, the book states "The woman was given two wings of a great eagle, so that she might fly to the place prepared for her in the wilderness, where she would be taken care of for a time" (12:14, NIV) As we have seen, eagles to the Nahua were a symbol of the true god. The juxtaposition of eagle and serpent was a familiar one to Nahua audiences, and survived right through to become included in the Mexican coat of arms – an eagle holding a snake standing on a cactus.

CULTURAL IMPACT

Guadalupe is not just a religious icon. She is political, socio-cultural, feminist, and has become a counterculture icon, as likely to be seen on the tattooed back of a prisoner as the family altar of a grandmother. She is as much an emblem of M*exicanidad* (Mexicanness) as of Catholicism.

The Guadalupe relic has been credited with many miracles. In

---

[22] Oleszkiewicz-Peralba 2007: 59

the early years of her cult, the tilma was carried through Mexico City in the hopes that it would stop the floods ravaging the city, which it was credited with achieving. Other tales tell of Guadalupe reviving the dead and dying. Due to her increasing fame, in 1737, Guadalupe was named the patroness of Mexico City and in 1746 of the whole country. A few years later, in 1754, Pope Benedict XIV established her feast day officially as 12 December. Nearly 150 years later, Pope Leo XIII granted her a canonical coronation in 1887 (just before the removal of the painting's crown, perhaps suggesting the reason for it) which took place in 1895. Popes of the 20th century have called her Mother of the Americas, Empress of the Americas, and Pope John Paul II named her Patroness of the Americas whilst also canonising Juan Diego in 2002.

As with other Black Madonnas, Guadalupe appears in times of crisis, her image being the figurehead for various armies and uprisings over the years. Her image appeared on the banners of the insurgents in the Mexican War of Independence from Spain (1810-21) whilst the Spanish bore an alternate Mary on their banners, the Virgen de los Remedios. It was not uncommon in earlier medieval warfare for opposing armies to claim the protection of differing iterations of Mary.[23] As it happened, Guadalupe proved stronger, and the first president of the victorious independent Mexico changed his name to Guadalupe Victoria in her honour. Guadalupe recurred on the banners of the brave during the War of Reformation (1854-57), the Mexican Revolution (1910-18), and the Cristeros Rebellion (1927-29).[24]

The pilgrimage to her basilica on December 12th is the largest in the world, dwarfing even the Polish one at Częstochowa, with the media reporting a record 6.1 million attendees at Tepeyac in 2009. One Mexican-American, Rubén Martínez, recording his first experience of the pilgrimage in 1994 describes it as more akin to Woodstock than a traditional Catholic ceremony. The faithful, the majority of whom are young people, assemble the night before the feast day, in a party atmosphere of dancing and fireworks.[25] Despite this, outside of the pilgrimage, the feast day of Our Lady of

---

[23] This is comparable to provincial India, where villages have their own Kali and Durgas, each claiming theirs is stronger than their neighbours (see Chapter 7).
[24] Oleszkiewicz-Peralba 2007: 60
[25] Martínez 1996: 107

Guadalupe is said to be of limited importance to Mexicans, because she is such a part of home life and spoken to on a daily basis.[26]

Martínez sees Guadalupe's influence in the USA too, and calls her the Undocumented Virgin, as she crosses all boundaries.[27] It is common for Mexican people making the crossing into the US to pray to her for safe passage and for good fortune in establishing themselves there. Guadalupe is a patroness of liminal spaces, of the in-between. Though she may at first seem like the opposite – being the product of the blending of Indian and European culture, she is as much 'neither' as 'both'. As such, she is particularly important to those of the borderlands, and to Mexican-Americans in the USA. It is important to remember that many Americans of Mexican heritage have had no choice in being on the US side of the border. Under the Treaty of Guadalupe Hidalgo, at the end of the Mexican-American war of 1846-8, the US expanded its borders, encompassing northern Mexican territories. Mexicans in the ceded lands, now US states, found themselves suddenly US citizens, with all the same rights in theory, but a colonised people treated as second-class citizens in effect. For those displaced people, Guadalupe stayed with them, a goddess in exile with her children. She is a useful representation of the feeling of being neither wholly belonging to one culture or one race more than the other.

Rodriguez writes that the psychological effects produced by the 'internal colonisation' of the northern Mexican states by the US were passivity, apathy and low self-worth amongst Mexican-Americans. The knock-on effect is sexism, through over-compensation and displays of machismo by men – Man believes that he must be the provider to show he is worthy to look after his wife and family; Woman must stay in the home. These accumulative cultural effects still impact upon mestiza women today.[28]

However, Rodriguez thinks that the stereotype of mestiza women as inferior, passive, and untrustworthy, dates back to when Aztec was the dominant culture.[29] Although all Aztec women were

---

[26] Rodriguez 1994: 138
[27] Martínez 1996: 108
[28] Rodriguez 1994: 71
[29] Rodriguez 1994: xxvii

educated, they were expected to be homemakers. This was compounded by two eras of conquest, first by Spain, and then by America. Pre-conquest, Aztec women also worked, had property and status, took part in war and in religion. This independence was removed when the Spanish destroyed their economic system, placing women solely in the home. Following the conquest, Spanish women were regarded as the highest class, followed by *Criollas* (women born in the New World), followed by mestizas (women of mixed Spanish/Indian race).[30] Former Nahua noblewomen were now domestic servants, but without the respect previously accorded to the servant class. All were brought down to the peasant level, having inferiority imprinted on them.[31]

Amidst these psychological and sociological inner struggles, Guadalupe has provided a rock to hold onto, and her presence hovers over the emergence of *Chicano*[32] culture amongst demoralized Mexican-Americans in the southern US in the 1960s. She featured on the banners of the United Farm Workers' Strike of 1965 which started the movement[33] and appears in Chicano murals and street art, which comment on the struggle for "civil rights, cultural equity, and self-determination"[34] for Chicanos/as.

Her image has been reproduced in countless ways within the artistic sphere – sometimes faithfully, sometimes with the colours altered to make her darker-skinned and clothed in the colours of the Mexican flag, sometimes in inventive and thought-provoking ways, to commentate on social injustice. Some artists have deconstructed her image, taking iconic and recognisable parts of it to portray a new message, particularly about women. In 1976, Ester Hernandez had Guadalupe breaking out of her radiant border and performing a martial arts kick in the piece 'Guadalupe Defending Xicano Rights'. In 1978, artist Yolanda M. López portrayed herself, her mother, and her grandmother as the Lady of Guadalupe in new ways: as a jogger, as a woman working at a sewing machine, and a woman sat on her cloak holding a snakeskin, respectively. As

---

[30] Rodriguez 1994: 65
[31] Rodriguez 1994: 6
[32] People of bicultural descent, identifying as neither totally Mexican or American (Rodriguez 1994: 64)
[33] Oleszkiewicz-Peralba 2007: 144
[34] Oleszkiewicz-Peralba 2007: 144

Oleszkiewicz-Peralba notes, "In these paintings, a number of Guadalupe's elements, such as the mantle, the angel, and the serpent, were retained, but recontextualized and infused with a new message".[35]

CHICANA WOMEN'S RESPONSES TO GUADALUPE

It is easy to talk about Guadalupe in terms of the legend, the miracles, her widespread popularity and visibility, but less easy to give an accurate experiential viewpoint from those who give their devotion to her. Mainstream theology, including Mariology, has long been the province of men, and of the privileged. Little is actually recorded from the perspectives of the impoverished or oppressed, especially women, who are amongst the Virgin Mary's greatest devotees. These marginalised women are equally 'doing theology' every day – they interpret the religious and transmit their faith through the activities of their home lives.[36] When theologising from our own limited standpoints, assumptions may be made on the beliefs of others. To combat this, extensive fieldwork is needed to seek out a multivocal approach. Luckily, there are researchers who have already begun his process. Within her study on Mexican-American women's relationship with Guadalupe, Jeanette Rodriguez gives these women a voice and explores their responses.

The responses in Rodriguez' survey are characterised by the women feeling they can relate to Guadalupe, primarily because she is female, Mexican, and a mother.[37] In her, these Chicanas find a mirror – of their own struggles and hardships, and their own aspirations. In one of the responses about Guadalupe, that she is "strong, but in a quiet sense",[38] the reader feels like the respondent may also be describing themselves. Another response reflects Guadalupe's endurance and loyalty. When asked what makes Guadalupe different from other apparitions of Mary, one woman answered simply "She stayed".[39] This could be construed in a literal

---

[35] Oleszkiewicz-Peralba 2007: 155
[36] Elizondo in Rodriguez 1994: ix-xv
[37] Rodriguez 1994: 121
[38] Rodriguez 1994: 124
[39] Rodriguez 1994: 128

sense – that her image remained on the tilma, but more significantly, that she continues to care for the Mexican people, her people.

The women were given a list of 300 adjectives to describe what Guadalupe is and is not. The answers showed that she is seen as supportive, stable, accepting and nurturing; not subordinate, critical, sceptical or attacking. In the adjectives selected, we find contradictions – she is both meek and strong-willed, dependent and independent, assertive and shy. Perhaps it is in these paradoxes that we define her best? Some readers may be reminded of the passage from the ancient Nag Hammadi texts, *The Thunder, Perfect Mind*, in which we see the Divine Feminine describing herself in these kinds of contradictions, defying definition, encompassing all: "I am the honored and the scorned. I am the whore and the holy".[40] Rodriguez relates the contradictory responses to the lives of the Chicana women who provided them. One adjective may derive from what they may be in their present situation and the other what they want to become – for example, from a passive individual to a powerful one. Therefore, in encompassing both, Guadalupe embodies transformation.[41]

The women of the survey describe her in terms of strength to endure suffering. In talking about her, they are filling in the blanks for themselves, of what is not intimately described in the Bible: how it feels to be a mother who experiences loss and hardship. This is a common factor in Marian cults. In fact, the miracles attributed to Mary in apparitions – such as freeing slaves, casting out demons, curing the sick – are all acts that canonically belong to Jesus, yet over the centuries, it is Mary, far more often than her son, who returns to talk to and watch over her people, and carry out such miracles.[42]

Although these women weave Guadalupe's story, not many of those questioned were very familiar with the detail of the account of Juan Diego and only vaguely knew of its significance, which Rodriguez attributes to women's exclusion from theological schools of thought. She writes that their experiences mirror Juan

---

[40] *Thunder, Nag Hammadi Codex VI* in Barnstone, W. & Meyer, M. W. 2005: 226-7
[41] Rodriguez 1994: 130
[42] Gebara and Bingemar 1989: 137

Diego only up to the second apparition. They recognise the Virgin and feel a familial bond and ease with her. Rodriguez asserts that they have been denied the chance to feel the empowerment, dignity, and mission felt by Juan Diego through their exclusion from theological conversation.[43] To many, however, delving into the texts of centuries ago is unimportant compared to interpreting Guadalupe for a new age.

LIBERATING GUADALUPE

Just as Guadalupe has been liberated by postmodern artists, so she has featured in the writings of feminist authors in new and surprising ways. Several authors have written about Guadalupe as a sex-positive role model for Chicanas and for lesbians in the modern era. In her short story 'Virgencita, Give us a Chance', Liliana Valenzuela writes about a girl waking from a dream in which she speaks with Guadalupe, and is in awe of the details of her female form. "Camila sees the Virgin's young body, her fresh skin, her wet vagina, everything you don't see in the holy cards. She sees herself as nude as well, sees her pubic hair, her tits. Sees La Virgencita. Sees herself."[44] The dream initiates a sexual awakening, as Camila explores her own body and that of the female friend in her bed. This kind of interpretation offers a striking alternative to the prescribed Catholic image of Mary.

In her youth, Sandra Cisneros always found Guadalupe to be an unachievable polarising role model of goodness, the only other option for mestiza girls being whoredom. She discovers a sexual role model in Guadalupe by delving into the Virgin's Aztec goddess antecedents, such as Tlazolteotl, patroness of sexual passion and the 'sin eater', who cleansed one of their transgressions, and Coatlicue, with her fearsomely solid, statuesque body.[45] For these modern women, Guadalupe assimilates the characteristics of those goddesses that have come before her, the traits that the conquistas rejected.

Gloria Anzaldúa, however, sees this division of the Feminine

---

[43] Rodriguez 1994: 162
[44] Valenzuela 1996: 95
[45] Cisneros 1996: 49-50

happening in Aztec culture even before the arrival of the Spanish. She sees the mother of the gods Tonantzin, who had once been whole, divided from her more monstrous aspects – serpent goddesses Coatlicue and Cihuacoatl, and filth goddess Tlazolteotl – by male-dominated Aztec culture. Thus, the Spanish adopted the characteristics that suited their Virgin and demonised all other iterations of the Goddess. Anzaldúa identifies the polarisation of the Feminine reoccurring between the chaste and docile interpretation of Guadalupe, and the whore/bad mother stereotype of other Mexican cultural figures La Malinche and La Llorona.[46]

LA MALINCHE AND LA LLORONA

Intimately tied to Our Lady of Guadalupe in the Mexican cultural subconscious is historical figure Doña Marina, also known as La Malinche. She is herself an important Black Madonna archetype, a strong female cast as a traitor, but in fact betrayed by her people instead; who kept her composure under abuse.

She was born Malinalli, a native Indian and a princess amongst her people but given as a slave to Cortés. Skilled in various dialects, she made herself indispensable to her captors in acting as the conquistador's interpreter. The Spanish gave her the name Doña Marina as an honour and mark of respect. It is believed that she also became Cortés' consort, and the first mother of the new mixed race that would become Mexicans. But rather than being revered as Mother of the Mestizas, her character in the story of the Conquest has been made into a traitor and a whore who gave her body willingly to the Spanish; the name La Malinche itself is something of a slur, roughly translating to 'foreign-lover'. Feminist interpretation, however, reminds us that this was a 14-year-old girl, who is unlikely to have given herself freely.[47] Her reaction to her new situation was an intelligent one, rather than one of passivity – she used her language skills to survive. The Spanish with their greater numbers would have conquered by force with or without her help, if they had not been able to converse with the Aztecs. In

---

[46] Anzaldúa 1996: 52-4
[47] Rodriguez, 1994: 74-5

helping the conquerors, she may have saved her people from excessive bloodshed.

We may wonder why La Malinche became the scapegoat, the woman who could be blamed for the downfall of the native ruling culture. One of the stereotyped qualities projected onto mestiza women is untrustworthiness. By making this single girl who mothered the first of their race an emblem of treachery, passivity, and mistrust, Mexican society makes her the progenitor of the untrustworthiness of mestiza women and uses her as justification for this stereotype. Society appears to have cast her as a Mexican equivalent of Eve, to blame for the Fall (in this case the Conquest). The juxtaposition makes sense; Mary is seen to be the antithesis of Eve, the mother of the human race, so the mother of the Mestiza race (unfairly) takes her place opposite the Mexican Mary.

The female scapegoat stereotype is expanded even further in the myth of La Llorona. She is the tragic figure of a native woman who, like Malinalli, submits to a conquista and bears his children, but is abandoned by him. In her grief she drowns her sons and then herself in a river, which she is said to haunt thereafter. It has been suggested that the myth is about La Malinche, but the character of the Weeping Woman pervades Mexican folklore and can be found pre-Spanish Conquest, including in the Aztec legend of the goddess Cihuacoatl. However, the tragedy and inequality of the 16th century became particularly attached to the myth as its backdrop. Other variants involve illegitimate pregnancy, rejection, and murder, nearly all ending with the Weeping Woman powerlessly wandering forever in search of her lost children.

We see a parallel of the juxtaposition of the beloved mother Guadalupe and the treacherous female Malinche in the Aztec myth of Coatlicue and Coyolxauhqui. The myth tells how the mother goddess Coatlicue gave birth to the sun god Huitzilopochtli. It was prophesied that the impending birth of the male god would bring war and bloodshed, so Coatlicue's daughter Coyolxauhqui tried to prevent him from being born. Huitzilopochtli, however, learned of the intended murder and leapt from the womb in full adult form, dismembering his sister and throwing her head into the sky where it became the Moon. The other 400 sons of Coatlicue who assisted Coyolxauhqui were also slain and became the stars. This shows us that the stereotype of the treacherous female was already present in society long before the Conquest. Whilst devotion continued to the Feminine in the form of the mother, a female scapegoat is created. Being a dark moon goddess and a forgotten wounded daughter, Coyolxauhqui contributes as much to the Black Madonna archetype (and thus Guadalupe) as Coatlicue does, a relationship echoed in that between Guadalupe and La Malinche.

We can talk about La Malinche being a 'shadow side' of Guadalupe, but to put it more bluntly, she reveals a damaging double standard. Guadalupe is seen as Mother of the Mestizas due to her appearance, but not in a physical, literal sense. The actual physical act by which Malinalli bears Cortés' children, the first of the race, is seen as shameful and traitorous. Guadalupe's form echoes both Indian and Spanish art, and is celebrated as the blending of their cultures, yet when Doña Marina finds respect amongst her captors, she is a 'foreign-lover'. The emergence of Guadalupe's cult ten years after the Conquest represents a rose-tinted take on the birth of the Mexican people, whilst the real mothers of the country have borne the curse of La Malinche down to the modern day.

Despite the harmful misogynistic stereotype created around La Malinche, Oleszkiewicz-Peralba reports that as well as Guadalupe, La Llorona and La Malinche are being reclaimed in Chicana culture in the 21st century, as emblems of opposition to patriarchal and Eurocentric oppression, and mothers of the dispossessed.[48] Coyolxauhqui too has been reclaimed by modern goddess culture, as a dark moon goddess, a reminder of the wounding of women committed by generations of patriarchal domination.[49]

SANTA MUERTE

As with the figures of La Malinche and La Llorona, Santa Muerte provides a shadow aspect of Our Lady of Guadalupe. In Mexican culture, Death is personified as female. She is sometimes called María Guadaña (literally 'scythe' in Spanish, or perhaps 'Maria Reaper'?). She and Guadalupe are regarded in folk culture

---

[48] Oleszkiewicz-Peralba 2007: 156-8
[49] Moraga in Castillo 1996: 68-71

as two flipsides of the same coin, like a descendent of the two-headed goddess Coatlicue.[50] However, Death is most popularly recognised as the polarising folk saint Santa Muerte, loved by her devotees and less so by the right-wing Government and Catholic Church. The fact that she is the only personification of Death in the Americas that is portrayed as female, unlike her Argentinian and Guatemalan counterparts, San La Muerte and Rey Pascual, makes her unique, and something that is accentuated through her attire and the nicknames given to her.[51] Sometimes she wears the attire of Guadalupe, identical except for her skeletal features. At other times, she is portrayed in a nun's habit, a queen's gowns, or a bridal dress. Mexican devotees often refer to her through affectionate pet names such as 'the Pretty Girl' or 'the Bony Lady'.

Like La Malinche, Santa Muerte has accumulated the darker elements of the pre-Christian goddesses discarded from the personage of Guadalupe. Whilst they may normally be honoured separately, when combined, the two figures of Guadalupe and Santa Muerte give a fuller picture of the Divine Feminine. Whereas La Malinche and La Llorona are not figures who are usually served or petitioned, Santa Muerte provides the Dark Mother alternative for Mexicans and Mexican-Americans to ask things for which they might not approach Guadalupe. Like so many of the countries and communities who venerate a Dark Mother, Mexico is a country where, for many, life is on a knife-edge, and the need for supernatural assistance in order to survive and prosper is often great. Those who serve her may still have faith in the Virgin Mary, but they may also regard Santa Muerte's power over life and death as even greater than hers, equal even to God.[52]

In investigating the origins of Santa Muerte, we can see that they are not that different from the formula of Guadalupe, both representing probable syncretism of Indigenous mythology with elements of Spanish Catholicism. Not much is known about her exact origins – as a folk saint, her devotees are less interested in them than your average scholar of religion is, and focus more on their everyday reciprocal relationship with her. There are colonial

---

50 Castillo 1996: 75
51 Chesnut 2012: 7-8
52 Chesnut 2012: 60

Above: "Santa Muerte". The extremely popular Mexican folk saint of death, sometimes depicted as a skeletal Guadalupe. Although her symbolism may have roots in a pre-Christian death goddess, the cult of Santa Muerte has only become public in the 21st Century, in an explosion of popular devotion.

writings dating back as far as the 1790s that mention her, but little is known about her cult before the 21st century.

The popular theory is that Santa Muerte arises from pre-Conquest underworld deities Mictecacihuatl and her husband Mictlantechutli who rule over the realm of the dead, Mictlan, blended with the European spectre of the Black Death, the Grim Reaper. In Spain, Death is personified as female too, called La Parca,[1] a concept that travelled to the Americas in the subconscious of the conquistas. La Parca derived from the Parcae, or Fates, of Roman mythology, specifically the eldest Parcae, Morta, who chose when to cut the thread of a person's life and how they would die. So, just as Mary was easily blended with Tonantzin, images of the female reaper were seamlessly merged with the skeletal goddess Mictecacihuatl, who was honoured at the annual Aztec festival of death.

Modern images of Santa Muerte are also influenced by the 20th-century depictions of elegant and jolly skeletons created for the Day of the Dead. These began as an illustration of a skeleton in a lady's hat from the 1910s called *La Calavera Catrina* by José Guadalupe Posada, a social satire mocking Mexicans who aspired to European standards of beauty and culture. The caricature has developed to represent the Mexican tendency to laugh in the face of death, and to celebrate *Día De Muertos* with as much life and colour as possible. Day of the Dead festivities have increased in popularity in recent decades, leading to it becoming an official public holiday in the 21st century and the tradition being included on UNESCO's intangible cultural heritage list in 2008.

Santa Muerte falls into the category of folk saints, who may be vastly popular but are not recognised by the Vatican. Folk saints are usually people who have died fighting for a cause, local heroes elevated to something similar to ancestor worship in death. Yet Santa Muerte is the personification of Death itself. She represents a universal concept and is therefore widely identifiable; so much so that she outranks most of the other saints, official or unofficial, in popularity in Mexico. If we look at store sales of Santa Muerte candles and statues translated into evidence of devotion, it has

---

[1] Chesnut 2012: 28

been suggested that she even outstrips Mexico's favourite official saint, Jude, in popularity.[2] When interviewed in 2009, Father David Romo, the 'godfather' of her church in Mexico, estimated 5 million followers in Mexico – 5% of the population.[3] Like death, she does not discriminate and welcomes all comers. She is popular with opposing sides on several fronts – including both prisoners and prison workers, and drug barons and law enforcement. This paradoxical appeal to both the assailed and assailants places her solidly in the same category as the Black Madonna, also making her difficult to comprehend and easily misunderstood.

Her cult has only been public since 2001. Along with David Romo, Doña Queta Romero is credited with being 'godparent' of the Santa Muerte cult. Doña Queta had prayed to the bony saint for her son's release from prison. After her prayers were answered, her grateful son bought her a life-size Santa Muerte statue. This was visible to the customers of the quesadilla shop she operated from her home and started to draw a following. On All Saints' Day of 2001, Doña Queta and her husband Ray installed the statue in a public altar outside of their house, the first to publicly display their devotion.[4] Doña Queta continues to hold gatherings and public devotions to the saint, attracting many young people, especially women. Meanwhile, David Romo had been researching the mysterious cult whilst ministering to an offshoot from the Catholic Church that he had founded in the 1990s, the Mexico-USA Tridentine Catholic Church. In 2003, on the feast day of the Assumption of the Virgin Mary, his church celebrated the incorporation of Santa Muerte worship. This not-so-subtle choice of day, seemingly putting Santa Muerte on par with Guadalupe, may be what provoked the Mexican government to revoke the licence of Romo's church.[5] Romo has since become Santa Muerte's unofficial spokesperson, and protested against blurred boundaries between Church and State. He particularly protested against the destruction of around 40 roadside shrines in towns on the Mexico-US border, by the Mexican army. The government's reason for

---

[2] Chesnut 2012: 9
[3] Chesnut 2012: 8-9
[4] Chesnut 2012: 38-9
[5] Chesnut 2012: 43

such action was the association of the saint with drug trafficking.[6] Despite the media's depiction of Santa Muerte's association with crime, advocates such as Romo have tried to distance themselves from these negative connotations. After it was reported that criminals had performed murders in front of her altar, which could be perceived as human sacrifice, whether or not that was the intention, Romo introduced a non-skeletal 'angel of death' statue at his church. However, it was not popular, and sales of the skeletal Santa Muerte paraphernalia persisted in popularity.[7]

Different coloured candles are dedicated to her for different reasons – red for matters of the heart, white for purity, gold for prosperity, purple for healing, green for justice, and black for nefarious uses such as revenge. Rainbow candles can be used for issues with multiple needs. Brown candles, although not amongst the higher selling colours, are used for matters needing enlightenment, discernment, and wisdom,[8] which is interesting considering the brown and black Madonnas' association with wisdom. There are areas of crossover in what people come to her for and what they ask of Guadalupe. Like Guadalupe, she is frequently petitioned by those hoping to make it safely across the border into the USA.

As with service to the spirits of death in Vodou, and other African diasporic religions, petitions to her are respectful and devotion to her is reciprocal. People make promises to her in return for miracles. She shares a liking for white roses with Guadalupe, which when placed on her altar must be kept fresh.[9] This strict protocol seems curious for a deity of death. In Vodou, food offerings to the Gede, the spirits of death, are often left to decay, where it is observed that the faster they decay, the more they have been taken by the spirits. But, like the Gede, she is intimately associated with the preservation of life, and is frequently petitioned for healing. Water is also present on her altars, as a cleansing element, and because Santa Muerte is literally parched and always thirsty. In Latin American folklore, water is also a symbol of death. The saint is often accompanied by an owl, not only an emblem of

---

6 Chesnut 2012: 45
7 Chesnut 2012: 18
8 Chesnut 2012: 20
9 Chesnut 2012: 71

wisdom, as in European culture where it is associated with Athene, but a symbol of death in Aztec culture. The lord of the underworld was crowned with tecolote (owl) feathers.[10]

CONCLUSION

In many ways, Guadalupe is the ultimate example of a Black Madonna. The Marian cult, and Guadalupe in particular, is appealing to the oppressed because of her unconditional love and the dignity she bestows. As we see in the Guadalupe myth and so many other Black Madonna stories, the Virgin is discovered by someone of the local ethnic group, usually poor, or a child. She affirms that she is as much their mother as that of the dominant culture, which serves to strengthen their resolve.

Devotion to her inhabits the realm of 'popular religiosity', which has its roots in marginalization and oppression.[11] She is most often contacted through spontaneous acts of worship not ordained or administered through the institutional Church. In fact, some churches retain an ounce of that Franciscan doubt in the authenticity of the Guadalupe apparition and do not allow devotion to her.

She is also problematic. For the women of Rodriguez's survey, Guadalupe is the antithesis of the inferior, passive, and untrustworthy mestiza stereotype. But for others this makes her an unachievable role model, too distant in her piety. In order to see her in a more balanced way we must acknowledge the figures of La Llorona and La Malinche who stand in her shadow, remnants of pre-conquest. They are the recipients of the qualities that are relegated and expelled from the Virgin as they do not fit the pious mould; just as the more challenging aspects of the Feminine have at times been projected onto the character of Mary Magdalene as opposed to being incorporated into the mother of Christ. Anzaldúa writes that, post-conquest, all three symbolic Mexican identities have been used to oppress: "Guadalupe to make us docile and enduring, la Chingada (La Malinche) to make us ashamed of our Indian side, and la Llorona to make us long-suffering people".

---

[10] Chesnut 2012: 67
[11] Rodriguez 1994: 143-8

Thankfully not all subscribe to the virgin/whore dichotomy and since the emergence of Chicano culture, Guadalupe and her shadows have been reclaimed, reimagined, and renewed by the people she has resolutely watched over since her inception in the Americas.

CHAPTER 5

The Black Madonna in Vodou

INTRODUCTION

Syncretism is one of the most important ways in which the Black Madonna's visual essence has come to symbolise something different in the modern world, and this is most visible in the realm of Haitian Vodou. Vodou is an ever-evolving system, more a set of practices than a codified religion, yet certainly no less rich in symbolism, myth, and the ability to mould cultural and social standards. Neither is it incompatible with Haiti's main 'official' religion of Catholicism. In a similar way to how the Japanese honour Shinto practices alongside Buddhism, many who practice Vodou do so alongside attending church as a Catholic. The name 'Haitian Vodou' is, in fact, more of an anthropological classification by outsiders for what most Vodouisants would call more simply *sevis Lwa,* serving the spirits. An important part of the development of the religion came in the identification of these spirits, the Lwa, with images of Catholic saints, when used on altars, in art, and in ritual. A simplistic interpretation is that in the early days of the religion within Haiti, these images were just used as a 'cover' by the Africans brought to the New World as slaves to hide their ancestral beliefs. The reality is more complex, and a blending occurred of the symbols and characteristics of the saints and Lwa until it became impossible to distinguish whether an image was chosen because elements of it fit the Lwa or whether they developed these characteristics influenced by the image.[1] In

---

[1] Marc A. Christophe believes that for the slaves to use the saints as a cover *en masse* would require them to have both visual familiarity with a host of Christian images as well as immediate knowledge about the characters depicted in them. In a land alien to both the African deities and European saints, a gradual fusion occurred to achieve order and balance, one of the most important tenets of Vodou (Christophe in Bellegarde-Smith & Michel 2006: 93-5).

this chapter we will look at how the image of the Black Madonna became one with the Lwa known as Ezili Danto.[2]

At the outset of this chapter I should relate my own level of experience with Vodou, which I feel is appropriate to do when it comes to being a Westerner and a White European talking about a people who have a history so indelibly marked by slavery at the hands of Europeans, and a religion which has disproportionately suffered from misinformation at the hands of the Western media. As neither a Haitian nor an initiate of the religion I am unable to speak on its behalf but will do my best to relate what I know with the care and respect it is due. Having lived with and been friends with several initiated Vodouisants in the UK I have had years of exposure to the practices and attended many fets[3] by invitation. Written sources on Vodou are scarce, due to the confidential nature and largely oral transmission of the practices, and aside from those quoted in this chapter, many are underinformed or deliberately incorrect to preserve the tradition's secrets. Therefore, I have relied largely on interviews with practitioners to relate their experiences. These people also stressed that they do not speak for the religion as a whole, due to its diversity, and because ideas and beliefs differ between houses or *sosyete* (societies).

HISTORY OF THE HAITIAN REVOLUTION

Vodou marries the ancestral beliefs and practices of the West Coast of Africa, believed to reach back 2,000 years, with elements of the rituals of the native Taino people who were first encountered on the island by Columbus in 1492, plus parts of Catholicism where comparisons were drawn with the enforced religion and integration naturally occurred. Upon colonising the island named Ayiti ('mother land' or 'mountain land') by the Taino,[4] the Spanish renamed it Hispaniola and wasted no time in exploiting its resources and people. Plantations were established

---

[2] Spelling of the creole name is various but the other most common spelling encountered is Erzulie Dantor.
[3] Literally 'parties' for the spirits involving the honouring of and conversation with the Lwa.
[4] Tann 2012: 18

Above: 'Our Lady of Częstochowa'. *The first Black Madonna that I painted and a favourite of many people. It is based on a combination of the famous Polish icon and the Santa Barbara Africana image used as a focus on the altars of the Vodou Lwa Ezili Danto. This solemn Black Madonna bears the scars on her cheek of the attack on Our Lady of Częstochowa when its monastery was ransacked. The marks carried over into the legends of Èzili, becoming an important part of her persona.*

once the Spanish discovered the island was not as rich in gold as they had first thought. However, they found themselves without a workforce due to European diseases like smallpox wiping out vast numbers of Taino who had no natural immunity to them. Slaves began to be brought to work the plantations from West Africa and from other Caribbean settlements, numbering 15,000 by 1516. Slavery from Africa was formally licensed by the King of Spain the following year and began in earnest, supplying sugar, cotton, coffee, and other luxuries to Europe, who in turn traded European wares to African kings in return for more slaves. By 1720 there were 8,000 slaves arriving on the island each year[1]. By this time, Hispaniola had been divided by the French and Spanish into the western French-ruled Saint-Domingue and the eastern Spanish-speaking Santo Domingo. By 1789, Sainte-Domingue held 500,000 African slaves, who vastly outnumbered the 20,000 White landowners and the 30,000 *gens de coleur* - freemen who were the mixed-race descendants of the colonists and the slaves. Prejudice abounded between the groups, the *gens de coleur* not wanting to be associated with the African slaves but neither receiving the equal rights they aspired to have in common with the Whites. The French government attempted to enforce these equal rights for the *gens de coleur* in 1789 but the landowners in Saint-Domingue rejected their order, fearful that this would open up the doors to slave rebellion. As it turned out, this is exactly what happened, although Maroon colonies of escaped slaves and surviving Taino living in the mountains had been making strides in raiding plantations and freeing slaves for some time.

Although brewing for a number of years, the Haitian Revolution is said to have officially begun on 14 August 1791 with a now almost mythologised ceremony happening at Bwa Kayiman. In one version, a Mambo (Vodou priestess) called Mayanét and a Houngan (priest) and Maroon leader named Boukman called upon Petro[2] spirits to lend their strength to the rebels. In some versions, a native black pig was sacrificed to the Petro Lwa named Ezili Danto, whereas in others, Danto was a human at the time of the ceremony, who only later became elevated to ranks of the Lwa after

---

[1] Tann 2012: 20-1
[2] A classification of Lwa typified as 'hot' spirits, which can manifest as a fiery temper.

death.[3] Although we may never know the particulars of that night, in the days that followed, chaos broke out in Saint-Domingue, with 4,000 slaveowners killed over the following two months. France once again declared all *gens de coleur* full citizens in the hope that they would make peace between the two groups and help put down the rebellion. However, the White colonists again refused to recognise the law and instead turned to Britain, offering to turn over the rule of the country to the British in return for their protection. The Spanish who still ruled Santo Domingo also sided with the colonists and the British, and in an extraordinary turn of events, France turned to Saint-Domingue's African slaves to maintain control. In 1793, the French military began freeing and arming slaves to fight for France in return for a guarantee of their continued freedom. This army, led by former slave General L'Ouverture were successful in driving the British and Spanish from the country, whilst the number of slaveowners was drastically reduced by the activity of the Revolution. In 1801, emancipation of the slaves was declared by L'Ouverture who also proclaimed himself governor. France was not happy to be losing the colony, so fought and eventually imprisoned L'Ouverture. However, his successor Jean-Jacques Dessalines was successful in finally routing the French after much bloodshed, and Haiti was declared independent on 1 January 1804.[4] The white stripe was removed from the French flag to create a new Haitian one and with this symbolic removal, a new nation was born.

Without going too deeply into the history of the proceeding two hundred years, it will suffice to say that life for Haiti has been far from plain sailing since it gained its independence. Corrupt governments, racial tension, coups, and debts all contributed to a tough existence in a country ravaged by blood and fire, not to mention the disastrous earthquake of 2011, the aftermath of which has lasted for years. Little wonder, then, in a country where daily subsistence is the primary concern of so many, that turning to a higher power has long provided the necessary strength to survive, and the pillar around which society is formed.

---

[3] Tann 2012: 24
[4] Tann 2012: 24-6

VODOU PRACTICE

In 19th and early 20th-century Western writings about Vodou, and the persistent stereotypes that have stemmed from them, its practice is seen at best as primitive animism and at worst as devil-worshipping, orgiastic, black magic. The truth is of course anything but, and only now is more being written by Haitians about Vodou's cosmology, cosmogony, its sophisticated ideas about the nature of the soul, and the purpose of ceremony and symbols in what is seen on the surface as a highly materialistic, animistic religion.[5] Guérin C. Montilus writes that whilst Christian theologians were debating whether Africans had souls and devising justifications for slavery, these people were continuing with their own view of personhood and affirming their place in the universe. He writes:

> *"The Vodou ceremony is effective because it provides the faithful with the structure for self- and collective expression. However, these practices are symbolic. The humanized or anthropomorphized universe is one that human beings have deciphered and one whose meaning has been fixed by symbols. All inhabited places are spaces codified by meaning. It is in this sense that Vodou is a civilizing agent. As with all religions it has the dynamism that helps organize societies and produce values. Its dogma explains the universe, and it explains human beings within it and their nature. There is a cosmogony in the religion which makes medicine, ritual, and divination work."[6]*

The areas where less has been written about Vodou concerns the particulars of initiation which are kept confidential within *sosyete,* although accounts where partial details are given do exist.[7] The first level of initiation is *hounsi*, and the ceremony, or *kanzo* involves several days of seclusion, and practice of a type of transcendental meditation which is said to open the initiate's minds to hidden worlds and potential revelations. The initiation is not undertaken lightly, as *sevis Lwa* for an initiate is a lifetime commitment that cannot be undone. Further levels of initiation may take the Vodouisant to the level of *Houngan/Mambo* (priest/priestess) although this role is better described by a term

---

[5] See Bellegarde-Smith & Michel 2006 *Haitian Vodou*
[6] Montilus 2006: 5
[7] Claude Planson, a French scholar wrote of his experience of *hounsi kanzo* in the 1987 book *La Vaudou*. (Crosley 2006: 10)

such as 'community leader' than the Eurocentric idea of the priesthood.

As mentioned, Vodou draws upon the traditions of Western Africa, brought over on the slave ships. These people came from numerous different countries, yet the conditions they found themselves in drove them to finding the commonalities in their beliefs in order to fashion new systems of worship that fitted their situation - in other words, to adapt to survive. In Vodou there are said to be 21 symbolic Nations – 19 parts African, one to honour European influence and one for the native Taino of Ayiti. We can trace the influence of the Taino in elements such as the *veve*, specific symbols traced for each Lwa which bear resemblances to Taino pictographs for their spirits, the *Zemi*.[8] Like the Taino, the Africans also had spirits that governed elements of nature and universal principles. Types of these spirits, or Lwa, are divided according to their nature as they require service in different ways. The Rada group of 'cool' spirits are seen as those most ancient with their roots in *Ginen Africa,* the homeland. Amongst them are the great white snake Danballah and his wife Ayida Wedo, the way-opener Papa Legba, the seafaring Agwe and his brides La Sirene and Ezili Freda, the sister of Danto. Their part of the rites is followed by a section for the Nago, a particular tribe who honour the Ogou family of Lwa. These are followed in service by the hotter Petro nation, with roots in the Kongo but who are more typical of the conditions that arose in the New World and embody the strength and courage needed to survive. Ezili Danto is amongst this section, embodying fierce protective motherhood. The order of service usually concludes with the Gede, the nation of the dead, as *regleman*[9] states that they should be kept separate from the Rada spirits who require cleanliness and purity (although this does not always stop Gede from turning up early in ceremony). Papa Gede, sometimes associated with Baron Samedi and sometimes separate from him, leads the ranks of the dead with his wife Manman Brigitte. Honouring the dead and particularly the ancestors is a vital part of Vodou ceremony. These Lwa are often mischievous and jovial, reminding people to live well and appreciate the things that

---

[8] Tann 2012: 53
[9] The protocol and order in which the Lwa are called during a service.

they themselves can no longer enjoy in death. Whilst some Lwa are ancient, others are said to be emerging all the time. All however act as intercessors for the one great, unknowable God, sometimes called Bondye in Creole. It is in this way that they are likened to the Catholic saints, which is why assimilation of their images happened with such ease.

Although service to the Lwa does include personal devotion through home altars, the majority of practice is communal. At a fet, altars are created with specially prepared food and selected items to honour various Lwa. They are saluted, sung, drummed, and danced for, and greeted in possession. The rhythmic atmosphere of the fet provides the ideal conditions for participants to enter a trance state wherein a Lwa is said to mount them (hence the possessed is called a 'horse'). During this time, they may greet their servants, converse, give out advice, eat, or perform seemingly superhuman feats that the horse would not normally be able to endure. Following the possession, the horse will have no memory of the experience and will have sustained no injury from the actions of the Lwa, although may feel exhausted. During the visitation it is believed that the consciousness of the person completely leaves the body to make room for the Lwa.

WHO IS EZILI DANTO?

Kingsbury and Chesnut write that the name of Ezili comes from the Fon word Azlí, meaning lake or lake spirit.[10] Several of the female African deities we will encounter in this book originate as water spirits, and some sense of the association with fecundity survived after the transatlantic crossing. Kingsbury and Chesnut tell us that 'Danto' comes from *D' En tort*, meaning Ezili 'of the wronged' which tells us a lot about her essence.[11]

Ezili Danto is usually described as an imposing Black woman, in peasant dress (specifically gingham), sometimes accompanied by her daughter or a black pig which is sacred to her. Her *veve* features a knife piercing a heart, which illustrates her anguish, and during

---

[10] Kingsbury and Chesnut write that Ezili absorbed some of the essence of the Taino water spirit Atabey, with whom the servants of Azlí found natural similarity in their new environment (2019a: 12)

[11] Kingsbury and Chesnut 2019a: 12

possession she favours knives, to handle or gesture with. She is also offered sweet red wine, baby dolls, and roast pork. The stories about the origins of Ezili Danto are various, but descriptions of her are consistent and we learn more about her from the words of those who have met her in ceremony. Interviewees described her as very powerful and very angry, and were in awe of her. This is how two Vodouisants described her:

> *"She is strict, absolutely, intense, absolutely, compassionate, absolutely. She is very 'tough love', that is the sense I get from her. She is certainly strict and certainly tough. I like her" (CJ).*

> *"Strength. Utter strength. There is not a single thing in this world one can't do if she is by your side. She is strength of will, strength of spirit, strength of heart, strength of body, and she has a stubbornness, a tenacity even, in overcoming of obstacles. She in that sense is a mother of the oppressed but also a mother of victors. Because in the end the victims become the victors through strength, through overcoming. And to me she is also a mother, not just of the oppressed but of those who serve her" (KH).*

She is seen as the mother of seven nations but she is by no means a gentle mother. Her connection with the start of the Revolution, either as human priestess or manifested Lwa shows that what she embodies is what was necessary at that time – pure rage at the indignities that the slaves were subjected to, their human rights stripped away.[12] Her fiery Petro spirit was what was needed to overturn the system, something that other Lwa, although powerful, did not embody. There are also other Ezilis – they form a family that spans the cooler Rada spirits as well as there being fiercer, hotter-still versions in the Petro nation such as Ezili Ge Rouge ('Red Eyes'). They are not, as some books claim, "all one Erzulie". Neither is Danto easily equated with deities from other pantheons. There are Western authors who simplistically describe Ezili Freda, Ezili Danto, and Gran Ezili as a maiden/mother/crone triad, or Danto as a triple goddess with Freda and La Sirene but this is the application of a foreign belief

---

[12] One of my respondents stressed that Westerners may not know just how horrific conditions were, and related an example used in Isabelle Allende's *Island Beneath The Sea* (2010, HarperCollins), where slave mothers were so terrified to bring a child into that world that they would kill their babies by pushing a pin into their brains, in order to leave no marks to show how they died, from fear of retribution by the masters.

system that has nothing to do with how the relationships between these Lwa function. One book on Vodou I encountered featured a table of corresponding deities in other pantheons which rather unhelpfully equated both Danto and Freda with 'Love' goddesses such as Freya and Aphrodite. Although both have been associated with love magic, this approach is reductionist and misguiding about who these Lwa actually are. As we will see, Danto and Freda are very different from each other, as well as from European goddesses.

Where we do find genuine syncretism is in the usage of a Black Madonna as an image for Ezili Danto - Our Lady of Częstochowa, the most famous Black Madonna of Poland, or variants of it.[13] We should however be careful not to state that Ezili *is* the Black Madonna. One respondent, when asked if they regarded the Black Madonna as a separate entity, one and the same, or a useful visual correspondence, replied:

> *"The two are separate. The saint image and the Lwa, from my point of view, are completely separate. I'm reminded of a saying 'All the saints are spirits but not all the spirits are saints'. I think it's important to remember that the images of the saints are images of saints, and they provide a useful correspondence but are not the same as the spirit. So I see them as a separate entity, the Black Madonna, Our Lady of Częstochowa, is a symbol of Dantor, a representation, but is not the same. And it's the same with all of the saints and Lwa." (CJ)*

As mentioned, images were often chosen which mirrored stories about the Lwa. Our Lady of Częstochowa has two scars upon her cheek, which themselves have their own legendary origin stories.[14] Some believe that this appealed to the Haitians as a reminder of the marks of scarification found in African traditions.[15] Vodouisantes often explain it as the scratches inflicted

---

[13] The most common image used for Danto is in fact a Black Madonna known as the Mater Salvatoris (or sometimes Santa Barbara Africana) that is based upon Our Lady of Częstochowa.

[14] In brief, when Hussites raided the Polish monastery of Jasna Gora in 1430, they struck the painting of Our Lady of Częstochowa with swords, causing the slashes to her cheek, an action which is said to have caused the offenders to immediately drop dead.

[15] Węgłowski 2015: 36-7

by her sister, Ezili Freda in a fight over a man.[16] Whereas most of the saint images used for Lwa are White, the one that is used for Danto is Black – significant in that it is the one that most mirrored Black Haitians' own appearance. Although the image would probably not have entered the country until after the Revolution broke out, as it is thought to have been brought to Haiti by Polish legionaries fighting for the French, its adoption is of importance. Here we have a Black maternal figure chosen to signify Danto,[17] the initiator of their rebellion. Haitians identified with her at a time when their will and self-determination was erupting into action.

THE POLISH IN HAITI

The presence of a Polish icon in a New World territory seems curious, and scholars have tried to identify how this Black Madonna became accepted and even popular in Haiti, rather than hated, seeing as her image arrived in the belongings of troops sent to oppress the uprisings. In fact, in the aftermath of the Revolution, the Polish, along with the Germans were the only European nationalities allowed by the constitution of 1805 to own property in Haiti.[18] Adam Węgłowski postulates that the Polish were tolerated more than the French because they did not disguise their dislike of the French, were less barbaric in their treatment of captured rebels, and a number of them (150-250) defected to the side of the insurgents.[19] Polish troops were also involved in the massacre of a battalion of 400 unarmed Black soldiers at St. Marc but their distaste for it is something remembered in Haiti. Sebastian Rypson finds that whereas European accounts present them as carrying out the orders to slaughter, no questions asked, Haitian historians describe the Polish as being unwilling and having their hands forced to act against those seeking their freedom, which is thought to be why Dessalines honoured them in the constitution

---

[16] One of my respondents explained the difference in the parts of the body each sister aims for: "For Freda the worst wound is against her sister's beauty. For Dantor, the worst wound is emotional – thus she stabbed Freda in the chest. This tells you a lot about their relationship!" (SF)

[17] Or in the words on one of the Vodouisants interviewed, chosen by her. "It's like she's almost asserted her will there because she wants to be seen for who she is" (SF).

[18] Rypson 2008: 68

[19] Węgłowski 2015: 27

following Haiti's formation.[20]

The Polish also had amongst their legions a biracial general, Wladysław Jabłonowski, which may or may not have affected the Haitians' preconceptions of them. Jabłonowski, however, succumbed to yellow fever, as did a large number of the 5,000 Polish sent by Napoleon; as many as 4,000 of them. Węgłowski suggests that with such a high number of funerals, public displays of the Black Virgin of Częstochowa may well have been a common sight, therefore increasing its visibility and familiarity amongst Haitians.[21] However, how public or individual the funerals were for victims of disease in a time of war is questionable. We do know though, that whilst around 700 of the remaining Poles left Haiti following the Revolution, up to 400 initially stayed and integrated with the Haitians.[22] Although mentions of the Polish in Haitian history are notable because of their curious nature, after the Revolution they disappear, the legionnaires and their descendants becoming mostly absorbed into Haitian culture.[23] The image of the Mother of God, Częstochowa, is the most enduring piece of evidence of their presence, one which became accepted amongst the legion of saints used as foci by Vodouisants in their ceremonies.

VOICE OF THE OPPRESSED

The image, both as Ezili in Haiti and as Mother Mary in Poland, has been used as a display of political defiance. In the Haitian military coup of 1991, images of Ezili were displayed and prayed to that the junta might fall.[24] In 1980s Poland, the same Black Madonna was used as the symbol of Solidarity, the trade union movement that opposed Communism. In 1983, Pope John Paul II visited Port-au-Prince, Haiti, a significant event for the country for

---

[20] Rypson 2008: 51

[21] Węgłowski 2015: 26

[22] The remaining Polish legionnaires were amongst the only Whites to survive Dessalines' slaughter, alongside French priests and doctors, and English and American merchants. It is thought, unlike the French prisoners of war, Dessalines did not harm the Polish prisoners, and recruited a number into his army (Rypson 2008: 62, 66)

[23] Sebastian Rypson searched for preservations of Polish culture in Haiti, particularly around the Poloné settlement of Cazale, but found that, much like the diasporic African clans, nothing survives such transplantation without serious modification. See Rypson, 2008.

[24] Węgłowski 2015: 40

which there was much preparation. The Pope paid homage to the Polish Legionnaires who he described as changing sides on arrival in Haiti and fighting for the liberation of the slaves. To the government of the time's dismay, the Pope went on to deliver a message which highlighted the struggles of the poor and inequalities under the current Duvalier regime and was taken as a direct criticism. To the people, this was taken as a sign of support, and some suggested was tied into the Pope's affinity to the Black Madonna of his homeland, which was also the symbol of their beloved Lwa.[25]

The Vodouisants I asked did not think Danto *herself* was political, as her focus is the immediate needs of those wronged, but it is impossible for her not to be an influential socio-political figure because she is a defender of the oppressed. Besides opposing slavery, she is also a defender of wronged women, and seen as patron of prostitutes and homosexuals. Some stories even suggest she is lesbian herself so may have first-hand experience of this kind of discrimination. It is in fact more common in Vodou Maryaj ceremonies for her to take wives than husbands as she prefers the company of women, and my respondents said that she is even known to appear in dreams as hermaphroditic.

To compare Ezili Danto to her Rada sister Ezili Freda is to compare night and day. Marc A. Christophe says: "In a country where the majority of the population lives in poverty, the two Ezilis exemplify the Haitian Vodouist's strength and courage (Ezili Danto) as well as his or her aspiration for material wealth (Ezili Freda)".[26] Whereas Danto is a practical and formidable mother figure, Freda is coquettish, genteel and easily upset. Danto plays mother to the children whom Freda pretends not to have. Freda is envisioned as a biracial woman who speaks French and likes dainty foods and trinkets. When faced with the realities of the world which do not live up to this idealised lifestyle, she weeps inconsolably. Because of this, she is depicted as the Mater Dolorosa, the sorrowing Mary. Often this is a white-skinned version of Mary clutching a knife that is piercing her heart. If we think about the Ezilis as a family who display varying degrees of

---

[25] Rypson 2008: 146
[26] Christophe 2006: 96

emotional response, Gran Ezili, at the Rada extreme, sorrows for the world on a grand scale whereas Petro Ezilis such as Ezili Ge Rouge embody unbridled anger. Both Danto and Freda sorrow for the world and its children, but, whereas Freda weeps when she sees wrongdoing, Danto screams.

In most cases, Danto is mute because her tongue has been cut out.[27] In possession she can only make guttural noises and is known to become increasingly frustrated if she is unable to get her message across.[28] Her mute status is variously explained as being retribution by male slaveowners for her part in leading the Revolution, for warning other slaves of danger, or by her own people in case she might give away secrets under torture. Another interesting possibility has been postulated, that being intertwined with a Polish icon, the guttural sounds she makes may represent what the alien language of the Polish settlers sounded like to the Haitians during the early years of integration.[29] Some modern activists wish to reverse Danto's mute status, seeing it as a symbol of neo-colonialism, but the Vodouisants I spoke to did not think it was something that humans could just decide 'for her' and that it would be arrogant to think we could change an aspect that is intrinsic to that Lwa:

> *'To me, part of her power, in the Haitian tradition, is that she's mute, because she's representing those who have had their voices taken, how can she represent them if she's talking? It's like if I was to go and start writing about domestic violence and how terrible it is but I have not experienced it. But she has experienced it to the point of having her tongue ripped out. So it's more powerful, and something people can identify, the idea of not being able to speak and getting frustrated because others won't hear.... I don't see it as a symbol of neo-colonialism, I feel that it's more of a kick against*

[27] Notably this is not the case in *21 Divisiones*, the version of Vodou practice in the neighbouring Dominican Republic. In *21*, Danto speaks. This is thought to be because of the differing histories and development of stories in the two countries. The Dominican Republic is a wealthier country with less of a history of oppression and revolution.

[28] When she is unable to express her message, her daughter sometimes also comes into possession to translate. Whereas the Black Madonna is depicted with the Christ Child, Danto's child is said to be a female called Anais. Anais should not be confused with Anaisa, a Lwa from the Dominican side of the island who is associated with the image of St Ann. Her name may be connected to the French for pineapple, *ananas*, as the Madonna's crown resembles one, and it has therefore become one of her offerings.

[29] Rypson 2008: 90

that actually. And also for me she is a real person, she's as real as me, so to say "let's reverse this" it's not like I chose that, like I can't change your eyes to brown, it's who she is in that aspect" (SF).

Even if it were possible, the respondents did not feel that it was necessarily something desirable, and that reversing her mute status would risk forgetting history:

"I think it's an important reminder, and I think if Dantor has no tongue then we are tasked with being her voice and therefore each of us is tasked with being a voice of the oppressed, and that's vastly important in today's world, because there's still so many people out there who do not have a voice, and even if they do have a voice, it's quiet, or people try to silence it, or it's in some part of the world we apparently don't care about" (KH).

They agreed that, even without a tongue, she can lend her strength to these people:

"Because she persisted. And there is a power to silence. And a power to silent rage. And I think it's uncomfortable for people to talk about that, and it's uncomfortable for people to acknowledge that silent rage as a useful force in our world. We are taught so often to turn the other cheek or be kind, or to speak with reason or logic in the face of the unjust, and time and time again we are shown that that does not work. Silent rage drives people forward, and silent rage in the end pushes things to the extreme. And that's when victory occurs" (KH).

IN HER IMAGE

Although Vodouisants would not agree that they create their deities, Kingsbury and Chesnut posit a nevertheless useful standpoint, that Ezili Danto is a creation of the female African slave 'in her own image', one not of weakness and passivity but one who frequently challenged and rebelled against the injustices of their world.

"It is women who made and to this today continue to be mounted by Ezili, a lwa whose complex, shifting, multifaceted persona goes beyond simplistic depictions of Black women... Ezili must not only be construed as a spirit who empowered women who had no rights

nor voice but also as a sentient, contemplative mode of self-generated resistance and expression.[30]

Rather than being a protector to helplessly cling to, she reflects their very selves – the women who both overtly and covertly were very much involved in the Revolution. Kingsbury and Chesnut point out the telling fact that the name Cécile Fatiman has been lost or purposefully omitted from nearly all accounts of the ceremony at Bwa Kayiman. This is thought to have been the identity of the priestess who embodied Danto that night, but the history of the Revolution has tended to remember only the men involved.[31] This puts another spin on Ezili's mute status, the fact that the very name of this key player in the Revolution has been silenced.

Despite female Lwa being honoured in Vodou in balance with the male, and Mambos having relatively equal status to Houngans, the touch of cultures which regard women as inferior has lingered, and as such, women today in Haiti are not without their struggles for equal recognition. Bellegarde-Smith and Michel in their book *Haitian Vodou* recognise this and interviewed ten Mambo in order to represent their truths in their own words. The women interviewed said that spirituality and Vodou is what they found to empower them in a man's world, which was also true at the time of the Revolution. It was women who kept the traditions passing down the generations, even in periods when it was illegal, such as during US occupation 1915-1934.[32]

Although outwardly, there may seem to be inequality between women and men in the religion, Bellegarde-Smith and Michel's interviewees did not view it as so. Many of the Lwa function in dyads of male and female pairings but these Mambo believed this dualism is present within every Lwa as well as every human being. Despite this perceived equality, one Mambo mentioned that they thought there were more Mambo than Houngan, and that many of the Houngan are homosexual or bisexual. This plays into society's perception that women (and gay men) are more perceptive, intuitive, and more natural adepts at religion, whereas male

---

[30] Kingsbury and Chesnut 2019a: 10
[31] Kingsbury and Chesnut 2019a: 7
[32] Michel, Bellegarde-Smith and Racine-Toussaint 2006: 74-5

arrogance can hinder contact with the spirit world.[33] Although this gender stereotyping is not without problems itself, it does allow women who have been largely excluded from professional or political roles to carve out a niche in a religion that provides them with role models such as Ezili Danto. Women and men alike know that with a Lwa like Danto by their side, anything is truly possible.

CONCLUSION

The persistent silent rage of Ezili Danto really encapsulates what the Black Madonna has come to mean in the modern world, not just in the streets of Haiti and Poland, but everywhere that a Black maternal figure has been adopted. We see it in the other Black Madonnas of Central and South American countries. We see it adopted into the Western feminist Goddess movement. And we even see similarities with Eastern traditions who honour a dark mother such as Kali and Tara. Just as Kali is seen as the Great Mother to whom all her followers return in death, Ezili, to some, represents the motherland, *Ginen,* and the cosmic womb to which all souls are reclaimed.[34] Claude Planson, the French scholar who wrote about his experiences of *kanzo*, said that during his seclusion he had a vision of a beautiful Black Goddess who he saw as the image of Mother Earth.[35] Although Vodou is technically a monotheistic religion with the distant Bondye a more-or-less equivalent of the Christian God, still, the idea of a Great Mother culturally persists. Bellegarde-Smith says that despite Haiti's fragmentary history, which has seen long-term division between Whites, Black Africans and mixed-race *gens de coleur,* "the link between all Haitians, however, is a Black mother, albeit with different fathers."[36] Although only one of many Lwa under Bondye, Ezili Danto is that powerful unifying force, the symbolic Mother of the Revolution that gave birth to a new country.

The current that runs through this archetype does not necessarily mean that all of the aforementioned entities/deities are the same, but the way this energy manifests in the world can be

---

[33] Michel, Bellegarde-Smith and Racine-Toussaint 2006: 79-80
[34] Christophe 2006: 96
[35] Crosley 2006: 12
[36] Bellegarde-Smith 2006: 30

compared from country to country and a common thread of righteous anger found. The Vodouisants interviewed certainly did not believe Danto to be just an embodiment of a universal force but rather an entity in her own right, yet one who exists to personify that very human quality of rage. Ezili Danto rose to prominence from a very specific set of circumstances at a certain time, yet is timeless in what she embodies, and her association with the Black Madonna ties her into a worldwide movement of inspiring Black Mothers.

CHAPTER 6

Syncretism and the Black Madonna in the Americas

INTRODUCTION

We have now seen how the Black Madonna has blended with both native deities and imported African ones, creating new modes of worship in the process. This is not limited to Mexico and Haiti, and happened throughout Central and South America, in differing regional variations. The act of colonisation and the slave trade produced these circumstances, and it is why so many Black Madonnas are, sometimes explicitly, linked to the fight for equality and freedom.

In Haiti, where a large number of the trafficked slaves hailed from Dahomey and Kongo, the particular practice that we know as Vodou developed based on the traditions from these regions, whereas in other parts of the Americas, Africans from Yorubaland and other regions developed similar but individual systems. Luísa Teish tells us that these New World variations were each determined by three things: beliefs and practices of their African ancestors, those of their oppressors, plus often the beliefs of the local Indigenes, with whom they often found natural commonalities. Teish thinks the latter has been downplayed by historians, and says some deities and practices cannot be traced back to Africa.[1]

In Cuba, African traditions developed as Lucumí, sometimes called Santería or Orisha. In Brazil, it is primarily Candomblé and

---

[1] Teish quotes an example from Maya Deren, who says the *ge rouge* (red eyed) family in Haitian Vodou originate from the native Arawak tradition of staining the area around their eyes red in order to look more fearsome to their enemies. Teish 1985: 112.

Umbanda. Puerto Rico has Spiritism, and in Trinidad, where emancipated slaves were replaced by indentured servants drawn from South Asia, we find forms of Hinduism and Kali worship. As some of these religions crossed into North America with secondary migration, we have practices such as New Orleans Voodoo and Hoodoo emerging, influenced by both Haitian Vodou and European magical grimoires. Black Madonnas can be found in all of these traditions, syncretised with some of the most powerful and popular deities. In this chapter, we will look primarily at two traditions – Cuban Lucumí and Brazilian Candomblé, and two Orisha – Oshún and Yemoja, to see how these two deities became entwined with Black Madonnas in both of these cultures. We will also approach the topic of syncretism – the association of African deities with Catholic saints, how it works in practice versus theory, why some wish to see an end to it, and why it is nevertheless of importance.

LUCUMÍ BELIEFS

As we have already spoken about Vodou, let us see how Lucumí/Santería differs in comparison. Whereas Vodouisantes serve the Lwa, Santeros serve the Orisha. We will later see how some of the Orisha appear similar to certain Lwa through their root deities in Africa, although the diverging development of their worship in the Americas has produced entirely separate beings.

The Orisha are served differently in ceremony. Each Orisha's presence is honoured in a bowl or vase containing *otánes* – stones and shells which together forms a representation of their physical bodies and spirits. Animal sacrifice forms a major part of the service, where particular fowl, goats, and other animals sacred to that Orisha, are offered to feed them. Their blood is spilled into the vessels, and then the bodies ritually prepared for consumption.

Opposite:: "Mothers of Water – Oshun and Yemaya'. This image depicts the Orisha known as Oshún and Yemoja in their native Yorubaland before they made the crossing to the Americas in the hearts of their people. Sometimes depicted as mother and daughter and sometimes sisters, here we see the moment freshwater meets saltwater, and Oshún asks Yemoja to take her with her across the sea.

The congregation will eat the meat of the animals, whereas the organs and blood are reserved for the Orisha – these contain the *ashé* or life force.[1]

Blood sacrifice is not the only kind of offering in Lucumí, and may include sweets, vegetables, grain, and libations. The type of offering is determined by divination using palm nuts, cowrie shells or coconut. Possession is also important in Lucumí, although it tends to be less spontaneous than in Vodou, with greater preparation of a particular Olorisha (initiate) to host a particular spirit, sometimes for an hour at a time.

As in Vodou, Lucumí has a singular godhead, Olódumare. Under him are Olófin, the aspect of God closest to earth and Olorún, ruler of heaven and dispenser of the *ashé*. Beneath them are the Orisha. Scholars disagree on whether the notion of God being distant and unapproachable is a European corruption or consistent with African beliefs, but the fact remains that, as in Vodou, Yorubans and Santeros pray to the Orisha as intercessors. Like the concept of a Vodouisante's *met tet*, Yorubans believe each person has an Orisha who resides in their head, the seat of the soul. The Orisha sometimes represent cosmic and environmental forces, such as Oya who embodies storms and Oshún and Yemoja who embody different forms of water, but also concepts closer to humanity, such as Ogun who presides over iron and warfare. Each of these Orisha has been paired with a different saint or form of the Virgin Mary on arrival in the New World.

---

[1] Ócha'ni Lele addresses the sensitive subject of animal sacrifice, which some find distasteful, in 'Sacrificial Ceremonies of Santería' (2012). Lele argues that the practice is not wasteful or orgiastic blood-letting; it is no worse than secular slaughter for human consumption, merely adding a spiritual dimension. City-dwelling Christians may pray over their plates but are removed from the act of sacrifice made to provide their meals. Blood sacrifices in Santería are performed humanely and respectfully, contrary to media propaganda. In occasional cases, such as for healing ceremonies, the meat is not eaten, as it is believed to have taken on the sickness from the patient, but these are still disposed of with care.

Above:: 'Iemanja Stella Maris'. Based on the traditional Brazilian image dating to the early 20th Century and used in Candomblé and Umbanda. Here the Yoruban water goddess Yemoya is Star of the Sea, patroness of seafarers and mother of the oceans.

HISTORY OF SANTERÍA

Centuries before the coming of the European slavers, the Yoruban Empire had developed a network of city states, with each city dedicated to a particular Orisha, although with temples to many other Orisha within it. By 1501, when the first slaves were shipped to Cuba, the city of Oyó was one of the most powerful. These slaves were probably prisoners of war from neighbouring cities.[1] It was not until Oyó was in decline in the latter half of the 18th century that large numbers of Yorubans started to be shipped to Cuba. After 1763, Yoruban slaves started to comprise a majority amongst the African population in Cuba,[2] and as such, their traditions began to shape the religious landscape.

In 1789, Charles IV of Spain issued a royal decree defining slavery in Cuba, the first of its kind issued by Spain. On the subject of religion, it stated that all slaves should be instructed in Catholicism, and a second law of the same year decreed that all slaves should be prepared for baptism within one year. Slave labour on feast days was forbidden so that they could attend mass (although landowners later found ways around the crown's decree). Lele writes that "Although meant to ensure total domination over the souls of the blacks, both the Royal Document on the Trades and Occupations of Slaves and the Fugitive Slave Law would, in time, actually have the reverse effect".[3]

Two priests, Father Juan Matienzo and Bishop Pedro Augustín Morrell de Santa Cruz, opted for a softly-softly approach to gradually ease Africans towards conversion, allowing the continuation of some of their traditional practices alongside the Christian.

They revived the Spanish custom of *cofradias* – group meetings each set up in a saint's name; lay brotherhoods providing religious instruction. These *cofradias* taught Counter-Reformation Catholicism which was folksier and more similar to magical practices than what the Africans were receiving in church, and it was here that they learned interpretations of saint stories that

---

[1] Lele 2012: 57
[2] Lele 2012: 59
[3] Lele 2012: 60

reminded them of their Orisha. They saw them as reinterpretations and used them as covers, successfully subverting Catholicism, but more than this, they saw them as parallel versions of the same *ashé*. Whilst acknowledging them as separate beings, they saw both the saint and the Orisha as humans who had led similar lives and were both representations of the same power.[4]

The *cofradías* evolved into *cabildos de nación*, which encouraged gatherings of Africans of the same ethnicity to supposedly strengthen their faith. It instead served to strengthen their secret worship of their ancestral deities, which in the case of Cabildo Africano Lucumí was the Orisha. Orisha feast days were changed to match those of the saints, whom they worshipped fervently, as a means of continuing their devotion to the Orisha. The emphasis on the saints earned the practice of Lucumí the name Santería, although this was originally coined as a pejorative by the ruling class, indicating a superstitious set of beliefs by those who they thought were not intelligent enough to 'get religion right'.[5] These practices were nonetheless allowed to continue, until cabildo meetings grew too large and became regarded as a nuisance so were banned from city centres. However, the lenience initiated by Father Matienzo and Bishop Morrell had allowed the religion to take firm root in Cuban culture, and various means were employed to ensure its survival during the latter 1800s leading up to the abolition of slavery in 1886. The old cabildos that had been repressed were replaced by new houses, and new practices were devised to provide more structure and to unite disparate ethnicities who had previously been kept apart. Intertribal and interracial marriage became more common, and an increasing number of Whites were initiated into the religion. Lucumí was no longer about tribal affiliations but cut across class and ethnicity.[6]

As the makeup of Lucumí became almost entirely Creole, it also became firmly tied to the culture of Cuba, though persecution of the religion did not cease. Throughout the 20th century, the art and music of Lucumí was celebrated, consumed, and exported, but its spiritual significance was downplayed. Increasingly severe

---

[4] Lele 2012: 61-2
[5] Lele 2012: 65
[6] Lele 2012: 71

government regimes drove Black spirituality underground, and eventually to begin migration to the United States, even before the Revolution of 1959. Conditions were no better for the religion under Castro, and many chose to leave and set up *Ilé* (religious houses) in the USA.[7]

MOTHERS OF WATER – OSHÚN AND YEMOJA

Water deities have already been briefly mentioned and, unsurprisingly, were of great importance to the first generation of the African Diaspora, all of whom had made an immense and dangerous ocean crossing to the Americas. The female Orisha of most importance in this regard were Oshún and Yemoja.

Oshún is associated with love, beauty and fertility and with the river Òsun in Nigeria. The last Orisha born, Oshún initially had no name, according to one story. Earth stagnated whilst she pined, until the sound of a boulder falling into water made the onomatopoeic sound *oshún*. Heeding this sign, the Orisha Obatalá declared this is what Oshún would be called, and Earth bloomed again with her happiness at receiving a name.[8] Lele tells us that the etymology of her name is linked to African sandalwood, *òsùn*, a red powder used in the sacred consecration of an initiate's head in Lucumí.[9]

Being mother to the other Orisha, Yemoja is most associated with motherhood, and praised as the Great Mother. She is also associated with rivers, primarily the Ogun, and all bodies of water. The etymology of her name suggests that it both means "the mother whose children are fish" and "the mother whose children are the world".[10] An ancient deity; it was from her womb that the first dry land appeared and where the Orisha who could not descend from Heaven on their own were birthed.[11] Like Ezili Danto, she is not only a fertile and nurturing mother but also a strict and fearsome matriarch, and she cares for her own children

---

[7] Lele 2012: 80, 88.
[8] Lele 2012: 40
[9] Lele 2012: 40
[10] Lele 2012: 42
[11] Lele 2012: 42

as well as those belonging to other Orisha who pretend to have none.

OUR LADY OF REGLA – YEMAYÁ IN CUBA

Once in the New World, Oshún kept her sweet-water associations but Yemoja transformed into more of a salt-water deity, becoming patroness of sailors and fishermen. The Lucumí tureens containing her *otánes* also often contain nautical items cast in lead, such as mermaids, boats and anchors.[12] In Cuba, whilst Oshún was syncretised with the Virgen de la Caridad del Cobre (Virgin of Charity), Yemoja became associated with Our Lady of Regla (Lady of the Rule). The Virgin of Regla's gowns are blue, a colour which is universally associated with depictions of Yemoja, spelled Yemayá in Cuba. Elizabeth Perez tells us that in Lucumí:

> *"Initiates pun on the Virgin of Regla's name to place emphasis on certain attributes of Yemayá: since in Spanish, regla means "rule" or "regulation," in Cuba one frequently finds straight-edged rulers and other instruments of measurement on altars dedicated to her. Regla also means "period" as a polite term for menstruation, encouraging the belief that Yemayá governs the cyclical flow of blood from women's bodies."*[13]

Of the four Virgins used to represent different Orisha in Cuba, the Virgin of Regla was the only one that was also a Black Madonna in Europe. The original statue, located in Chipiona, Cádiz, is associated with the Rule (Regla) of St Augustine of Hippo, having been 'rediscovered' by members of the Augustine order. In order to account for her black visage, and because of this connection to the African saint, a legend developed, recorded in the 17th century, that the Black Madonna was carved by Augustine in North Africa.[14] Shortly after Augustine's death, Hippo was besieged, and Cyprian and some other African saints were able to flee the city by ship to Spain, taking the statue with them. Our Lady of Regla protected the saints during violent sea storms, leading her to becoming the Spanish patroness of seafarers.

---

[12] Perez 2010: 207
[13] Perez 2010: 207
[14] Perez 2010: 203-4

Whereas Chipiona was the departure point for many ships to the New World, the Bay of Regla in Havana was the first point of landfall for both ships from Spain and slave ships from Africa and was therefore a fitting spot for the cult of this seafaring saint and ocean mother to grow. The current Church of Regla, built in the Bay of Havana in 1811 and dedicated to the Virgin, is one of Cuba's most visited. The statue itself, however, preceded the church. The people of the town, formerly called Guaicanamar, worshipped an oil painting of the Spanish Virgin of Regla in the sanctuary of an old sugar mill from 1687 until 1692, when both chapel and painting were destroyed by a hurricane. Another shrine was hurriedly built on the site by a Spaniard who had escaped a shipwreck after praying to Our Lady of Regla, and a copy of the Spanish statue was donated soon after.[15]

She is definitively black, and Bishop Morell noted in his 1755 account (the first written mention of that statue) that "she had never accepted touch-ups with white colour",[16] a prominent feature of the legends of many Black Madonnas. One of the notable features of the original statue is that the Black Madonna holds a White child. When it was examined in the 1930s, it was determined that the statue was probably early 14th-century in origin, from a single block of wood, but it was impossible to determine her original colour, following numerous restorations. It is thought, however, that the Madonna and child were probably originally one colour, as evidenced by the colour of Jesus' feet, and that the difference is due to various stages of restoration.[17] This current appearance dates back at least to the 17th century, by which time she was already being depicted in print as racially Black whilst holding a White Jesus.

Symbols which accompany the Spanish Virgin of Regla in paintings also held significance in her new Cuban home. The crescent moon, often associated with depictions of the Virgin Mary, and the anchor, symbol of her seafaring patronage, are also associated with Yemayá. Her golden key was mirrored by the key to the city with which the Cuban Regla was symbolically gifted

---

[15] Perez 2010: 211
[16] Perez 2010: 202
[17] Anderies 2006: 10-11

when crowned Patroness of Havana. And the significance of the slave chains, which appear in 19th-century depictions of her, need no explanation in the Cuban context. Julie Parella Anderies writes that the unshackled chains, which first appear in two 19th-century Spanish engravings, represent her granting the Spanish freedom from the Moors,[18] but could this possibly be another case of reverse influence, as we saw with Montserrat, symbolism from the New World influencing European depictions?[19]

The Black Virgin of Regla was first celebrated on her feast day, with the installation of her statue in 1696. Annual celebrations started in earnest after 1714, by which time Regla had been proclaimed Patroness and Protectress of the bay of Havana.[20] The first festivities lasted eight days, with the statue taken out of her church and down to the ocean, to be floated on a raft in the Bay of Havana. The tradition gradually dwindled, along with the town's reputation, but was revived in the late 19th century by two of the *cabildos,* with pilgrims visiting in great numbers every September 7th. Rather than parading the official Black Virgin, the Santeros carried their own statue of the Black Madonna of Regla to be received and blessed at the church doors by the parish priest then down to the ocean where followers cleansed themselves with seawater, threw coins in for luck, and passed Yemayá's animal, a duck, over their bodies to remove negative influences.[21]

The processions were not only about honouring Yemayá but about Afro-Cuban visibility. Once representing over 30% of the population in Regla, their numbers had reduced significantly by the 20th century. The processions stopped at various important municipal landmarks: "By crossing the threshold of government agencies, the cabildos symbolically gained possession of the town that, by 1921, had become the site of bigotry and frequent racist violence",[22] says Perez. A race war in 1912 had forced many Blacks to flee Cuba, including Pepa Herrera, director of Cabildo Yemayá, one of the procession organisers. She returned in late 1920, and the

---

[18] Anderies 2006: 15-16
[19] Elisa Foster presented the argument that New World works of art sent back to Spain depicting racially Black Virgins influenced how the Spanish thought about the ethnicity of their Black Madonnas. See Chapter 3.
[20] Perez 2010: 211
[21] Dianteill 2002: 129
[22] Perez 2010: 214

annual procession restarted in 1921.[23] Thereafter, besides being a celebration, it would forever be intertwined with the struggle for racial equality.

Yemayá as a voice for the plight of Black slave women is visible in the literature of 19th-century abolitionist Cirilo Villaverde. His novel, *Cecilia Valdés,* set in Cuba's slave society, features a character called María de Regla, clearly named after the Black Virgin and based on Yemayá's nurturing characteristics. She is the wet nurse who breastfeeds both her own child and that of her slaveowner and is the book's only source of maternal love and guidance.[24]

Racially-codified perceptions of intelligence are at play in the novel, and the fact that Mariá is well-spoken and "knows how to talk" proves doubly-problematic for the slaveowner, thus leading to Mariá's exile. On her return, Mariá is able to plainly tell her story, that she was exiled for knowing the particulars of Cecilia's birth, the details of which the narrator has skirted around. One of the sisters refuses to believe Mariá's story, denying her authority on the matter.[25]

The technique of having Mariá be the mouthpiece for the things the narrator won't say is a reflection on the views of the author and how they evolved between 1839, when his first version of the story was released, and 1879, when the final version was published. The original was written at the urging of slave abolitionist Domingo del Monte, to add to the cause for reform put before the International Tribunal of Justice. However, Villaverde turned from reform to conspiring for Cuban independence. He was caught and jailed for six months before escaping to the US where he continued to support Cuban freedom. He gradually came to believe the lesser evil would be annexation

---

[23] Perez 2010: 216

[24] In the novel, the mulatta character of Cecilia Valdés is born of the liaison between a White plantation owner and a Black woman, a fact that he covers up. Cecilia later embarks on an incestuous affair with her half-brother Leonardo, without either of their knowledge (although he does comment on her similarity to his sister). Mariá de Regla, having been employed to nurse both the legitimate and illegitimate daughters of the master, is exiled because she 'knows too much'. She is separated from her husband Dionisio, the house cook, and only allowed to return years later, when she is able to tell her tale to the daughters.

[25] It is this "racially-restricted listening" (Sommer 1994: 41) by the privileged that causes their downfall. Cecilia had been warned earlier in the novel by Dionisio, after she rebuffs his invitation to dance, but his words fall on deaf ears, as her focus is on the aspirational courting of the White man who turns out to be her brother.

under the US, reflected in his White narrator's attitude.[26] The narrator is the voice of those who do not want to give up their White privilege, and who do not want to recognise the Afro-Cuban voices that were maintaining that independence was the only means of true freedom.[27]

> *"Conscious of his complicity with privileged compatriots, Villaverde repeats their defensive blindness and deafness in his narrator… The whites simply decline legitimate intercourse with blacks. And Villaverde's text keeps pointing to the white narrator who draws blanks in order to preserve the colour-fast fabric of slave society."*[28]

So, whilst recognising himself in his narrator, Villaverde provides the alternative voice through Mariá de Regla, and "throughout the novel, Maria assumes the role of advocate played by Yemayá in her mythology, defining the boundaries of morality and declaring her solidarity with those at the social margins."[29] She is the archetypal Black Madonna who has been wounded, discarded, yet exudes motherly tenderness and wisdom. Villaverde was still in support of abolition, and through Mariá's words about the inhumanity of slavery, he was able to voice it.

CARIDAD DEL COBRE – OCHÚN IN CUBA

Dressed in gold and yellow, the Cuban Ochún is syncretised with the Virgen de la Caridad del Cobre. The statue of Caridad del Cobre is not technically a Black Madonna, though she may once have been under the layers of paint on her face. Depictions of her often portray her as darker-skinned or biracial to match her people, and one folk tale gives an explanation for this. When the slavers came and took their people away, the Orisha found ways to travel with them to Cuba, in objects or through the elements. But Oshún was dismayed because she could follow no further than where her river met the salty sea. She called out to Yemoja for help who granted her the power to travel with her in the form of rain. Oshún asked Yemoja about the people of Cuba and on learning about their range of skin colourings, wished to become like them in order

---

[26] Sommer 1994: 30-1
[27] Sommer 1994: 35
[28] Sommer 1994: 43
[29] Perez 2010: 211

to reflect them. Yemoja, in her great power, granted her wish, straightening Oshún's hair and lightening her skin, although only as a 'glamour', saying those who gazed upon her would see what they regarded as most beautiful.[30] In this way she is able to appeal to biracial people by mirroring their appearance and giving them divinity in their own image.

Besides her own racial appearance, Caridad del Cobre is intimately tied to the identity of Cuba, through the three men or boys in a boat often depicted below her which relate to the origin story of the statue. Often called 'the three Juans', these figures were traditionally two Indians and an Afro-Cuban (and one of the Indians was originally called Rodrigo). In later years, depictions changed to make one of the figures White European, to represent the trinity of races that went into making modern Cuba. One version of the story has the three fishermen in the ocean when a storm hits. They pray to the Virgin Mary to spare them. As the storm suddenly clears, they spot the statue floating in the sea, which when hauled in is seen to bear the inscription "I am the Virgin of Charity". It is thought that it originated from a Spanish shipwreck. Much to their surprise, the statue remained completely dry. There follows typical Madonna origin details with the statue repeatedly disappearing from the church in which she had been placed, until one was erected at the spot where she was discovered, where the boat landed in El Cobre. As with Guadalupe and other Black and Brown Madonnas, she chooses to appear to those with the lowest social standing and becomes their champion. As well as representing the diverse races of Cuba, this Madonna became associated with the emancipation of slaves, when an edict freeing slaves from the El Cobre copper mines was read in front of her, which was interpreted as her will. Copper items are brought to be blessed by her, and the red-gold metal is connected with Ochún's traditional association with gold.

At the request of veteran soldiers of Cuba's war of independence, Pope Benedict XV declared Nuestra Senora de la Caridad del Cobre the Patroness of Cuba on 10 May 1916, and she continued to be honoured by popes throughout the 20th century.

---

[30] Lele 2012: 68-70

Besides being associated with the patroness of Cuba, Oshún is also associated with the patroness of Brazil.

SOME BACKGROUND ON AFRO-BRAZILIAN RELIGIONS

African-rooted religions, including Candomblé, Tambor de Mina, Batuque, Xangô, Umbanda, Quimbanda, and Macumba,[31] developed in Brazil in a very similar fashion to those of Cuba and Haiti. When the Portuguese colonised Brazil, just as had happened elsewhere, they brought with them European diseases which killed much of the native population, their initial workforce. Needing a replacement to work their sugar plantations and dig their gold mines, the Portuguese turned to African slavery. Slaves were brought to Brazil in their millions from the mid-1500s up until the late 1800s when slavery was abolished. Slaves were drawn in waves from various different locations, meaning that slightly different, but interlinked traditions found their way to Brazil. Yoruban Orixá (the Portuguese spelling of Orisha) worship, developed into what became known as Candomblé in Brazil, though variants came from Angola/Congo, Benin/Dahomey and elsewhere. Although the most well-known branch, the emphasis on 'Nago' (Yoruban) Candomblé has provoked resistance – "*inquice* worship (Bantu or Kimbundu-speaking peoples) and *vodun* worship (Fon or Gbe-speaking peoples)—are also asserting themselves and reacting against what they view as "nagô-ization"".[32]

Being Yoruba-based, Candomblé bears a lot of similarity to Santería. Devotees believe in the spiritual power *axé* (the Portuguese spelling of *ashé*) meted out by the creator and cared for by the Orixá, who are appealed to as intercessors by their devotees. There are both priests (*pais-de-santo*) and priestesses (*mães-de-santo*), who head up community house groupings called *terreiros*, the oldest being *Ilê Axé Iyá Nassô Oká* in the state of Bahia, founded in the 1830s.[33] Divination is used, namely the *jogo de búzios* and *ifá* oracles, and ceremonies are held during which the priests and priestesses

---

[31] Gledhill 2012: 10
[32] Gledhill 2012: 13
[33] Gledhill 2012: 13

will embody the Orixá. These celebrations are larger and more public than, for example, a Vodou fet, and even permit tourist attendees, if they respect protocol.[34]

In addition to Catholic and African influences, Candomblé features the most Native American elements, particularly the ritualistic use of herbs and focus on animistic local spirits of place. To the contrary, Umbanda, the latest of the religions to develop, has Spiritist influences from the White middle classes and has been said to aspire to a more 'civilized' and intellectual approach (and therefore more acceptance by White society). As opposed to the sometimes fleeting and unexpected possessions seen in Vodou, possessions in Umbanda and Candomblé are longer (sometimes one to two hours) and more planned, with specific initiates prepared to take certain Orisha. This is shared by some branches of Santeria, where only consensual planned possession by trained initiates is acceptable as opposed to horsing. The longer possessions in Candomblé and Umbanda allow for pauses to dress the initiate in ritual garb such as Oshún's bright yellow skirts, and Yemoja's beaded masks.

OXUM AND IEMANJÁ IN BRAZIL

In Brazil, Yemoja absorbed the characteristics of Mami Wata, a West African mermaid Orisha, along with another siren-like Native Brazilian deity, Iara, before being further blended with the Virgin of the Immaculate Conception, and becoming Brazil's most popular deity, Iemanjá.[35] It is notable that the most iconic and commonly reproduced image for Iemanjá here is not one of the Madonna but that of a light-skinned, dark-haired woman walking on the waves in the moonlight. This image became prevalent in the 20th century due to the newest Brazilian religion, Umbanda.[36] Like the Virgin, she is dressed in blue/white with the moon and stars about her and hands in an open, giving gesture. Yet her hair is unbound and her dress clings to her form in a way that would not be seen in a traditional Marian image. She has also absorbed associations from Mary's other forms, the Stella Maris (Star of the

---

34 Gledhill 2012: 12
35 Oleszkiewicz-Peralba 2007: 83
36 Oleszkiewicz-Peralba 2007: 108

Sea) and Our Lady of Navigators, important icons for Spanish and Portuguese sailors, which also serves to remind us of her saltwater associations and her dangerous nature as siren. Mermaids in the African Diaspora religions (such as La Sirene in Haitian Vodou) have a dual nature, having both the power to guide or to draw a ship beneath the waves.

In the Brazilian state of Bahia, Iemanjá is honoured on the feast days of both the Madonnas with whom she is associated – 8th December for Our Lady of the Immaculate Conception, and 2nd February for the feast of Our Lady of Seafaring. The festival for the latter bears many similarities to the procession for Yemayá in Havana, with offerings floated on rafts in the Bay of All Saints, Salvador. However, her most celebrated time is probably New Year's Eve, when Brazilians in their droves flock to the shores wearing white, making offerings to the sea and wishes for the New Year.

Whilst Iemanjá may be the most popular Orisha in Brazil, Oshún is associated with the official patroness of the country and holds her own in terms of popularity. Oxum, as her name is spelt in Brazil, is venerated for her beauty, femininity, and powerful magic. Worship to her is carried out near or in bodies of water, where her devotees make their offerings and cleanse themselves with her waters. Just as in Cuba, she is associated with the colour yellow, and with copper and gold. She welcomes gifts of gold jewellery and fine perfume, and in possession may behave like the Vodou Lwa Erzulie Freda, weeping inconsolably and longing for love. Kingsbury and Chesnut believe that her desire for lavish gifts "should not be seen as a dream of luxury but rather a memory and mimicry of the excesses of the colonialists whose opulent lifestyles came at the expense of the backbreaking toil of slave labour."[37] Her association with gold reflects the Portuguese gold rush in Brazil; their mines of course manned by Oxum's people.

Whereas in Cuba, the statue of Caridad del Cobre was found in the sea, in Brazil, Oxum is syncretised with a Black Madonna which was found in a river, which better suits Oxum's sweet-water origins. The Madonna is named Nossa Senhora Aparecida,

---

[37] Kingsbury & Chesnut 2019b: 6

meaning 'Our Lady who Appeared'. Her statue, a small clay version of the Virgin of the Immaculate Conception turned black by the water, was found in 1717 in the Paraíba River by fishermen who had prayed to the Virgin Mary for a good haul. Following this, they retrieved the body, then the head of the statue in their net. Afterward, the men caught a multitude of fish and praised Our Lady who had 'Appeared' from the waters. Theories arose about her origin, one being that the statue of the Immaculate Conception was thrown into the river to drive away a serpent terrorising the local population,[38] or perhaps she was merely disposed of. However accurate, it is a significant analogy – a White Virgin, discarded by her people (the Portuguese) but transformed by her years underwater and recovered as a Black Virgin by the poor Black and mixed-race inhabitants of the area. Her connection with the river, besides associating her with Oxum, patroness of rivers, is important. Its name, Paraíba, can be interpreted to mean "useless river" (para'iva) but her appearance makes it bountiful. The native and slave population, also treated as useless, their personhood discarded, rediscover their dignity through her. She emerges as a reflection of these people, a miraculous blessed image in their own skin colour. [39]

A series of further miracles followed her discovery which led to her increasing status, and by 1931 she had been declared Queen and Patroness of Brazil by the Pope. Gebara and Bingemar believe the many papal endorsements and consecration of Latin American countries in the name of Mary to be primarily about those in power winning over the masses for their own interests rather than honouring those favoured by the Madonna's various apparitions.[40] Whether accurate or not, there is no doubt Aparecida has remained popular with the common people, and like Caridad del Cobre, she also has an association with the liberation of slaves. One particular folk legend has a slave asking if he can pray at a shrine to Aparecida that his master was passing. On being permitted to do so, the chain around the slave's neck broke and fell from him. This was interpreted to be the will of the Black Madonna, and opinion began

---

[38] Gebara and Bingemar 1989: 156
[39] Gebara and Bingemar 1989: 156
[40] Gebara and Bingemar 1989: 135

to spread that she disapproved of slavery in Brazil.[41]

Despite Aparecida's popularity with the cause for slave liberation, other less noble reasons than her apparent disapproval may have played a part when the final act was signed in 1888. The fact that Princess Isabel, regent at the time, paid a visit to the basilica in Aparecida to present Nossa Senhora with a crown has been interpreted by some as proof that her mind had been changed by the miracles wrought by the statue, prompting her to sign the freedom act. In fact, slavery had been on the decline for most of the century, after peaking in the 1820s, with estimates then ranging from a third to half of the population being slaves. The reasons behind its decline include external pressure from Britain and financial benefit to the ruling classes. Abolitionism started to gain ground after Brazil achieved independence from Portugal in 1822, but unlike in Mexico and elsewhere, where Mary adorned the banners of independence movements, the Brazilian Black Madonna did not become an emblem for national liberation. Unlike in Spanish-occupied America, independence did not occur due to proletarian action but due to royal disputes with Portugal. Don Pedro I, the man declared first Emperor of Brazil, was himself of the Portuguese royal family.[42] The Lei Áurea (*Golden Law*) which finally ended slavery in 1888 was succinct and unconditional, leaving no doubts about its totality, but also not providing those freed any form of assistance in making new lives for themselves. Sadly, many had nowhere to go, and no education to help them provide for themselves.

LUCUMÍ AND VODOU IN THE US

Historical upheavals, such as the Cuban Revolution, provided the impetus for many initiates of African-based traditions to relocate or in some cases even flee to other countries, primarily the US. Here, some Santeros broke with tradition and rejected Catholic elements whilst others further blended with influences of other traditions creating new hybrid practices. Besides orthodox Lucumí, other variants can be found in the US, such as one labelled

---

[41] Gebara and Bingemar 1989: 157
[42] Gebara and Bingemar 1989: 134

'Santerismo', heavily influenced by Puerto Rican Spiritism, which uses different saints for the Orisha and does not practice blood sacrifice. Another, commonly called 'Orisha-Voodoo', was started as an African Nationalism movement by Walter King (Osejiman Adefunmi). He broke with the traditions of the Cuban Houses and set up his own Yoruban Village in South Carolina, proclaiming himself king of the Yoruba in America. King wanted to remove the saints and any Catholic influence, keeping Orisha worship for the descendants of slaves only and not admitting Whites.[43] We will return to the topic of de-syncretisation towards the end of the chapter.

Whereas many Santeros went initially to Florida, and then New York, Vodouisantes from Haiti commonly found their way to Louisiana prompting the rise of New Orleans Voodoo. In the bigger cities, Theosophy, Spiritualism, and West Indian Obeah all contributed to the make-up of late 19th and early 20th century Vodou in the US. In the largely Protestant Bible Belt of the South, it was hard for syncretic religion to flourish, due to the Baptist churches' intolerance of saint devotion. It was only within pockets of Catholicism, such as in New Orleans, that devotees of the Lwa and the Orisha were able to find any expression. One of the famous figures credited with keeping this strong connection is Marie Laveau.

A free biracial woman born in the late 18th century, Marie Laveau stepped into a tradition that was already highly matriarchal, picking up the mantle of 'Voudou Queen of New Orleans'. Descendants of Nago, Fon, Ibo, and Congo people had gathered together under these queens to perform ceremonies, drink, eat, and dance together. Laveau held what appeared to be ceremonies in Congo Square which drew much attention from their White neighbours, but these were decoy entertainments; the real ceremonies being held privately at Bayou St. John.[44] Teish tells us that in her position as a hairdresser for the wealthy of the city, Laveau was able to pick up useful information to influence and manipulate the right people.[45] Coupling her knowledge with the

---

[43] Dianteill 2002: 130-2

[44] Teish 1988: 176

[45] Teish 1988: 176

magical practices of her tradition, Laveau was able to turn Vodou into a successful business as well as create a legend around her own person.[46] This was not solely for her own gain, however, but for the benefit of her congregation.

Despite her dedication to Vodou, it is asserted that Marie Laveau was also a committed Catholic. Records show that she was baptized, married, attended mass, and had her children baptized at St. Louis Cathedral, as well as acting as a godmother.[47] Morrow Long tells us:

> *"Earlier journalists and popular historians could not reconcile the idea of Marie Laveau as a virtuous and exemplary Christian with her leadership of the Voudou congregation. If she were indeed good, she could not have been a Voudou priestess; if she were a Voudou priestess, she could not have been good".[48]*

Yet she appears to have succeeded in being both simultaneously. Martha Ward credits Laveau's success to her interest in Mariology:

> *"Laveau's focus upon the goddess, Mary, was central to many of her rites and prayers. Laveau's adoption of Mary aptly blended the two religious faiths by creating a divine female deity from her understanding of Mary, the mother of Jesus. Laveau's gravitation toward Mariology is one of her most significant theological innovations."[49]*

Laveau made herself a figurehead of her community, a beacon, just like the Virgin. Her nephew, a witness of one of the ceremonies at Bayou St. John, described her emerging from the water of the lake "with a great communion candle burning on her head and another in each hand",[50] a veritable Stella Maris come to life. It seems likely that Laveau leaned into the Catholic imagery of her morning services in creating her Vodou ceremonies by night.

The Marian influence, however, was not just in terms of

---

[46] It is said that Marie Laveau rebirthed as a younger woman, but most likely her daughter, bearing a startling resemblance to her, took over her name and the organising of congregations after her death.

[47] Morrow Long 2009: 59

[48] Morrow Long 2009: 64

[49] Dolan: 13

[50] Teish 1988: 178

spectacle. Laveau is credited with many acts of kindness[51] and in a way, was a living breathing Black Madonna within her community. She tended the sick and opened her house to women, orphans and dispossessed Native Americans. She visited and prayed with prisoners on death row and intervened with the courts where she could, on behalf of the Black community.[52] Her actions, plus her near-mythical status saw her elevated to the ranks of the Lwa following her death.

The Catholic Church were generally tolerant of Laveau and the Vodouisantes but the growing Protestant presence in the region was not. By the turn of the 20th century, the movement had mostly gone underground but the Laveau legend continued to inspire and inform the tradition for decades.

SYNCRETISM – HOW IMPORTANT IS IT?

We come now to an extremely important question, one of the most crucial in the book. Just how important is the act of syncretism in defining the worship of deities who originated in other religions, specifically, the use of Catholic icons such as the Black Madonna in the worship of African Lwa and Orisha? Since around the 1980s, after these religions became more globalised, there have been movements within Vodou, Lucumí, and Candomblé to remove all Catholic elements, seeing them as unnecessary and relics of slavery. I am, however, going to argue for the continued importance and relevance of syncretism in the Diaspora. But before going into de-syncretisation, let us look at the study of syncretism versus its actual presence within the practices of these cultures.

Discourse on syncretism is often more problematic than syncretism itself. Some scholars on the subject argue that seeing and commenting on the parallels between African deities and Christian figures is a Western imposition akin to the Roman Empire's absorption and reappropriation of the Greek and Egyptian pantheons. To an extent this is true, especially in the

---

[51] Most of her obituaries recalled her in this way, but much of the journalism of her time despised, ridiculed and sensationalised her, which further contributed to her legend.
[52] Teish 1988: 183

books that will label the equivalences of 'love goddess Ezili' or 'war god Ogun' in a neat table which has little use or relevance other than to fascinate Western minds and to make an alien tradition fit into their outlook on the world. Critics of this kind of scholarship point to its belittling of African tradition in comparison to the reader's Western perspective. Too often, divergent traditions are oversimplified and lumped together as 'primitive religion', reflecting a history of racism and privilege. As Eric James Montgomery says:

> *"A problem with syncretism as an analytical approach is that it often misses the universality of the processes it studies: all cultures and religions of the world are syncretic, borrowing from one another. When marginalized groups or disempowered cultures of postmodernity are tagged as syncretic, they are stigmatized by negative implications that they are somehow inauthentic or impure and thus inferior."*[53]

I would argue that, rather than syncretism itself, it is being labelled a 'syncretic religion' and being perceived as inauthentic or as a primitive subset of Christianity which the proponents of de-syncretisation wish to escape.

Syncretism itself as a concept was developed in the 1920s/30s by Melville Herskovits[54] but was happening in the Diaspora long before then, and longer still within the Abrahamic religions. The difficulty comes in that the concept has been used as an anthropological tool to classify the practices with which the Christian and the colonial have come into contact during their dominant expansion, as a way of pointing to the 'other'. However, those cultures that actually incorporate syncretism into their beliefs usually do so from a sympathetic rather than an adversarial position. As Montgomery found in his study of Gorovodu[55] in Togo:

> *"Some refer to Muhammad and Jesus Christ as themselves "Vodu spirits" with supernatural abilities. They are not acknowledging Christ or Muhammad so much as they are respecting their essence,*

---

[53] Montgomery 2016: 5
[54] Montgomery 2016: 10
[55] Gorovodu is a religion of the Ewe people of southeastern Ghana, southern Togo, and southwestern Benin. It developed in the early 20th century and bears similarities with the Diaspora religions.

and seeing traits and symbols in them that begin and end with their
own home-grown spirits… followers are not mixing oppositional
forces as much as they are conjoining parallels."[56]

The same spirit of recognition can be found throughout the Diaspora religions that adopted Christian symbols. On arrival in the Americas, the pantheon of the saints would be only one aspect of new environments, foods, and manufactured goods that would be figured into African belief systems.[57] This was not Catholicism forcing syncretism on them, this was natural adaptation at work.

There is no denying that the Christian pantheon was forced upon African slaves, but the belief that syncretism of the Catholic saints was adopted as no more than a mask for the African gods to hide behind is an over-simplification. Whilst in Vodou, the Lwa and the saint are viewed as different beings, in Santería, the saint and the Orisha can be seen as the same spirit in different manifestations. Just like the saints, in Yoruban mythology many of the Orisha began as humans, and Santeros see no conflict in the spirit having more than one human life. After death, the saint and Orisha can be said to have combined, and it makes little difference which name they are given in worship.

The way in which images and statues of the saints are used varies. Mary Ann Clark finds in the early Western descriptions of Santería et al. that equate syncretism with a corrupted form of Catholicism there is prejudice and confusion about the use of idols and fetishes: "One critique of such religions is that they confuse what is profane (the natural or manufactured object) for the sacred (God)."[58] This is far from the truth. The icons and statues of saints on a Vodou altar, for example, are not what the Vodouisante is praying to. They, along with other items on the altar are visual reminders, associations that tell a part of the overall story of the Lwa's identity. Actual saint imagery is not used across the board, however. Clark, in her research into Santería discovered "that not only do many Santeria altar displays contain no representations of Catholic saints but many contain few or no anthropomorphic

---

[56] Montgomery 2016: 9
[57] Clark 2001: 26
[58] Clark 2001: 22

figures at all",[59] a critical difference that Clark was not expecting, based upon traditional scholarship's insistence that Santería was a religion full of superstitious paraphernalia.

The presence or absence of saint images may depend on the audience and whether they are initiates or not. Without doubt, the key part of a Santero's altar is the pots containing the stones known as the *otanés* or *fundamentos* of the Orisha, in much the same way as the Communion wafer and wine of Catholicism.[60] Perez, on the importance of the *fundamentos*, states that:

> *"According to initiates, visual contact with these stones depletes them of the vital energy called ashé and compromises the security of the immanent oricha"*

Therefore, when images of the saints are used as substitutes, it is to provide a way for the uninitiated to 'read' these illegible objects without polluting them with their gaze.[61]

The relative lack of saint images on Santería initiates' altars may reflect West African ideas on anthropomorphism in sacred spaces. Yoruban altars feature little in the way of anthropomorphic figures and those that did appear, which the early European missionaries named 'fetishes' and assumed to be images of African gods, are in fact usually depictions of worshippers.[62] These are models of 'horses'; the wide-eyed, fixed stares of the figures signifying the arrival of an Orisha in the body of a medium. Once in the Americas, "confronted by Roman Catholic images with prominent eyes and unsmiling countenances, Lucumi followers chose to read the saints as fellow devotees surrounded by the preferred accoutrements of the deities in question"[63] and indeed, where saint images are used, the main function of the image is to read it for its symbols as one might read a tarot card. In this form of decoding, items and colours hold more significance than the gender or personality of the original saint. This method provided a useful visual record to accompany oral transmission about the nature of

---

[59] Clark 2001: 23
[60] Clark 2001: 28
[61] Perez 2010: 206
[62] Clark 2001: 29-30
[63] Perez 2010: 206

the Orisha at a time when it was vital to hang on to information by any means necessary.

DE-SYNCRETISATION

As Diaspora religions have become more globalised and moved towards recognition as 'world religions', a de-syncretism movement has grown, particularly within Candomblé.[64] This has occurred in tandem with a Re-Africanisation movement which seeks to reunite descendants of Africans in Brazil with the languages and traditions of the Yoruba. Both movements reject Catholic elements of Candomblé and seek lost fragments of knowledge to reconstruct a supposedly pure African religion.[65]

Advocates of these movements are not in fact rejecting all forms of syncretism, just the Catholic parts of their religion. Sharing amongst Diaspora religions is encouraged as ""good" syncretism between "sister religions", allowing other Afro-Brazilian religions, such as Umbanda, to rediscover their African past and worldview through connections with, and ritual borrowing from other African-derived religions."[66] This fulfils their objective of piecing together a lost African religion. However, this approach plays into the mythologised concept of a United Africa, the mythical homeland of *Ginen*, which itself arose from slavery. It does not acknowledge the diversity present in the western part of the continent from which these religions were drawn, and gives ammunition to those that criticise the 'Nagoization' of Candomblé, where focus is unequally placed on Yoruban heritage as representative of the whole of West Africa.

The cause for uniting disparate faiths under one Orisha religion has been driven by The International Congresses of Orisha Tradition and Culture (COMTOC) since their first meeting in 1981. Capone writes that "The main discussion topics at these

---

[64] De-syncretisation with Catholicism has already happened to an extent within Santería in non-Catholic countries such as the US. Clark, in meeting members of Houston's Santería community, found little to no evidence of Catholic saint statues. This is, however, less of a conscious uncoupling and more about the fact that members have been raised in Protestant or other upbringings, to whom the saints are not familiar (Clark 2001: 27).
[65] Capone 2016: 473-4
[66] Capone 2016: 474

forums are tradition, standardisation of religious practices, and the fight against syncretism, topics that are common across different regional variants of the "orisha religion"".[67] One of the most affirmative actions against syncretism came at the second meeting of COMTOC in 1983 where five famous *mães-de-santo*, priestesses of Candomblé, presented their manifesto. According to Capone:

> "*This petition urged the end of Afro-Catholic syncretism – the association of Catholic saints with African orisha – and the rejection of all Catholic rituals "traditionally" performed by Candomblé followers, such as masses attended on Catholic saints' days corresponding to orisha, the iyawó (new initiate) pilgrimage to churches at the conclusion of initiation, and the washing of the steps of Salvador's Bonfim Church.*"[68]

Mãe Stella of Axé Opô Afonjá who led the petition said "A true religion is valued on its own account. It does not need to use another as a crutch to prove that it has value", asserting Candomblé to be a true religion, not a "syncretised sect".[69] She did not, however, agree with *terreiros* breaking with tradition and advocated de-syncretisation only, not Re-Africanisation.[70] For many *terreiros,* seeking religious authority in Africa would mean also giving up their power structures built over several generations. Worshippers were urged to seek spiritual purity in Afro-Brazilian traditions – just without the Catholicism.

Discussions on syncretism often revolve around the theory of the 'mask', largely developed by Roger Bastide in 1978, which asserts that African spirits were only hidden behind Catholic faces. His theory suggested that the descendants of Africans 'compartmentalized' their spirituality, being simultaneously Catholic and Candomblé, whilst not mixing the two, in a kind of 'mosaic syncretism'.[71] Whilst often cited in the argument for de-syncretisation, his view has been challenged with research into new perspectives. Bastide's theory hinged on the presence of two 'religions'. However, the idea of what the Africans practised being understood by them as a religion has been debated. For the Yoruba

---

[67] Capone 2016: 475
[68] Capone 2016: 476
[69] Gledhill 2012: 13-14
[70] Capone 2016: 481
[71] Ogunnaike 2020: 150

"the word *ęsin*—most commonly used now as a translation for "religion"—could more accurately be characterized as "form of worship."[72] Ayodeji Ogunnaike compared Candomblé and Lucumí practices to the modern-day and historic Yoruban practices from which these religions claim origin. In pre-colonial Yorubaland, deities ceded their areas of influence to other more popular Orisha or were merged with them if these spheres of influence were similar enough. This practice carried over to the Americas, with Yemoja, formerly associated with the Ogun river, taking on Olokun's domain as Orisha of the ocean.[73] The ease with which deities were combined into each other is precisely because it was the form of worship that was important, not the belief system that it came from. Rather than being rulers of their domains, they are the embodiment of these domains (eg. iron, water) – calling them by a different name would not change their inherent makeup. This is why adopting names of the saints was not contradictory or a new dynamic for the Africans in the Americas. Rather than what their origins are, the important component is the practical one, what it is that they 'do'.[74] It is easy to see how, for example, the Black Madonna swathed in the blue of the ocean who cradles her infant and protects seafarers would be the obvious expression of Yemoja in the New World.

Ogunnaike found priests and initiates on both sides of the Atlantic who were of the opinion that non-Yoruban deities, whether Christian, Muslim or even Ancient Greek could not be just masks, as they are cosmologically the same as their Orisha, according to their function.[75] It would however be interesting to compare this attitude to the de-syncretisation movement's comparisons between Afro-American religions. One of my respondents in the Vodou community said that, for example, whilst sharing similar imagery, one would never give La Sirene offerings favoured by Yemayá, as they are distinct beings and the spirit could well find this offensive. Whilst absorbing the traits of beings from new cultures may be easy, reversing a deity to find its beginnings may not. Clearly, the cosmology of the Diaspora is far

---

[72] Ogunnaike 2020: 154
[73] Ogunnaike 2020: 156
[74] Ogunnaike 2020: 157
[75] Ogunaikke 2020: 160

more complicated than can be reduced to a single African 'root religion'.

CONCLUSION

The argument that Christian icons like the Black Madonna were 'just a mask' and of no spiritual value suggests that they were held in contempt by those praying to them in churches, following them in parades, or displaying them on their altars. The evidence suggests far to the contrary. Ogunnaike found that not all freed slaves who returned to Africa rejected Christianity once there, and many set up Catholic places of worship; clearly it had been more than just a mask to them.[76] Truly, some people may fit the model of 'mosaic syncretism', able to worship separately as a Catholic and a Santero, but this is not always the case. There will be many people who are 'Catholic' in name but who follow practices that do not conform to High Church dogma; and there will be Candomblé initiates too fond of Nossa Senhora Aparecida to see her iconography removed from their daily worship. Just as there is a spectrum of ethnicities present in these New World countries, so too is there a spectrum of belief and practice. For many mixed-race inhabitants, Catholicism is as much a part of their ancestral heritage as Orisha. These religions have not been carried by people of solely African heritage.

A significant argument not made is how the spirits themselves might feel about de-syncretisation? It is all very well to focus on who has the most authentic traditional practices but, to look at the issue from a theological standpoint, what about the Orisha and Lwa who have adapted for and along with a racially shifting people? The spirits are ancient but ever-changing. They, like their people, have become accustomed to New World offerings; would it not be considered offensive to strip them of these, to forcibly revert their personalities? This is not to argue that they have become more civilised or bettered through interaction with White European culture but that they have lived with elements of it for so long that they have become accustomed to its offerings and the eclectic methods of service. Has it not been considered that Ezili Danto

---

[76] Ogunnaike 2020: 155

may be angered if you take away her icons, or take from Yemaja the celebration she has enjoyed annually on the feast day of the Virgin Mary? Would Oxum not have already made her displeasure known at being honoured under the veil of Nossa Senhora Aparecida? The argument may remain that they no longer need to wear these masks, but to rip them from their make-up and discard them may prove as uncomfortable for the Orisha and Lwa as for their supplicants.

For the de-syncretisation movement, the acceptance of Catholic elements would appear to mean acceptance of the validity of slavery or that Orisha religion is a subservient religion to Catholicism. It is true that the Diaspora religions would not exist without the tragedy of the slave trade, but their traditions also represent the ingenuity, bravery and sheer fortitude of whole generations in adapting to their new surroundings and carving out a spirituality to suit it. Rather than denying what necessitated it, why not honour it? [77] The retroactive removal of Catholicism will not erase slavery from history, only the unique variants of African traditions that developed following it, which have a right to their individuality. Just as the Vodou initiates I spoke to were opposed to reversing Ezili Danto's muteness because of it being intrinsic to her part in the Revolution, the scarred face of the Black Madonna is a reminder of history. A face that stood up to the centuries of oppression and who held her children close through it. Her image is ingrained in the cultural memory of all of these societies, whether she appears as Danto, Oshún, Yemaja, or an Indigenous American deity. I would argue that of all the syncretised saints, the Black Madonna is the most important because of what she represents, and to try to remove her warning from history would surely be a mistake for future generations.

---

[77] Luisa Teish writes that in Our Lady of Guadalupe she recognises the African earth mothers Ala and Nana, and the mother of wind – the warrior Oya, because of Guadalupe's untiring place amongst her people during warfare and natural disaster. (Teish 1996: 140). In doing so she honours the ingenuity of her ancestors in recognising the correspondences with the saints that would keep their religion alive.

CHAPTER 7

Mother Kali:
Black Madonna at the Periphery, Dark Goddess at the Centre

INTRODUCTION

We have seen how Black Madonnas in Central and South America have been the foci of worship by members of the African Diaspora. However, they are not the only diaspora in the Caribbean, nor are they the only ones to venerate a Black Madonna. On Good Friday, in a Catholic Church in Siparia, Trinidad, thousands of descendants of the Indian Diaspora converge to celebrate La Divina Pastora, a Black Madonna they call Siparee Mai and consider to be the goddess Kali. The tradition has lasted 150 years, going back to the period of indentured servitude to the British Empire. Subtle historical differences here mean that the Virgin was not syncretised in the same manner as with the Orisha of Africa, but the Christianity of the ruling classes still had an enormous impact on the remodelling of Hindu tradition in a new environment. This saw Kali rejected by the majority who subscribed to the new form of 'orthodox' Brahminical Hinduism, along with the practices associated with her – animal sacrifice, fire walking, and trance possession.

Although exiled to the margins, Kali worship has never ceased in Trinidad, and has seen a resurgence since the 1970s in a new form that blends old traditions. In this chapter we will look at the worship of Kali in Trinidad and Guyana, her association with La Divina Pastora, and then look at the Kali of India, where, despite the Brahmins of Trinidad's disapproval of her, she is still a goddess central to the Hindu pantheon.

AN INDENTURED HISTORY

The twin islands of Trinidad and Tobago sit at the south of the Caribbean only a few miles from the mainland of Venezuela. As of 2011, the population stood at 1.26 million with roughly 35% of South Asian descent and 35% of African descent, with mixed races making up the rest, plus a minority of White and Chinese inhabitants. In terms of religion, in 2018, Hinduism accounted for 18.2% whereas varying forms of Protestantism including the growing number of Pentecostals accounted for 32.1%, and Catholicism for 21.6%. Originally discovered by Columbus in 1498, Trinidad was a Spanish colony until 1797 when it was invaded by the British who held it until the country gained independence in 1962.

Like other colonies, Trinidad was rich in sugar, coffee, cocoa and cotton. As more and more Caribbean countries abolished slavery, the colonial landowners found themselves once again without a workforce and turned to a new system called indentureship, which was in reality not much different from slave labour. During the period of indenture, which lasted from 1838 to 1917, over half a million South Asians were brought to work on British West Indian Sugar plantations[1] including mainland countries such as Guyana. Although slavery in Trinidad ended in 1838, indenture there began later, with 144,000 labourers disembarking between 1845 and 1917.

The system of indenture involved a nominal wage and a term of service set at three and then five years but which could be renewed more than once. The Indians were not classed as free during their servitude and if they wished to return to their homeland at the end of it, they had to pay for their own passage. Shameful living conditions and harsh discipline earned indenture the description "the new system of slavery".[2]

Unlike the previous African slaves, the East Indians did have the freedom to practice their own religion, despite Christian missionaries' efforts to persuade them otherwise. Nonetheless, decades of close contact with the ever-present Christianity and the

---

[1] McNeal 2003: 226
[2] McNeal 2013b: 176

colonial social system had a reshaping effect on Hinduism in both Trinidad and Guyana. An orthodoxy grew in the early 20th century following the end of indenture, based on the Brahminical system of India and partly inspired by an Indian movement called *Ārya Samāj* (association of nobles), which valued a textual approach to worship and rejection of religious imagery.[3] Although wanting to remain distinct from the Christians, the Brahmins emulated their values in order to increase their own social status. Influenced by what Christians regarded as inferior or backward, the leaders of this orthodoxy exiled elements of worship that could be seen as pagan or superstitious – including animal sacrifice, spirit possession, and the 'fire-pass' ceremony of testing one's faith by walking on hot coals. Most of these traditions were associated with *shakti* worship[4] – veneration of the Great Goddess and a means of raising power in the body, though not all were originally associated with Kali. This division between orthodox and unorthodox practices came with a dose of racism. Folk practices were labelled as 'Madrassi'; those who had migrated from the southern Indian port of Madras (Chennai) rather than the lighter-skinned, more 'sophisticated' Indians from the northern city of Calcutta (Kolkata). Whilst making up the majority in the beginning, overall Madrassis were a minority, only making up 6% of indentured labourers.[5] 'Madrassi' was used as a generalised term for the darker-skinned people from southern India who were scapegoated as a backward, embarrassing remnant of Hinduism's past in the new orthodoxy and stereotyped as uncultured heavy drinkers with loose morals.[6]

This new attitude, influenced by Christian morality, saw a majority of Hindus in Trinidad reject Kali, despite her importance during the period of indenture, and her continued importance in the homeland. Previously, Kali puja[7] would take place publicly for the benefit of a whole village, even if the whole village did not attend.[8]

---

[3] Bakker 2003: 5
[4] McNeal 2003: 227
[5] McNeal 2003: 232
[6] Despite these stereotypes, Kali puja in fact requires abstinence and fasting as a means of prior purification (Tsuji 2009: 71).
[7] Ritual or worshipful act, ranging from small devotions at home to large public ceremonies over several days.
[8] McNeal 2003: 233

Facing: 'Kali'. This painting was inspired particularly by the writings of Ramprasad, who was the first to really describe Kali in more than her dreadful form. Whilst her fearsome side is still important to her iconography, she is also the Cosmic Mother. Therefore, I painted the pathway leading back to her cosmic womb. Ramprasad puts particular emphasis on feet, and being touched by the 'lotus feet' of the Goddess. There we see the footprints of her devotee, and the dancing feet of Kali, ever moving in her frenetic dance of creation and destruction. The shape of the spiral within her body and the outer spiral follow the Fibonacci sequence of creation.

The Goddess is self-arising – Here we see her rising out of the brow of Durga, rather than the more common depiction of her stood on the prostrate form of Shiva. Her skin is black and glittering, like the depths of space. Round her neck is the Kali yantra (the essence of Kali in symbolic form), and around her waist is the red serpent. Her palms and soles are red, and the hands of her right side (her benign side) are in the boon giving and fear removing postures. Her left hands hold the sword and severed head of the annihilation of illusion and the ego, and the release from the cycle of birth and death. Her favoured red hibiscus flowers cascade from her body.

As Kali moves in her wild dance, the string of skulls around her neck swing with her. The skulls represent the letters of the Sanskrit alphabet, and each is inscribed. She is every possible combination of sound and is the sound of creation, like the Om or the Logos. Her three eyes represent the Sun, Moon, and the sacred fire at the end of the Universe. Many commentators say that her red tongue, white teeth, and black skin represent the combination of all three gunas; she is Sattva, Rajas, and Tamas, inclusive[1].

Collections of offerings were made throughout the week and the meat of ritual sacrifice was cooked and passed around as *Prasad*.[1] By the mid-20th-century, this tradition had fallen out of favour and its elements of ecstatic possession and animal sacrifice seen as circumspect.

INFLUENCE FROM GUYANA AND KALI REVIVAL

The orthodox movement was common to all West Indian communities, not just Trinidad, and developed in much the same way in Guyana and Suriname. Christian influence can be seen in the presentation of Guyanese temples, and particularly in their preference for the word 'church' over 'mandir' (temple).[2] The Madras traditions that had been ousted from the orthodoxy, whilst not being welcomed back into the mainstream, were revived following various political upheavals including Guyana's independence from Britain in 1966 and the Black Power Movement of the 1970s. The latter helped consolidate and reinvigorate Orisha religion amongst Afro-Creoles and served as inspiration for South Asians to do the same with Madrassi traditions.[3] A particularly influential leader, the Guyanese *pujari*, Jamsie Naidoo helped spread the revival to Trinidad through exchange relationships and strengthened the traditions in both countries. Kali temples began to increase in number and there were thought to be eighty to a hundred in Guyana by the turn of the millennium.[4]

Anthropologist Keith McNeal has closely studied the Kali temples in Trinidad,[5] which he estimated as fifteen to twenty in number. Most temples contain a *murti* (statue) of Kali at their centre,[6] flanked by altars holding statues or chromolithographs of other *deotas* (deities). This includes both deities commonly

---

[1] Food offerings made to a deity and then consumed by the congregation to gain blessings.
[2] Kloß 2016: 88
[3] Kloß 2016: 97
[4] McNeal 2003: 237
[5] See McNeal 2003: 228-31 in particular
[6] Usually in the form of *Dakshinakali* with the goddess stood on the supine form of Shiva. (McNeal 2013a: 954)

worshipped by orthodox Hindus, and lesser-known *deotas* who may have originated from regional gods. Kali pujas are held weekly, usually on a Sunday night. Devotees typically bring offerings of milk, fruit, and flowers and circumambulate the shrines making their offerings to the *deotas* before coming together in front of the main Kali *murti* of the temple. Despite the Madrassi stereotype perpetuated by both Hindu and non-Hindu outsiders, modern Kali temples in Trinidad rarely perform animal sacrifice.[7] Ecstatic spirit possession still forms a central part of puja, and those present go to Mother Kali through the voice of her medium to solve a range of problems, and cure illness or infertility. Mediums take flaming cubes of camphor in their mouths to prove the manifestation is real, whilst lay people may also become possessed by *shakti* energy during puja for limited bouts in what is locally termed 'catching power'. During the annual three-day 'big puja', the purity and authenticity of members' devotions are tested by lashings or fire walking whilst under the influence of *shakti*.[8] This Madrassi fire-pass ceremony was not associated with *shakti* worship in the time of indenture, but being one of the practices which were excluded, it has been welcomed into Kali's fold since the 1970s revival.

SIMILARITIES AND DIFFERENCES WITH AFRO-CARIBBEAN PRACTICES

It must be recognised that modern Kali worship in the West Indies does not compose so much an unbroken tradition as a rearrangement of traditions and in this way bears similarity to Afro-Caribbean religions. Kloß writes that since the 1970s: "The Madras tradition has been revitalised and standardised, consolidating what may be labelled an invented tradition. However, this invention... should not be regarded as marking the tradition as inauthentic, for indeed there exist no 'genuine' cultures."[9] As Orisha devotees had done with their ancestral practices, Kali worshippers blended local and universal Hindu beliefs into a reconfiguration of ritual. In the

---

[7] It is more common to still find animal sacrifice performed in Guyana where Kali churches are also more numerous. Those that do enact it hold to a rule that it must be a beheading with a single stroke. (McNeal 2003: 231)

[8] The feminine life force, discussed later in this chapter in relation to the goddess.

[9] Kloß 2016: 107

British colonies, the Afro and Indo-Caribbean traditions grew alongside each other, no doubt influencing each other in small ways. Kali pujas welcome attendees of all religious backgrounds whilst Trinidadian Orisha worship (commonly called 'Shango' in Trinidad) incorporates Indian and Chinese names for the spirits besides their African and Catholic ones, as well as some that are specific to Trinidad and Tobago.[10]

General similarities between Indo-Caribbean and Afro-Caribbean traditions include the sharing of food blessed during the ceremony, and the performance of extraordinary bodily feats whilst the practitioner is under possession. The main similarity is the centrality of ecstatic mediumship as means of problem-solving. However, during an Orisha possession, the medium's eyes will usually be open and engaging with their petitioner; in a Kali rite they will remain closed as they speak.[11] Another difference comes in how the manifested deity is identified. In Shango, little iconography is used, and if the Orisha does not speak, cues are taken from their behaviours, such as Yemanja miming oaring through the ocean, her domain. Indo-Caribbeans make more use of their *murtis* and typically will only manifest deities in front of their specific statue.[12]

Due to the commonalities involving possession and animal sacrifice, comparisons between Kali puja and Shango have also been made by their detractors, who will often say it is all *Obeah* ('black magic'). Hindu folk magic known as *Ojha* did indeed cross over with Afro-Creole *Obeah*, in their clientele as well as types of practice, which traditionally include exorcisms, love potions, and spells to find lost items. Both cultures perform *jharay*, ritual fanning for healing, but other than this, *Ojha* practices had mostly faded into obscurity by the 21st century.[13]

Another obvious similarity is the use of syncretism, which, as we have seen, can be a method of adapt-to-survive, as well as the recognition of compatible forms of worship. Christian hymns and imagery have found their way into Kali temples that also include

---

[10] McNeal 2012: 496
[11] McNeal 2012: 498-9
[12] McNeal 2012: 500-2
[13] McNeal 2013b: 179-80

space for the ecumenical devotionalism of Sai Baba, the Indian guru.[14] Just as the Orisha and Lwa adapted to their new environs and incorporated Christian symbols, "Kali has had to look after her children in a range of innovative ways given their ever-present, and yet ever-changing, New World context".[15] *Shakti* worship is ever-evolving and shifting, and Kali's inclusivity and embracing of outcasts and other races and cultures rather than maintaining 'Indian purity' is exactly what the Brahmins despise about her worship, and exactly what makes her an ideal figure to be represented as a Black Madonna.

SIPAREE MAI/LA DIVINA PASTORA

Nobody is entirely sure why Hindus began making a pilgrimage to a church containing a Black Madonna in a remote town on the south coast of Trinidad, but it is thought to have been spontaneous rather than through Catholic conversion attempts. Since at least the 1870s when it was first recorded, Hindus have flocked to pay homage to the Virgin of Siparia, whom to most is Kali, though is also sometimes petitioned as Durga, Lakshmi or other forms of the Goddess. She is however best known as Siparee Mai. In the 1871 church records, Rev. Fr. Cornelius O'Hanlon states that Siparee is a type of seed in India and the name of a Hindu saint, which is why Indians adopted her, but there is no apparent evidence for this, and it has since been accepted that 'Siparee Mai' is simply translated as Mother of Siparia.[16]

To the Catholics of the island she is La Divina Pastora, the Holy Shepherdess. The statue is in fact a bust with jointed moveable arms that appears to be a full figure when dressed. She is 2.5 feet high, made from African cedar painted a dark brown and has an enviable supply of dresses, donated mostly by wealthy Hindus.[17] Her origins are as mysterious as her cross-cultural popularity, and various stories give different versions of how she arrived on the island, ranging from her being the prow of a native Warao canoe from Venezuela, to her being dug up in Trinidad

---

[14] MvNeal 2003: 240
[15] McNeal 2003: 234
[16] Mahabir: 6
[17] McNeal 2002: 75

itself. Most likely is that she originated with the Cappuchin monastic order of Southern Spain. They formed a mission to Venezuela in the early 18th century but fled persecution from the Warao in 1730, coming to Trinidad, and reportedly, bringing the statue with them. Another account says that the statue was a figurehead from the washed-up boat carrying a later group of Cappuchins from the mainland in the 1870s,[18] though the cult appears to have been already well established by this time.

Despite wanting their Holy Shepherdess to be a conversion tool, the Catholic priesthood also kept their feast day as a separate occasion from that of Siparee Mai after Hindu attendance proved too much of an 'intrusion'. By the 1910s, the Hindu pilgrimage was moved to Holy Thursday and Good Friday whereas the Catholic pilgrimage took place on the second Sunday after Easter. Due to the huge volume of Hindus coming to make their devotions to the statue, it was brought out from the church on Good Friday to the yard[19] where offerings of rice, olive oil, flowers, money and candles are made in return for healing and answering prayers. McNeal observed that "they also make *aarti* to her – a respectful offering of a lit flame – and *charawe* her by touching her arms and feet and then transferring her power to themselves with a touch to their foreheads."[20] Oil offerings are blessed and redistributed to supplicants (in both the Hindu and Catholic traditions). On Good Friday, the area surrounding the church is alive with the hubbub of stalls selling wares and barbers offering children their first haircut, a Hindu rite of passage seen as auspicious when in the presence of Siparee Mai.[21] By comparision, the Catholic festival is a no more solemn affair, and has grown into a week-long celebration of carnival proportions with feasting and music.

Despite the conspicuous similarities in the devotional practices of the Hindu and Catholic pilgrimages, the Catholics have staunchly drawn a line between the festivals. At one point in the 1920s, they even attempted, unsuccessfully, to outlaw Hindus from the shrine. Notably, the church was still happy to receive the more

---

[18] McNeal 2002: 77
[19] By 2000 the statue was placed in the local church hall for security on Good Friday (Tsuji 2008: 149)
[20] McNeal 2003: 239
[21] McNeal 2002: 79

valuable gifts of jewellery and dresses from the Hindu community. Unease at the Black Madonna's popularity and association with Kali even prompted the Church to set up an alternative White Divina Pastora. A Dominican friar set up a mission in East Dry River, on the outskirts of the large town of Port-of-Spain in 1873, even christening the location Siparia Hill, or 'New Siparia'.[22] Attempts to launch a rival pilgrimage to this White Madonna to eclipse that of Siparee Mai ultimately failed, even after a holy apparition was witnessed in its presence in 1917. Unfortunately for the Catholics, this White Madonna was herself eclipsed by the much more famous apparition of Our Lady of Fátima in Portugal that happened the same month.[23]

Unsurprisingly, the *pandits* (priests) of the Hindu orthodoxy disavow any association with La Divina Pastora, labelling those that go to petition her as superstitious and not true Hindus.[24] Excluded by both the Hindu *pandits* and the Catholic congregation of Siparia, Kali's devotees do not seem to be troubled. They have their Mother and they belong to her alone. That said, Kali temples have gone some way to standardise in order to avoid stigmatisation from both camps. Rising to the criticisms of the Brahmins that their traditions have no scriptural foundation, some temples have started printing devotional songs formerly only shared in the oral tradition.[25] The *Devi Mahatmya,* the story of Kali's origin, is also quoted, which we examine in further detail in this chapter. Efforts have been made to emulate Christian churches by replacing the temporary structures of the past with more permanent concrete Kali temples whilst also taking influence from contemporary Indian Kali temples.[26] Some have even gone as far as painting their Kali *murtis* pink so as to appear 'less scary' to outsiders and potential devotees than her traditional black skin.[27] This is reminiscent of the efforts of churches and governments in Europe to remove the 'esoteric mystery' and otherness of some Black Madonnas by painting them white. But, just as pilgrims to Black Madonna shrines seem undeterred, Kali's worshippers recognise

---

[22] Tsuji 2016: 4
[23] Tsuji 2016: 10
[24] Tsuji 2008: 153
[25] Kloß 2016: 104
[26] Kloß 2016: 104
[27] McNeal 2003: 241

her in any colour and by a variety of names. The following description of Kali resonates with the characters of the Black Madonnas, goddesses and spirits we have met so far:

> *"She is a lone female warrior, her many arms loaded with weapons and ready for battle... Her outside detractors selectively focus upon her ostensibly "negative" characteristics—her ferociousness, her thirst for blood, her breaking of taboos, her subversive feminine power—and then castigate her through a studied effort at misinformation and willful ignorance of her more elusive profundities. But armed with a deeper understanding of Kali's complex personality, her devotees are able to appreciate shakti's sacred polarities... Indeed, she is the shakti of bondage and the shakti of liberation."*[28]

Like the Black Madonna with which she has come to be associated, Mother Kali turns no one away, because she is the mother of all. She shelters the outcasts, and welcomes the curious, if they can see past her unnerving imagery. This holds as true in India as the West Indies. For a more complete picture of the goddess, we must turn to her original context, her myths and the practices of her devotees.

KALI IN INDIA

To western observers, Kali is at first a shocking goddess of contradictions: "simultaneously understood as a bloodthirsty demon-slayer, an inflictor and curer of diseases, a deity of ritual possession, and an all-loving, compassionate Mother."[29] Her frightening appearance of lolling tongue, garland of heads, skirt of human arms and blood-soaked weapons initially make us wonder how on earth she could be affectionately worshipped as Mother.

The first thing to overcome when looking at Hindu deities from a Western perspective is the centuries of misinterpretation and misunderstanding. Examination of any colonial British writings on Hindu religious and folk practices, particularly Shaktism (devotion to the Goddess and interaction with the female principle), will show a dismissive and superior take on this

---

[28] McNeal 2003: 243
[29] Kripal and McDermott 2003: 4

'primitive' religion as they saw it. The 1928 *Encyclopaedia of Religion and Ethics* speaks of Shaktism – "the most debased side of Hinduism" in such unfavourable light: "In Bengal, again, the worship of Durgā is accompanied by wearisome puerilities and gross idolatry. The cult of Kālī-Devī is also associated with the horrors of Thagi"[30] (Thuggery[31]). Kali was identified as the pinnacle of depravity, a mixture of naked lasciviousness and bloody violence that both repulsed and enthralled the Victorian imagination.[32]

Behind the startling iconography, Kali has a complex character that has developed over a period of at least 2,000 years in India. During the Puranic period (350-1700 CE), the triune of gods Brahma, Vishnu, and Shiva who personify creation, sustenance, and destruction were joined by Devi, the Goddess in her various forms. The Puranas were arranged into four sets according to the nature of these gods, with Devi encompassing all three. The first appearance of Kali is in the Puranic epic, the *Devi Mahatmya*, the key myth for Kali worshippers, written around the 6th century CE. In this text, Kali is the terrifying personification of rage, the ultimate expression of the goddess Durga's wrath. Later Tantric philosophy (circa 8th to 16th century) elevated Kali to "the greatest of all deities or highest reality"[33] from whence Brahma, Vishnu and Shiva arose. Later still, from the 17th century, the development of devotional poetry, *shakti bhakti*, has seen a shift to praising Kali in the form of benevolent mother whilst not removing any of her contradictory characteristics. In the modern age, as information about world religions has become more widely available, Kali's striking imagery is still fascinating Western audiences but is now being appropriated by feminist and social justice causes.[34] We will examine the impact of this perspective towards the end of the chapter.

---

[30] McDaniel 2004: 14
[31] Kali has been known to be notoriously favoured by impoverished robbers who worship her in the form of Dacoit (Bandit) Kali.
[32] Urban 2003: 169-70
[33] Kinsley 2003: 29
[34] Kripal and McDermott 2003: 4

THE KEY GODDESS TEXT –
THE *DEVI MAHATMYA*

The *Devi Mahatmya*, part of the larger *Markandeya Purana*, is one of the key texts relating to the Goddess in India and sacred to her followers, known as Shaktas. Its significance is proven through the fact that it has been translated and distributed separately from the rest of the purana countless times, being sometimes titled the *Durga Saptasati* (700 Verses to Durga) when presented separately.

The text is divided into three sections, which all deal with the Goddess aiding the gods in some way in overcoming demons. During the first part of the text, the goddess is less tangible, being Mahamaya – goddess of illusion and reality, and Yoganidra who, as the goddess of sleep, resides in Vishnu's eyes, keeping him under her spell. When two emergent demons threaten the order of the universe, Brahma praises the Goddess and implores her as the only one able to rouse Vishnu so he may kill the demons. She comes forth, manifesting for the first time, and releasing Vishnu from sleep to perform this task. The various demons throughout the text represent different vices and traits that impede spiritual growth. The two in this section are called Madhu ('honey') and Kaitabha ('bitter'), representing attachment and hatred.[35]

The second episode is much more dynamic, and describes how Durga (who is variously also called Candika and Ambika in the text) is born from the combined powers of the gods. The chief of the Asuras (demons), Mahisa, has overthrown the gods, and the gods congregate to decide what to do. From their shared rage, a fiery mass comes into being, which forms into the shape of a woman. The parts of her body and her various weapons are each the gift of a different god. The Goddess rides a lion into battle and annihilates the millions of demons who assail her. When faced with Mahisa himself, she slays him several times over as he changes form, from buffalo to human and back again. Whilst she is fearsome, unstoppable, and could be interpreted literally as rage personified, she is also described in beautiful and delicate terms, when the gods gather to praise her victory. The name Durga can

---

[35] McDaniel 2004: 218

be roughly translated as 'unattainable'; virgin in the sense of beholden to no man.

We may ask ourselves, why is it the role of the Goddess to destroy the demons, not that of the male gods? One explanation is that, in Indian philosophy, the female principle is always seen as the active one whereas the male is stationary, which may seem an inversion to Western minds. In Yoga, this is depicted as the female Shakti rising as kundalini in the body to meet the male Shiva at the crown. The gods cannot act without their feminine Shaktis, the source of their power. The Goddess and the demons are also intimately linked, as she, being the creator of all, is also their creator.[36] Like the Virgin Mary, she is the redemptress for all levels of creation.[37] In Durga we do not just have the female counterpart of any one god, but the culmination of the power (Shakti) of all of them.

In the third section of the *Devi Mahatmya*, the narrator tells how Kali comes into being. Although taking place in a different time, the text states that the goddess is one and the same as she who saved the gods from Mahisa, and she who is Vishnu's *'maya'* (illusion). On this occasion, the gods have again been conquered, this time by the demon Sumbha and his brother Nishumba. Sumbha is described as a collector of the world's riches, and is informed by his generals Canda and Munda of the beauty of the goddess. Desiring to possess her, Sumbha sends a messenger to impress her with his offer of marriage. From his description of her as the greatest 'jewel amongst women', it is clear that, firstly, he regards women as possessions, and that in regarding the Goddess as a 'mere woman' he has no idea what he is dealing with.

Durga's response is that unfortunately she promised that only one who overcomes her in battle would be fit to be her husband, and invites Sumbha or Nishumba to come and attempt it. This angers the messenger who threatens to drag her into their presence by her hair. The demon king, on hearing the Goddess' reply, sends another general, Dhumralocana, and his army to do just as was threatened, to drag her before him by her hair. No sooner does he

---

[36] Brahma actually names her in the first episode as, amongst other things, the great demoness (*Mahāsurī*).
[37] Coburn 1991: 158

attempt to attack the Goddess, does she reduce him to ashes with sound - a single powerful HUM, and destroys his army from astride her lion. The increasingly angry Sumbha sends Canda and Munda along with their demon army to take the Goddess by force, which evokes the fearsome black Kali:

> *"7.4 Ambika then uttered a great wrathful cry against them,*
> *And her face became as black as ink in anger.*
> *7.5 From the knitted brows of her forehead's surface immediately*
> *Came forth Kali, with her dreadful face, carrying sword and noose.*
> *7.6 She carried a strange skull-topped staff, and wore a garland of*
> *human heads;*
> *She was shrouded in a tiger skin, and looked utterly gruesome with*
> *her emaciated skin.*
> *7.7 Her widely gaping mouth, terrifying with its lolling tongue,*
> *With sunken reddened eyes and a mouth that filled the directions*
> *with roars.*
> *7.8 She fell upon the great Asuras in that army, slaying them*
> *immediately.*
> *She then devoured the forces of the enemies of the gods."*[38]

Having slain Canda and Munda, Kali brings their heads to the Goddess from whom she emerged, and she (here named Candika) bestows on Kali the name Camunda (slayer of Canda and Munda). According to assertions already made in the text, we are to believe that all of the individually named goddesses with their own personalities are in fact one great Goddess. It therefore appears strange to see Candika converse with Kali-Camunda like a benevolent ruler addressing a subordinate and a separate individual. It may be that the various names given to the Goddess, like Camunda, belong to local or ancestral deities assimilated into Durga and Kali for their similar qualities, and the text seeks to incorporate them in this way. It must be remembered that the Puranas, like most Hindu literature, were put together over hundreds of years and may have featured countless interpolations.

At this point we may be confused as to how the terrifying, ghoulish Kali described above could relate to the benevolent Mother, but as the Devi Mahatmya closes, the all-pervading nature

---

[38] Coburn 1991: 61

of Mahakali is described:

> *"**12.35** O King, this whole egg of Brahma is pervaded by her,*
> *Who is Mahakali at the end of time, having the form of the great*
> *pestilence.*
> *****12.36** She herself is the great pestilence at one time; she herself,*
> *unborn, becomes the creation at another;*
> *And she, the eternal, provides support for what is created at yet*
> *another time.*
> *****12.37** In times of well-being, she is the good fortune of men,*
> *granting them prosperity in their homes.*
> *In times of privation, she exists as ill-fortune, for the sake of*
> *destruction.*
> *****12.38** Praised and worshipped with flowers incense, perfumes, and*
> *the like,*
> *She grants wealth, sons, an auspicious mind, the pathway to*
> *dharma."*[39]

This makes clear her role as the creator, sustainer, and destroyer of life; all is within her.

OTHER ORIGIN STORIES OF THE BLACK GODDESS

The question of the Goddess' skin colour is not an insignificant one. In contrast with Black Madonnas, we do not find stories of statues changing to black over time but rather stories of the goddess herself changing colour, and receiving a new name on her transformation, usually signifying a change of state and temperament. Kali's black colour seems to play a significant part in her stories. As we see in the *Devi Mahatmya,* her blackness is often representative of anger. In a story in the *Linga Purana,* Parvati undergoes a change to emerge as the ferocious black Kali to overthrow a demon who can only be defeated by a female. In this instance, rather than being a weaponised goddess created by all of the gods, Parvati turns herself black after drawing poison from Shiva's neck. The colour change also happens in reverse; Kali returning to the calmer Parvati. In a story in the *Skanda Purana,* Parvati is teased by Shiva for her black colour. She goes away to

---

[39] Coburn 1991: 82

the Himalayas to practice asceticism in order to change her colour. Before she goes, she stations her son Viraka outside their home to prevent any other women approaching her lusty husband. A demon disguised as the Goddess does gain entry (and is slain by Shiva) but Parvati, hearing this, thinks that her husband has cheated and her son failed her. In rage and despair she manifests a ravenous lion that leaps from her mouth. The Goddess is prepared to jump into the lion's mouth and end her own life, but Brahma arrives to stop her and banishes her angst by allowing her to become golden. However, rather than just changing colour, she sloughs her skin and steps out of it as the gold-skinned Gauri. The black-skinned goddess she shed remains an entity in her own right who becomes known as Kaushiki.[40] This Kaushiki is sent away by Brahma to kill the demon generals that we are familiar with from the *Devi Mahatmya*, with the newly manifested lion as her mount, whilst Gauri returns to her husband. Brahma makes clear that Kaushiki is one and the same with the Goddess in her entirety, not merely a part of her.[41]

The Puranas give us these examples of Kali arising from the Goddess' anger, usually for the purpose of battle. The oral tradition, however, gives a slightly different nuance; the generation of Kali happening through grief or shame.[42] McDaniel recorded a couple of these versions: In the first, a variant on the birth of Ganesha, the Goddess creates her son out of dirt. She places him on guard so no one may enter whilst she is bathing, and when Shiva tries to get past him, Ganesha refuses three times before having his head struck off. This grief causes Durga to transform into the bloodthirsty Kali, killing and eating men as she roams the earth for her son's missing head. Only after Shiva replaces Ganesha's head with that of an elephant and lies on the ground so that Kali steps on him, is she placated. It is through shame for touching her husband with her feet that she is returned to her original form but in the second story it is shame that motivates her transformation into Kali. In this version of the fight with the buffalo demon, Mahishasura, Durga realises that the fast-moving demon only

---

40 Chandola 2007: 63
41 Doniger 1975: 259
42 Folk traditions vary from the 'high literature' of the Brahminic class in that they are often taken more literally than metaphorically, and often exhibit inconsistencies.

leaves himself open to attack when he pauses to stare at her genitals. Having realised she has been created in this form to be a sex object, her shame evokes the wild, destructive dance of Kali. In both cases she is only reverted by Shiva lying beneath her and penetrating her.[43] These emotions of anger, grief, and shame, are ones that feature prominently in other goddess mythology and whereas we may have thought that these stories exhibited a feminist message, it appears somewhat defunct when social order is restored by the Goddess submitting to her husband, and we are reminded not to lose sight of the social reality faced by many women in India, despite this interpretation of its mythology.

FOLK PRACTICES

Kali worship is not only the domain of the high mythology and theology of the Puranas and Tantras. In India, as in the West Indies, Kali is favoured amongst folk traditions. Folk Shaktism[44] features tribal goddesses and ancestresses who are generally amoral, and have seemingly no divide with the more famous Hindu goddesses; very localised deities often being worshipped under the names of Durga or Kali. Those who follow Folk Shaktism practices do so for pragmatic reasons, rather than simply for the love of the goddess. The deity is propitiated for fertility, healing, magic, and prevention of disease. The deities invoked have human personalities and the range of emotions that come with them, so may be unpredictable in their reaction to ritual or may appear unannounced outside of ritual space. In this oral tradition, a goddess might appear as an old human woman needing assistance, a mother, or a warrior.[45] They are also shapeshifters and have a range of forms, including natural objects. Local statues and rocks are worshipped as a deity, their significance usually being revealed in a dream.[46]

There are different folk theories concerning goddesses in rocks

---

[43] McDaniel 2004: 236-8

[44] For those wishing to understand the nuanced differences between folk, tantra, Shakta, and bhakti practices and their subdivisions, see *Offering Flowers, Feeding Skulls* by June McDaniel which offers a detailed discussion with regard to West Bengal in particular.

[45] McDaniel 2004: 8-9

[46] Although a phenomenon open to exploitation, this apparently does not happen often, as people are mostly fearful of the wrath of the gods.

- Sometimes they are said to have always been there; sometimes they have been transformed and await the right person to wake them up. The rock might be a statue that has worn down, run away, or maybe been hidden from invaders, replaced with a decoy and forgotten.[47] This is comparable to the multiple stories we have of lost and found Black Madonnas, usually discovered by a simple villager, in a place that becomes a new cult centre. Statues of Kali are sometimes said to have once been the goddess in the form of a human girl and have stories attached to them. She becomes a wandering goddess when her statue or her people are displaced. It seems, no matter the origin, folklore loves a sentient statue or a *genius loci*.

Kali's domain is the burning ground, which is where she is worshipped by Folk Tantrikas, a group outside of society and misunderstood by many. Here she is *Dakshinakali*, the form most commonly found in Trinidadian temples, with Kali stood on the corpse of her husband Shiva. Whereas Classical Tantra places importance on understanding the metaphor of sacred texts and seeking liberation from illusion, Folk Tantra is much more experiential. Its followers are largely illiterate, and place emphasis on the literal enacting of ritual practices to commune with the Goddess. These practices gain Folk Tantrikas a bad reputation for drinking, drug-taking, fornicating, and devil-worshipping,[48] which leads them to be feared and viewed as degenerate by many from the Classical school and other outsiders,[49] just as the Madrassis are in the West Indies.

Curiously, in Folk Shamanism, Kali is viewed as a goddess of lowly standing. Shamans dedicate mantras associated with the *guna* of *tamas* (the quality of darkness) to deities such as Kali for the purpose of ill will, or protection against it. The aim of the folk shaman is to overpower the deity and order them to do their bidding.[50] Folk mantras to Kali actually insult the goddess to provoke anger and action from her, to prove she is powerful.[51]

---

[47] McDaniel 2004: 30-1
[48] McDaniel 2004: 72
[49] McDaniel 2004: 10
[50] Chandola 2007: 109
[51] Chandola 2007: 113

RAMPRASAD SEN AND SHAKTI BHAKTI

At the other end of the spectrum, *bhakti* practices are very loving and devotional. Largely an oral and experiential tradition, *bhakti* uses songs rather than sacred texts to inspire love and devotion to the Goddess in the form of the Mother. Shakti Bhaktism is a devotional practice that is said to owe a lot of its popularity to the early-modern Puranic writings attributed to Ramprasad Sen. This 18th-century saint devoted himself to Kali and wrote thousands of verses to her in praise and in prayer. To Ramprasad, she is a Goddess of Wisdom, with much in common with the Biblical Wisdom that has been linked in modern literature to the mysteries of the Black Madonna. Kali is neither solely a nurturing mother nor the destructive terror she is made out to be in Western readings of her iconography. She is a warrior, for certain, but the demons she fights are self-inflation of the ego, not an external 'enemy'. In this mode of thinking, Kali's purpose is not solely creation and destruction but enlightenment and illumination.[52]

Ramprasad was born around 1723 in Bengal. His work was acknowledged in his own lifetime, gaining him imitators and detractors, and offers from both a Hindu king and a Muslim prince to become their court musician – which he declined, preferring a life of simple devotion. Only 250 of the estimated 100,000 poems he wrote survive, but their popularity continues right up to this day in Bengal.

Ramprasad emphasized that there was no need to go on pilgrimage or make offerings – a large part of Hindu practice – other than offering heart and mind, which is the essence of *bhakti*. According to Ramprasad, one does not need to go to sacred sites or try to attain absolute truth. The answers are within and the path itself is the goal. His ideas almost approached iconoclasm:

> *'Do you not feel foolish adorning clay statues with wooden ornaments painted gold?... Why create finite images and concepts of the living Goddess who is infinite?... Only ecstatic love and selfless meditation can be offered to the Goddess of Wisdom. External*

---

[52] Hixon 1994: 23

forms of worship and propitiation are bribes she will never accept."[53]

Ramprasad addresses her blackness on many occasions and does so in terms of power and beauty, and in much the same way as our Black Madonnas have been addressed. It is a radiant, luminous black that attracts the soul of the mystic, whether Hindu, Muslim, Christian, or otherwise, a blackness that has transcended the boundaries of culture and time. The familiar physical description of Kali that he mentions on various occasions is highly detailed, yet it is asserted that in her translucent blackness she is unknowable. As she incorporates all of nature, Ramprasad likens her to the vast blackness of the cosmos, and the depths of the ocean. The imagery he uses of black and fertile soil is reminiscent of the symbolism of the Greek goddess Demeter, but here, rather than earthly fertility, it is a metaphor for the cultivation of the soul.

He also addresses the meaning of her nakedness, which for many is a challenging aspect of her image. She is completely transparent which is what makes her fearsome. He writes: "O Mother of the Universe, this child is terrified by your naked truth, your unthinkable blackness, your sheer infinity. Please cover your reality with a gentle veil".[54] This gives an interesting contrast to the Western concept of Wisdom, which is regularly described as veiled. Like some of the Black Madonnas of Western Europe and the Americas, statues of Kali can become so heavily adorned with fabric, jewellery, and flowers, that the statue itself is barely visible beneath them. This seems antithetical to the concept that she is unable to be covered, that she is all-pervading. Quite possibly it is the desexualising of the Mother (in both cultures) that causes her worshippers to prefer her as heavily clothed.

Textual evidence for Kali does not go back nearly as far as some of the other Hindu deities and evidence of her worship is not vast until relatively recent times. Ramprasad was one of the first of the famous visionaries of the early-modern age to popularise Kali worship. Other major figures followed in the ensuing 19th century to bring Kali the Mother to the masses.

---

[53] Hixon 1994: 106
[54] Hixon 1994: 135

RANI RASMANI, SRI RAMAKRISHNA, AND SRI SARADA DEVI – DEVOTEES OF THE MOTHER

One of the most significant cult centres of Kali is the Dakshineswar Temple outside Kolkata, built in 1847. The founder of the temple, Rani Rasmani was a remarkable woman who truly embodied our idea of the 'Black Madonna spirit' in her defence of the poor, and bravery in the face of the establishment. She was born into a poor caste, but her fortune changed when a rich man in his boat saw her bathing and was so overcome by her beauty that he came back to marry her. After his sudden death, the Rani found herself in charge of his estate. People were sceptical that the Rani could deal with his finances, but she did so adeptly. When the British imposed a fishing tax which was extremely prohibitive to local fishermen, she bought the fishing rights to a section of the river then proceeded to barricade it with chains so that the British boats could no longer pass. She only agreed to remove them when the British repaid the hefty sum for the rights and abolished the tax. Other stories abound about her turning the lives of the poor around and defying the British, who were obstructing religious processions. The money and supplies she had been planning to spend on going on pilgrimage she instead distributed amongst the poor after having a vision of the Mother telling her to create her own shrine on the Ganges. The Kali temple was built in eight years at a great cost but the Rani astutely had bought land to support the upkeep of the temple after she passed (until 1947 when the land, and therefore the funds, was sadly taken by the Empire). One stumbling block to fulfilling the Rani's mission was her low birth, which meant higher caste Brahmins would not worship and eat at her temple. This was overcome when Ramkumar, who was of the Brahmin caste, suggested consecrating the temple in the name of a Brahmin and officiating at the ceremony himself. In this way, the liberal Rani Rasmani found a way to welcome people of all castes and religions to worship at the feet of the Mother.[55]

The younger brother of Ramkumar, Sri Ramakrishna was a mystic and devotee of Kali, born in Bengal in 1836. Rather than seeking a career, he was only interested in broadening his spiritual

---

[55] Harding 1993: 159-65

experience, and spent much time at Dakshineswar Temple where his brother led worship, eventually joining him to be a priest around age 20. After the sudden death of his brother, Ramakrishna's spiritual quest became increasingly introverted and unorthodox, detaching himself even further from the material world. He longed for a glimpse of the Divine Mother to whom he had devoted his being, experiencing the separation from her as a real, physical agony. One day this culminated in him finally snatching up the sword that hung above the altar of Kali, with the intention of ending his own life. It was at that moment that the infinite consciousness of the Goddess was revealed to him, and he passed out in reverie for several hours. Following this epiphany, he was unable to carry out his priestly duties, instead spending countless hours in meditation or reeling around intoxicated with worship. His actions had become so irregular and sacrilegious that he was suspected of insanity by temple officials, but the Rani recognised his true devotion and decreed that he should be free to continue in his own manner. This all happened before Ramakrishna reached the age of 23.

At around this time, Ramakrishna's family arranged his marriage to a child of 5 years old (not unusual in Indian culture). Sri Sarada Devi lived with her family until the time came, when she was 18, to move to live with her husband at Dakshineswar. The marriage, however, was never consummated; Sri Ramakrishna never being able to comprehend touching the female body which he could only see as the Great Mother to whom he was devoted.[56] He addressed Sri Sarada Devi as Holy Mother, and his disciples began to worship her as the Goddess in human form.

Sarada Devi herself was a quiet, shy individual who wore a veil and shied away from the divine status and attention bestowed upon her, whilst remaining aware of how Ma Kali had touched her life. She had received various visions of the Mother since childhood, and it is told that she once went spontaneously into possession by Kali when in danger. Whilst travelling, she was separated from her companions at night and confronted by robbers who were stunned when Kali manifested in the frightened girl. Rather than scaring the

---

[56] Harding 1993: 268

robbers, she spoke sweetly to them, asking them to deliver her to Dakshineswar safely, which they reportedly did, under the influence of the Mother's love.[57] Whilst Ramakrishna worshipped his wife as Goddess, Sri Sarada Devi in fact worshipped him as an incarnation of Ma Kali, so pure was his devotion and his expression of her.

Ramakrishna turned to gurus to further his experience, becoming learned in first Tantric and then Vaishnava and Vedanta disciplines. He learned but rejected the Tantric practices that involved alcohol and sexual intercourse, remaining chaste and dismissing these features as undesirable and unnecessary. During his Vaishnava period, Ramakrishna nurtured his own motherly instincts, caring for a statue of the child god Rama as if it were his own child, and actually spending time dressed and living as a woman in order to feel closer to the Divine Feminine.[58] Ramakrishna drew the attention of great leaders and thinkers, but rather than spend time with them, preferred to surround himself with lay disciples from all walks of life. Like the biblical Wisdom, at sunset, Ramakrishna would stand on the rooftop crying out "Come, my children! O where are you? My tongue is parched from talking to the worldly-minded. O come, I long to talk to you!"[59] Significantly, over the following years, Ramakrishna took on a synergistic and agnostic view of religion, practicing Islam and Christianity for a while, before coming to the conclusion that all paths lead to the same God. His teachings – a mixture of bhakti devotion to the Mother, Vedanta philosophy, and the belief that all religions' deities are *Brahman*,[60] became known as Shakta Universalism.

WESTERN PERSPECTIVES ON KALI

If we look at the text of the *Devi Mahatmya* through a modern, western cultural lens, an obvious interpretation would be that the (exclusively male) demon collective represent oppressive patriarchal forces. The repetition of the notion of dragging the

---

[57] Harding 1993: 286
[58] Harding 1993: 262-3
[59] Harding 1993: 269
[60] The formless, unknowable creator.

Goddess by her hair reinforces an all too familiar image we associate with domestic violence. The passage describing Kali's emergence has, in feminist circles, be seen as a depiction of anti-patriarchal rage, especially in relation to the attempt to force the Goddess into marriage, and the threat of physical violence if she resists. In response, a more fearsome form of defence and retribution is unleashed. In its historical context, however, the intention of the composer to present such a strong feminist theme is unlikely. There has been, without doubt, continued sexism and suppression of women within Brahminical Hinduism throughout history. Nevertheless, in the modern age, the power of the Devi has inspired Hindu women in the West who wish to make a stand.

The Bengali Women's Support Group was set up in 1985 in Sheffield, UK, to support and inspire isolated Bengali women. Although the group has feminist members, they do not describe the group as feminist. Unlike some feminist groups, they do not shy away from religious pluralism, and celebrate Eid, Christmas and Durga Puja with their Muslim, Christian, and Hindu members. In relation to male violence, they directly quote the Durga myth in harnessing their *shakti* as a force for change.[61] In 1979, the Southall Black Sisters was set up in London as an organisation for women's rights and the needs of Black and Minority Ethnic women. With both Hindu and non-Hindu Indian members, they campaign on issues inherent in the Brahminical tradition such as domestic violence.[62] In some cases, Hindu women have gathered their own following in Britain, not just of other Hindu women, but men and non-Hindus, in an embodiment of the Goddess or administering of her rites in a neo-Hindu feminist synthesis. One such woman was Prabhadevi Chauhan, who held public gatherings and welcomed visitors to her house in Leeds, UK, in the 1960s, offering blessings and healing whilst in possession.[63]

In India itself, *Kali for Women* was set up as a feminist publisher in 1984, to make women's voices heard; the goddess Kali becoming an emblem of female independence. Not only Kali, but the likes of Durga, Shakti, and other manifestations of the goddess have lent

[61] Chatterjee 1995: 93
[62] Knott 2012: 100
[63] Knott 2012: 100

their name to self-defence programmes for young women in India over the past few decades. In 2013, Save the Children India ran a powerful advertising campaign called Save Our Sisters, depicting iconic goddesses such as Durga sporting the cuts and bruises of domestic violence, to bring home the hypocrisy of harming women within a culture that worships the Divine Feminine.

An example of the divergent perspectives of East and West is made by Roxanne Kamayana Gupta who writes that because Kali is worshipped by the most outcast and oppressed it is easy, from our Western perspective, to presume she is a representative of repressed rage. The desire to use her for self-empowerment and to bolster our own effectiveness is quite antithetical to the Tantrika who surrenders in the face of her almighty power.

> *'Within a Hindu framework, this surrender to transcendent inevitability… can look a lot like the egoless state needed to attain enlightenment. To the Westerner, it can look a lot like powerlessness.'*[64]

CONCLUSION

Over the course of the 20th century, the West has struggled to shake off the negative colonial interpretations of Kali, but even in repositioning into an idea of her as a feminist, sex-positive counterculture icon, we are still subverting her Eastern interpretation, making her unrecognisable to many Hindus. Does this, therefore, make these interpretations completely invalid? I would argue not, just as I would say that the modern archetype of the Black Madonna as a fearsome and maternal defender of social justice is not 'wrong' even if it is not centuries old. The blended 'Madrassi' ceremonies that have grown around Kali in the West Indies are, as Kloß pointed out, invented but not inauthentic.[65] As cultures spread across the world, increasingly faster in the age of the internet, new renditions of gods and goddesses appear, and patterns emerge threaded throughout seemingly disparate religions. It is not up to us to appoint ourselves the adjudicators of what constitutes the 'right' and 'wrong' ways to carry out a religion. It is

---

[64] Gupta 2003: 139-41
[65] Kloß 2016: 107

our duty to acknowledge their similarities and differences and recognise what is reinterpretation versus Indigenous tradition so that we do not fall into the trap of thinking that the lens we currently use is the only correct one. If we ignore and replace Kali's contextual history with our own interpretation, we fall into neo-colonialism that only consumes and reappropriates rather than celebrates Kali's plurality.

CHAPTER 8

The Romani Saint
and the Magdalene

INTRODUCTION

We now travel back full circle, from India to France where we began, in the company of the Romani. On a hot May afternoon every year, thousands of Romani travellers gather alongside locals and tourists to celebrate the procession of a Black Madonna from the church of Les Saintes-Maries-de-la-Mer down to the sea. However, this is not a statue of the Virgin Mary. Instead, this Black 'Madonna' is a representation of Saint Sara, or Sara la Kali as she is popularly known. The beach is said to be the spot where she came ashore in the company of the three Marys: Mary Magdalene, Mary Salome, and Mary Jacobe, as well as other biblical refugees fleeing the Holy Land after the Resurrection of Christ. In some versions of the story, Sara is the maidservant of the Marys, come from Egypt; in others she is a Romani queen who instead welcomed the Marys to Gaul. Even stranger theories cast her as potentially the daughter of Mary Magdalene and Jesus, brought to Europe in the womb of the Magdalene, which some regard as the real Holy Grail. The popularity of such legends, elaborated in modern books such as the fictional *Da Vinci Code,* have contributed to the growing market of spiritual tourism in the south of France to reclaim the lost Feminine on the trail of the Magdalene, who some regard as the real identity of the Black Madonna...

THE PILGRIMAGE OF LES SAINTES-MARIES-DE-LA-MER

The town of Les Saintes-Maries-de-la-Mer sits on the coast of

Provence, south of Arles in an island delta known as the Camargue where the Rhone meets the sea. Every year, in the weeks leading up to the 24th May, an estimated 10,000 to 15,000 Romani descend upon the small town of 2,500 inhabitants to celebrate their saint, Sara la Kali. They are joined by a mass of tourists and media bringing the attendance to an estimate of between 25,000 and 40,000.[1] All have come to witness the blend of local and Romani culture, led by 'Les gardians', traditionally dressed French cowboys on horseback, and a group of Romani carrying the statue and relics of Sara down to the seashore.

The procession starts at the town's fortified church, built to repel raiders from the 9th century onward. Its bell tower and crenellated battlements stand out over the houses. Inside, statues of Mary Jacobe and Mary Salome, the half-sisters of the Virgin Mary stand in a boat in the nave. Twice a year the relics are lowered from a window in the Choir to be paraded through the town,[2] the first of these occurrences being 25th May, the original pilgrimage date. Whereas these statues enjoy the prominence of the Choir, the black statue of Sara is relegated to unsanctified ground in the church's crypt, for she is not recognised as canonical by the Catholic Church. As at other subterranean Black Madonna shrines, a curious concurrent devotion is 'allowed' to continue alongside the prescribed rituals of the Church above. This relegation is somewhat telling of the racial hierarchy instigated during the pilgrimage's history.

The crypt itself is filled with candles, offerings, and crutches left as prayers or thanks for healing. The statue of Sara stands about 5-foot-tall next to an altar of pre-Christian origin containing her reliquary, no doubt lending weight to the legend that she inhabited this land before the coming of the Marys. The small statue is covered in layer upon layer of cloaks. Various writers have described visiting the shrine and witnessing Romani families praying, conversing with the statue, tending to her clothing and diving beneath the layers to kiss her feet.[3]

---

[1] Hayes 2010: 408
[2] Hayes 2010: 407
[3] See Hayes, p408 and Galland, p175-179 in particular for descriptions.

Above: 'Sara la Kali'. Patron saint of the Romani, Sara la Kali is bound up in the legends of the Three Marys – including the Magdalene – coming to southern France after Christ's crucifixion. Her black statue is ritually taken down to the sea every 24 May.

The procession on the 24th May for Saint Sara comes with much pageantry and spectacle, an event that has bloomed alongside a growing spiritual tourism trade and those seeking alternatives on the margins of Christianity. As Hayes eloquently puts it: "While French churches have been emptying, crowds and the media have been flocking to these annual interfaith, multi-ethnic, over-the-top, theologically aberrant, civic, religious, touristy happenings". The white statues of Mary Salome and Mary Jacobe are taken down to the sea the next day, and the local tourist board follows it up with a range of local heritage entertainment such as folk dancing and bullfighting in an attempt to hold onto the tourists in town for the festival.[1] And just like that, the Romani depart in their motor homes for another year. But how did they come to celebrate this annual tradition in Provence in the first place?

THE HISTORY OF THE ROMANI

Due to linguistic similarities between Indian and Roma language, it has long been suspected that the Romani people originated from India. Genetic studies in 2012 confirmed that the Romani came from a single group who left northwest India in the 6th century.[2] Romani are commonly known in English as gypsies, short for 'gypcian', a misnomer based on the belief that they originated from Egypt due to their dark skin. Medieval people commonly conflated dark-skinned people who were not 'Saracen' with 'Egyptians'.[3] Gypsy, unsurprisingly, is widely considered a slur and avoided where possible in this text. 'Romani' is also something of a catch-all and does not fully represent the many sub-groups of these people, but it is the most accepted title in the modern day. The genetic findings have helped this global community become recognised as members of the Indian Diaspora; the Indian Minister of External Affairs declared that the Roma community are children of India at the International Roma Conference of 2016.

Linguistic and legendary evidence points to the Romani being comprised of "itinerant clans of musicians" who made their way to the Persian Kingdom after leaving India to find work as

---

[1] Wiley 2005: 151
[2] Bhanoo 2012.
[3] Foster 2016b: 8

entertainers.[4] The Romani reached the Balkans by the 12th century, and by the 15th had found a new means of survival besides music – the pastime of pilgrimage. "Upon entering Europe in large numbers in the 15th century, they understood that Europeans had been conditioned to grant privileges to travelling strangers",[5] meaning that the established tradition of pilgrimage granted safe passage to those travelling as Christian pilgrims. The Romani declared themselves pilgrims and invoked the protections that came with it, similar to those that they had enjoyed as musicians in the Middle East.[6] Many believe that assuming the role of Christians was just that – a role played by those who were used to a life of performance art. Angus Fraser says "In the entire chronicle of Gypsy history, the greatest trick of all was the one played on Western Europe in the fifteenth century".[7] Whatever the case in the beginning, they kept to this faith after pilgrimages declined in popularity and today are largely a deeply Catholic people.

The first Roma recorded in France were in Paris at the start of the 15th century, and in 1438 they arrived in Arles, Provence. By this time, the cult of Mary Magdalene had already become established in nearby Saint-Maximin-la-Sainte-Baume which claimed her relics. In 1448, René of Anjou ordered excavations to look for more relics at the outpost fortress-church at the mouth of the Rhone where the party had come ashore and, sure enough, two bodies were found in the crypt which were identified as Mary Salome and Mary Jacobe. It was for them that the town was later renamed Les Saintes-Maries-de-la-Mer.[8] Hayes says that the relics of Sara la Kali were unearthed there in 1496 and claimed by the Romani as their saint,[9] though most authors state that the earliest we hear of her is in *The Legend of the Saintes-Maries* of 1521 by Vincent Philippon. The origins of Saint Sara remain unclear, though the legends contain several flaws. Her identification as 'Sara the Egyptian' no doubt comes from her adoption by the Romani, a people who medieval Europeans believed as coming from Egypt. The alternate story of Sara being a royal ancestress of the Romani

4 Wiley 2005: 141
5 Wiley 2005: 142
6 Wiley 2005: 142
7 Fraser 1995: 62
8 Hayes 2010: 284
9 Hayes 2010: 285

who lived in the region at the time is of course anachronistic as the Romani people had not even left India in the 1st century CE. Although not a belief commonly stated by the Romani now, many scholars believe the saint to be a metamorphosis of the goddess Kali; the 'Sara' part either coming from the goddess Saraswati or, more convincingly from one of the names of Kali/Durga mentioned in the *Durgasaptashati* which was composed around the time the Romani were leaving India.[10] It could also be merely linguistic. 'Kali' means 'black' or 'dark' in both Hindu and Romani dialects and *Calé*, a derivative of it, is an alternate name for the Roma, thought to be a euphemism for their dark skin. It is likely, just as we have seen with other Black Madonnas favoured by marginalised peoples, that the Roma are drawn to this saint who appears 'in their image', which is rarely found in official Church iconography.

The origins of the statue itself are perhaps even harder to trace. Marc Bordigoni states that there is no evidence of its existence before the 20th century, though the Romani were recorded as present on the pilgrimage at Les Saintes-Maries-de-la-Mer from at least 1852. To the contrary, Bordigoni believes Sara's presence in the crypt follows the Romani presence there, not the reverse, and delving into the pilgrimage's 20th-century history seems to evince this.[11] A shrine in the crypt held human bones that would have been believed to be Sara, but an engraving of the crypt by Canon Lamoureux in 1897 shows Romani gathered at the shrine with no statue to be seen. Further descriptions of the crypt in 1911 and 1927 make no mention of the statue and it seems likely that one was introduced in line with the advent of a pilgrimage day designed specifically for the Romani in 1935.[12]

The recollections of eyewitnesses at the start of the 20th century include Romani families sleeping overnight within the church, a fact that the media used to try to provoke outrage with tales of the crypt being given over to them to enact black masses, the election

---

[10] The ritual bathing of the statue in the sea also bears resemblance to aspects of Durga Puja practiced in India. However it is also a relatively common practice in Christian history, so is more likely to stem from other pilgrimage traditions than far removed Indian ones.
[11] Bordigoni 2005.
[12] Bordigoni 2005: 3-4

of a gypsy queen, and even sacrifices.[13] In actual fact, the Romani were relegated to the crypt as the growing popularity of the pilgrimage had meant that the Eucharist was being disturbed by the noise and activities of the Roma, talking loudly and lighting candles. Seen as a disruptive force rather than 'real' Catholics, the Romani were segregated during the years between the World Wars, with entry and exit to the crypt through a separate door which kept them apart from the 'respectable Christians' who viewed these intruders with contempt.

This all changed when in 1935, the Marquis Folco de Baroncelli-Javon, a supposed advocate for the Romani, instigated a separate pilgrimage day just for them. Whether this was purely for their benefit or to ease the pressure on the church of Les-Saintes is unknown, but it was a success. The Marquis negotiated with the Archbishop of Aix and Arles for an authorised procession to be held on 24th May specifically for Saint Sara,[14] and it was he who instigated the anachronistic legend of Sara being a local 'gypsy queen',[15] seemingly to legitimize this people's ancestry in the Camargue. It is around this time that the black Sara statue must have been introduced to provide a focal point for the parade. Bordigoni surmises that the plaster statue may have been donated by one of the Romani vendors that sold pilgrimage paraphernalia including such statues.[16]

ETHNIC TENSIONS

The clergy did not initially participate in the Romani procession. Alan Hayes writes: "Until the 1950s the church kept an official distance from the ceremony but then it appointed chaplains to the gypsies (partly in reparation for their suffering under the Nazis and partly to foil the Pentecostal missionaries); since then priests have joined in the annual procession, and when the statue is brought to the sea, a priest ritually washes her as she is partially submerged."[17] The testimony of one of the priests at the time

---

[13] Bordigoni 2005: 6
[14] Bordigoni 2005: 8-9
[15] Bordigoni 2005: 14
[16] Bordigoni 2005: 4
[17] Hayes 2010: 409

reveals that there was talk of banning the procession, and when rumour got out, he had to reassure a town square filled with agitated Roma that it would still be going ahead, and indeed announced the clergy's participation.[18]

The pre-war bigotry towards the Romani never really went away. Wiley reports that some locals find the pilgrimage a nuisance, and that it also reveals "intercultural tensions that persist in modern relations between European villagers and Romanies".[19] Despite the Romani suffering atrocities at the hands of the Nazis and persecution in Eastern Europe, attitudes towards them by the locals have never improved above 'tolerating' the festival, according to Pepe Le Fleur, leader of the Romani pilgrimage in the 2000s.[20] Wiley describes it as a non-threatening form of foreign occupation, with an unspoken law between performer and spectator which ensures the Romani's safety as much as the villagers'.[21] It is on one level, like many counterculture pilgrimages, about visibility. Similar to the Afro-Cuban pilgrimage of Caridad del Cobre that we came across in Chapter 6, this misunderstood and mistrusted minority are stating "we are here, witness us, we are proud of our heritage". And like the Afro and Indi-Caribbean cultures who reinvented and reinterpreted their beliefs in a new setting, "the procession is at once artificial and authentic, a deliberate creation by one person that was given life when successfully grafted onto an ancient pilgrimage tradition".[22] It re-enacts the performance marvel of the 15th-century height of pilgrimage and invents it anew.

Despite the annual recurrence, there is no bonding between pilgrims and locals, many of whom lock up their houses at night or board up their businesses for the duration. The warnings of the locals are downplayed by the local Tourist Office, who occupy a curious position that promotes the pilgrimage but allegedly does nothing to improve local relations. Wiley reports that the imagery of the pilgrimage seen in the media is false; Romanies recruited by the Tourist Office to dress anachronistically and pose for photos

---

[18] Bordigoni 2005: 14-15
[19] Wiley 2005: 138
[20] Wiley 2005: 149-50
[21] Wiley 2005: 139-40
[22] Wiley 2005: 152

to create a romanticised 19th-century impression of the town and festival.[23] He compares it to the sanitized heritage tours of plantations in the US that do not show or talk about slave conditions. The promoted images sweep under the carpet the atrocities and vilification these people have faced for centuries.[24] Like the Black Madonna pilgrimages in the Americas, the Romani pilgrimage has become as much if not more about the spectator than the culture celebrating at its heart.

THE COMING OF THE MAGDALENE

Mary Magdalene is not particularly celebrated at the place she came ashore at Les Saintes-Maries-de-la-Mer and neither has the town ever claimed her relics. These were already established some 150km east at Sainte-Maximin-la-Sainte-Baume. Here, local tradition holds firm that Mary Magdalene lived out her remaining years in Sainte-Baume, despite the writings of Gregory of Tours in the 6th century stating she died at Ephesus. No consecration to Mary Magdalene was made in France until the establishment of a monastery in Vézelay, Burgundy, around 1040. This abbey claimed her relics yet refused to show them. It became named the start of the St James Way, the Camino de Santiago de Compostella and became a large wealthy pilgrimage site.[25] Apparently driven to prove how the bones of the Magdalene might have come there, Vézelay sent a monk to the south coast, the only place she could have entered Gaul, to look for clues. Coming to a priory of Saint Maximin, the monk found an ancient sarcophagus with a relief of the anointing of Jesus' feet. As this was commonly regarded as being carried out by Mary Magdalene, the monk must have concluded that the sarcophagus once held her relics, and that they must have been taken north to protect them during the Saracen occupation of Provence in the 8th century. However, this unwittingly gave Provence the opportunity to stake a better claim on Mary Magdalene. By the early 13th century, Provence was claiming the relics of Mary Magdalene (and her companions, though theirs were not unearthed until later). By 1279, they were

---

[23] Wiley 2005: 149-50
[24] Wiley 2005: 153
[25] Hayes 2010: 279

claiming Mary's relics had always been there and never went to Vézelay. Charles of Salerno, future Charles II of Anjou and king of Sicily supported the claim and in 1294, the new pope, Boniface VIII, confirmed it.[26]

Saint-Maximin's fortunes began to outstrip Vézelay's. Charles II had the basilica built and, at his request, the Pope had it put into the hands of the Dominicans. This was followed by the convenient discovery of the relics of the other two Marys at Les Saintes-Maries-de-la-Mer. Vézelay, once the preferred starting point for the Camino de Santiago was now rivalled by the resting place of Saint James' mother, Mary Salome, and Les-Saintes became a popular departure point.[27]

Saint-Maximin-la-Sainte-Baume, with a modern population of 16,500, sits below the Sainte-Baume mountain that was said to be Mary Magdalene's final home. The impressive basilica of Saint-Maximin holds the relics of Mary Magdalene in its crypt. A Gallo-Roman sarcophagus serves as an altar, and the relics are housed behind it. A gold and silver reliquary contains her skull and a crystal tube houses a bone tissue fragment found undecayed in 1279, said to be where Jesus touched her. On her feast day of 22nd July, hundreds of people follow a procession of her reliquary. Although the pilgrimage is not as well attended as Les Saintes-Maries-de-la-Mer, the crypt still draws 100,000 to 200,000 visitors a year.[28]

A 40-minute walk through the forest leads to the cliff where, 150 steps above, perches the monastery built around the cave that was believed to be Mary Magdalene's resting place. The tradition, recorded in *The Golden Legend*, compiled by Jacobus de Voragine, Archbishop of Genoa, in 1275, states that Mary Magdalene, along with Lazarus and Maximin preached Christianity in the Marseilles region. Whilst the latter two went on to become legendary founding bishops in the region, Mary Magdalene demurely retired to the cave in Sainte-Baume and spent the last thirty years of her life as a hermit. This part of the tale had been conflated with the life of Mary of Egypt, a desert hermit, when the Magdalene's *vita* was first being composed in Europe.

---

[26] Hayes 2010: 281-3
[27] Hayes 2010: 284
[28] Hayes 2010: 411

According to Hayes, Sainte-Baume draws far fewer 'traditional' Catholic pilgrims – there were around 150 worshippers on her feast day in 2009[29] - but receives many 'New Age' pilgrims. Anthropologist Anna Fedele travelled with some of the groups of Magdalene pilgrims in southern France and gained significant insight into understanding the intentions, behaviours and beliefs of these New Age or 'energy pilgrims'.[30] But what draws these seekers and how do they relate to the Black Madonna?

Fedele found that her pilgrims, whilst trying to escape from the constrictions of Catholic doctrine, were still heavily influenced by it, particularly the portrayal of the Magdalene as a sensuous sinner.[31] Since the early days of the Church there has been debate over the identity of the Magdalene, with some early Christians combining her with the unnamed sinner who anoints the feet of Christ in the Gospel (Luke 7:36-50) and Mary of Bethany who anoints Jesus' feet at her home (John 12: 1-8). It was Pope Gregory the Great who in 591 definitively declared Mary Magdalene, Mary of Bethany, and the anonymous sinner to be one and the same, colouring the portrayal of her in the Western Church forevermore.[32] Modern feminist scholarship has accused the Catholic Church of maintaining a 'virgin/whore dichotomy' (Despite the Gregorian allusion to the Magdalene as a penitent prostitute being retracted by Pope Paul VI in 1969). Marina Warner writes: "Together the Virgin and the Magdalene form a diptych of Christian patriarchy's idea of woman. There is no place in the conceptual architecture of Christian society for a single woman who is neither a virgin nor a whore",[33] and this, despite the retraction, has held mostly true in the mainstream.

The preponderance of Black Madonnas in southern France

---

[29] Hayes 2010: 413

[30] Fedele began to refer to her travelling companions this way after learning that many regarded the term 'New Age', which they once might have been labelled, as a negative description with connotations of shallow, easily purchased spirituality. In order to find an umbrella term for the various movements, Fedele chose a term, 'energy', which is commonly used by the pilgrims themselves – whether Pagan, New Age, or Goddess worshipper – to describe the quality of pilgrimage destinations. The 'energy' of these places is what draws the pilgrims and, according to them and their guides, is what drew our ancestors to build temples and churches there. Fedele 2018: 116

[31] Fedele 2014: 74

[32] Beavis 2013: 24

[33] Warner 1976: 235

along with the popular veneration of Mary Magdalene in the area has led to the development of a theory in the late 20th century that these statues in fact represent the Magdalene rather than the Virgin Mary. In this theory, the virgin/whore dichotomy is literally laid out as black and white. The theory goes hand in hand with the idea of Mary Magdalene being the secret Bride of Christ, a fact supposedly covered up by the Church, which was expounded in popular literature. For these theorists, the Black Madonna is the symbol of the repressed Feminine in the Bible, Magdalene the lost Bride, whose womb was the literal Holy Grail. In these depictions, the Black Madonna's child is not Jesus himself but his progeny (sometimes said to be Saint Sara).

THE DEVELOPMENT OF A NEW LEGEND

The 21st-century perception of Mary Magdalene has arisen from a complicated set of circumstances, beginning with the discovery of the 'Gnostic Gospels' at Nag Hammadi in 1945. These 'alternate' books of the Bible, thought to have been hidden after their rejection from canonical scripture by the early Church fathers contain more focus on the Feminine, placing Mary Magdalene in a much more central role amongst the Apostles. Renewed interest in non-canonical interpretations of the Bible led to the publication of the notoriously popular *The Holy Blood and the Holy Grail*. Introduced to the world in 1982, the book caused shockwaves in its hypothesis that Jesus and Mary Magdalene had been married, and that their bloodline was preserved in the Merovingian dynasty of French monarchs. Filled with conspiracies, the main theory hinges on the claim that a secret order called the Priory of Sion, installed in 1099 and associated with the Knights Templar, had been secretly working to return the Merovingian line to their rightful throne and domination of Europe. It was not until 2005 that it came to light that the existence of the Priory of Sion was an elaborate hoax started in 1956 by Pierre Plantard, a Frenchman who had apparently commissioned forged parchments relating to the Priory's medieval existence, and an author to write a credible-sounding book about them. Baigent, Leigh and Lincoln, the authors of *The Holy Blood and the Holy Grail,* were led to this information which saw the production of three BBC documentaries and the subsequent book. However, Plantard's claims centred around him being a descendant of the Merovingians, and made no mention of the bloodline of Christ, an element that the authors introduced independently.

Despite *The Holy Blood and the Holy Grail* being generally considered debunked, it had by this time already inspired other works of scholarship, namely Margaret Starbird's *The Woman with the Alabaster Jar* (1993), and fiction, with the publication of the bestselling novel *The Da Vinci Code* (2003) by Dan Brown and subsequent movie adaptation. *The Da Vinci Code* cited the research of the other two books, bringing renewed interest in them by the general public.

Starbird's *Alabaster Jar* and her subsequent works show little interest in the Merovingian bloodline aspect. For her, the detail of importance is Mary Magdalene's role as the mother of the offspring of Christ and the goal being the reclamation of the lost Feminine. In her *The Goddess in the Gospels* (1998), Starbird details her own feelings as a Catholic reading *The Holy Blood and Holy Grail* for the first time and feeling shaken to the core by the claims that all she thought she had understood about the relationship of Jesus and Mary Magdalene was potentially incorrect. Starbird began her own analysis of Biblical and post-Biblical texts as she became increasingly convinced of the veracity of this claim. Her books have been instrumental in Mary Magdalene being claimed by the Goddess movement, with the Magdalene treated as somewhat of a representative of the Goddess herself, and numerous tours dedicated to visiting the sites associated with her taking place every year.

In much the same way as Fedele's energy pilgrims sought an energetic response from a place to test out their prior expectations of it,[34] Starbird's verification of the 'proof' of her theories comes from noticing synchronicities and applying her intuition. Although a valid method as the steer for her personal spiritual quest, it unfortunately does not confirm the truth of her historical research, which others scholars have contradicted.

Mary Ann Beavis in particular has demonstrated why some of

---

[34] Fedele 2018: 121

Starbird's assertions are far from watertight. Starbird follows the accepted Church assumption that Mary Magdalene and Mary of Bethany were the same person, meaning that it was the Magdalene who anointed Jesus. Using 12th-century French abbot Bernard of Clairvaux's equation of Mary of Bethany with the Bride in the *Song of Songs* and elsewhere with the Magdalene as proof, plus the fact that the Catholic church calendar does not have a separate feast day for Mary of Bethany and "French tradition explicitly calls the Magdalen "the sister of Lazarus"",[35] Starbird accepts that they are one and the same. However, the fact that something was widely accepted in the Middle Ages does not mean it was invariably true, and the influence of Pope Gregory's proclamation cannot be underestimated.

Starbird finds in the act of anointing an echo of an ancient erotic 'sacred marriage' ritual since it is theorised that the *Song of Songs* is based on the fertility rites of the goddess Inanna and 'the shepherd' Dumuzi. *The Gospel of John* does indeed feature enough parallels with the *Song of Songs* for the connection to be made, but Beavis argues that in John the lines between Mary of Bethany and Mary Magdalene are so blurred that they cannot be confidently asserted as one.[36] There is enough indistinction for the conflation of Mary to have occurred in the early years of the Church and endured enough to influence medieval tradition.

The Gnostic Texts are also quoted by Starbird and other authors to show Mary Magdalene's prominence amongst the apostles and Jesus' special love for her. As Beavis finds: "Few of these texts, however, refer clearly to Mary Magdalene. *The Gospel of Thomas* mentions a figure called "Mary" twice (21, 114), neither specified as "Magdalene," as well as a female disciple called Salome (61). Similarly, the document frequently referred to as the *Gospel of Mary Magdalene* features dialogues between various male disciples and a woman called Mary (5.2,4,5,7; 9:1,5), but the title "Magdalene" does not appear."[37]

Furthermore, the Cathars of medieval France are given as evidence of the tradition of Jesus and Mary Magdalene's marriage,

---

[35] Starbird 1993: 28
[36] Beavis 2012c: 288
[37] Beavis 2012c: 290

despite the only writings we have on them being from their detractors. The Cathars, a 12th/13th-century Christian sect considered heretical by the Catholic Church, are written in *The Holy Blood and the Holy Grail* as keepers of the secret knowledge of the marriage. Starbird takes it further, suggesting they harboured the secret of Jesus and Mary's offspring, Sara.

The Cathars were largely wiped out by the Albigensian Crusade against them. The Cathars of Béziers were massacred on the feast day of Mary Magdalene in their church, the charge levelled at them of saying that Mary was Christ's concubine. This might seem quite conclusive of their beliefs but was more than likely a fabricated charge, particularly, as Beavis points out, they would not have celebrated a concubine. Cathars were known to value chastity and live in gender-segregated communes.[38]

Further audacious claims were made against the Cathars by 13th-century Catholics, that the Christ who had the Magdalene as his concubine was an earthly, fully human, and therefore innately evil Christ. The real Christ never took on corporeal form but only appeared to his followers in a spiritual body. As Beavis points out, if this is what they believed, "neither the "wife" or the "concubine" variant represents Mary Magdalene as a faithful disciple or spiritual equal of Christ; both seem to be influenced by the Western medieval tradition of Mary as the repentant prostitute who "gave herself up to all the delights of her body," crystallized in the Golden Legend of Jacobus de Voragine".[39] It is therefore hard to see where the evidence that the Cathars honoured this 'hidden tradition' comes from.

Despite the difficulties in finding sound historical proof, Starbird's work has helped grow a patchwork of modern myth around Mary Magdalene as the female equivalent of Christ and the embodiment of Holy Sophia (Wisdom). Heavily influenced by Starbird, Lynn Picknett, for example, in *Mary Magdalene: Christianity's Hidden Goddess* (2003) is fully committed to the idea that the Black Madonnas in southern France are not only representations of the Magdalene rather than the Virgin but are visual confirmation that she bore Christ's offspring because they

---

[38] Beavis 2012b: 422
[39] Beavis 2012b: 424

all hold a child.[40] Ultimately the narrative of Starbird has proved popular because it provides an antidote to the unobtainable: "Rather than being an impossible ideal (the Virgin Mother), a disembodied abstraction (Sophia) or an all-powerful goddess, she is *both* an image of the divine female *and* has a human story to which women can relate."[41] The idea of Magdalene as Black Madonna and equal with Christ, going against established Church doctrine, is a potent psychological balancing of God as Black and female rather than White and male that serves as a balm for the modern soul, weary from patriarchal rule. Popular attraction to the concept is unsurprising.

Whilst questioning Starbird's reasoning, Beavis' work is not a hatchet job; she nevertheless believes the growing interpretation of Mary Magdalene as Christ's equal and the discourse being created on the feminine Divine as welcome and healthy.[42] The same can be said for my own feelings on scholarship around the Black Madonna. Whilst presenting attractive theories centred on uncovering secrets and pondering mysteries, much of it veers off into fantasy fulfilment rather than presenting an alternative take on the available evidence. This is not to say there is no worth in addressing the subject from a spiritual or archetypal point of view, but one of the reasons that the Black Madonna is presented as such an enigma is because of all of the misinformation presented as historical fact. I would argue that since the finding of the Nag Hammadi Library, there has been a popular penchant for uncovering hidden wisdom, and this is mirrored in the 20th-century interest in Black Madonnas, often unearthed after centuries in the ground to point to some esoteric mystery. Jodi Eichler-Levine points out that the public love to consume a book promising hidden wisdom, which is of course not so hidden once it sits on bestseller lists.[43] However, they prefer the evocative and empathetic approach as opposed to dry analysis of gnostic gospels (and all the misogyny that they actually contain). A return to the 'lost sacred Feminine' that may or not have existed, but isn't explicitly present textually, is more about dreaming up the

---

[40] Beavis 2012b: 420
[41] Beavis 2012a: 151
[42] Beavis 2012:b: 428-9
[43] Eichler-Levine 2013

antithesis of our modern situation and the destruction that millennia of patriarchal domination has wrought. Dreams of the Black Madonna as the transformation of an ancient goddess, as secret portrayal of Magdalene/Sophia or the daughter of Christ are preferable to there being no mystery at all. Just because these theories may be unfounded, does not take away from the Black Madonna's iconic and spiritual importance in modern-day events such as the Romani pilgrimage. However, I would say that there needs to be a distinction between the facts and the fiction. In my final chapter I will approach the historiography of the Black Madonna and try to elucidate what is fact and what is coincidental.

CHAPTER 9

The Historiography of the Black Madonna

INTRODUCTION

In this chapter we will examine some of the major modern influences that have been an inspiration for and product of the growing interest in the Black Madonna. These are texts in the popular realm as opposed to those within the pages of journals, some of the latter which we have already quoted: the likes of Foster and Scheer. Although arguably just as valuable, if not more so, those articles have had less of an impact on the public imagination than the titles to be found in esoteric and general bookshops. These 20th-century titles have been influential in the modern resurgence of interest in the Black Madonna.

The first major studies into the Black Madonna were published in the 20th century in French – *Nos Vierges Noires, Les Origines* by Emille Salliens (1945), *Etude sur l'origine des Vierges Noires* by Marie Durand-Lefèbvre (1957), and *L'Enigme de Vierges Noires* by Jacques Huynen (1972), all of which are untranslated and difficult to obtain today. The French sources were a big influence for Ean Begg's *the Cult of the Black Virgin*, (1985, rev. ed. 1996) important for being one of the first major sources in English and for featuring a gazetteer. With Begg, the lines are blurred between historical information and legendary accounts, so as to weave a far more enthralling story of the history of these figures. Because of this, it is a book that proves difficult to use critically, but which is nevertheless one that has been quoted widely.

Another key name in bringing the Black Madonna to the attention of the English-speaking world is Leonard Moss, who, with Stephen Cappannari, gave an address to the American

Association for the Advancement of Science in 1952. When they presented their hypothesis on the origins of the Black Madonna, it is said that every priest and nun in the audience walked out. Nevertheless, their theory was published in a scientific journal the following year, and in 1983 was repeated in a more widely available form in *Mother Worship: Themes and Variations*, an anthology of essays edited by James J. Preston.

The subject became popular with feminist authors who were keen to connect the Black Madonna to matriarchal theory of a goddess-based ancient religion that draws on the work of Marija Gimbutas. Two such authors are Italian-Americans Lucia Chiavola Birnbaum, who published her *Black Madonnas: Feminism, Religion and Politics in Italy* in 1993 and the more wide-ranging *Dark Mother: African Origins and Godmothers* in 2001; and Alessandra Belloni, who spent years on fieldwork researching the Black Madonnas of Southern Italy and learning and teaching its local Black Madonna songs and dances, before publishing the story of her work in *Healing Journeys with the Black Madonna* in 2019.

Male authors on the subject have tended towards a more patriarchal analysis, such as Jean Hani, whose 1995 *La Vierge Noire et la Mystère Marial* put the responsibility for her cult in the hands of a monastic intellectual elite, for whom the Black Virgin is an alchemical allegory. Hani, along with other 20th-century male authors leans into a Jungian psychological interpretation of the Virgin that is not without its flaws, which are rooted in sexism. Despite this, it has been an influence on the Goddess Feminist response.

BEGG AND THE LEGENDARY APPROACH

Ean Begg's work has been heavily quoted innumerable times and is widely named as the primary source for Black Madonnas in the English-speaking world. It is undoubtedly a trove of mythic information; however Begg unfortunately chooses not to reference his sources directly. In his preface he acknowledges that "it has not been my concern to differentiate historical fact – always difficult to establish – from legendary material". Sadly, other writers, especially on the internet, who mine his work for 'facts' do not make

Above: *'Isis Black Madonna'. This image acknowledges the similarities of the statues of Isis nursing Horus and the later Virgin and Child. It features reverse influence from the Black Madonna of Ostrabrama in Vilnius, Lithuania, projected onto the image of Isis.*

this distinction. One may wonder how many of those quoting his work notice this caveat in the preface before repeating the legendary elements of his research as historically accurate.

Begg's enthusiasm for Baigent, Leigh and Lincoln's *The Holy Blood and the Holy Grail*, and its theories about the Priory of Sion shines through in his work. *The Cult of the Black Virgin* was published only a few years after *The Holy Blood and the Holy Grail*, years before anything came to light about allegedly forged documents being placed in the path of its authors (see previous chapter). Despite *The Holy Blood and the Holy Grail* not actually mentioning Black Virgins, Begg's book is littered with references about what this (now believed to be fictional) 'Priory' allegedly knew. These references date the text, yet such claims are still repeated on websites that talk about the Black Madonna today.

Another instrumental source for Begg is the address by Leonard Moss and Stephen Cappannari. He mentions the much-talked-about walkout by the clergy at Moss and Cappannari's initial lecture of 1952[1] as a starting point for musings on the clerical opinion of Black Madonnas. Begg, and others, have commented on the Church's diffidence about the statues, usually based on impromptu questions asked of clergy in attendance at Black Madonna shrines. To my knowledge, no larger surveying of clerical opinion has been carried out. Begg believes the reticence he experienced when it comes to talking about the Black Madonna's significance is due to the perhaps unorthodox nature of her enthusiasts.[2] This theory may hold merit; many Christian sites today express difficulty in understanding the actions and intentions of both 'alternative pilgrims' and secular tourists, yet in many cases have shown a willingness to try to extend appropriate welcomes.[3] Begg suggests the clergy's hesitance is marked by suspicion, however it could equally be a lack of experience in how to relate to different audiences and unexpected questions.

Begg says that little has been written on the Black Madonna because it falls into the gap between art history and ecclesiology,[4]

---

[1] Begg 1996: 9
[2] Begg 1996: 11
[3] See the University of York's 2017 Pilgrimage and Cathedrals project, www.pilgrimageandcathedrals.ac.uk/
[4] Begg 1996: 1

and that "Early textual references to the blackness of the image are rare". As we saw in Chapter 2 of this book, this absence, according to Elisa Foster, was due to the importance of the statues not being about race or colour but concerned with their purported Eastern origins and miracle-working properties; therefore colour went unmentioned. Begg, more concerned with evincing that the statues *were* black in the 12th century, inadvertently confirms the claim that racial connotations were only introduced much later, in that the pieces of evidence he quotes are 16th or 17th-century.[5] Begg considers and rejects the 'coloured dark by smoke' theory, and lists other possibilities, but notably misses the hypothesis of the dark colour being intentional to denote age and authenticity.[6]

In his Foreword, Begg states that "Increasingly, Black Virgins are being whitened, stolen, removed to museums, or withdrawn from circulation".[7] I do not have figures on how frequently this has actually occurred but it would be interesting to know if it has seen an increase since Begg's time of writing (1985), particularly in light of the prominent whitening of the Chartres Virgin in 2014 and the uproar caused by it. He mentions a similar reaction to the whitening of Our Lady of Einsiedeln at the end of the 18th century and the concern that she would lose her cultic appeal.[8] We may wonder whether the reaction at the time went more than skin-deep – a worry of upsetting the faithful's familiarity with her appearance. I think that it is doubtful that the same fears expressed in 21st-century Chartres about the whitening being racially motivated or silencing the alternative voice would have been considered in an earlier age.

Begg states "That early images of Madonna and Child were based on those of Isis and Horus is generally accepted".[9] But when were they copied? The vast majority of known Black Madonnas are confirmed to be 12th-century sculpts with legends that claim much more ancient origins. It seems to make sense that in order to aesthetically match their legendary origin stories, they might mimic the 'in majesty' seated or *Xoanon* standing poses of statues from

---

[5] Begg 1996: 5
[6] Begg 1996: 6-8
[7] Begg 1996: xiii
[8] Begg 1996: 5
[9] Begg 1996: 13

antiquity. In some cases, it is possible that 12th-century statues replaced earlier versions, but it appears far more likely that this was a contemporary stylistic choice that connoted the ancient world. This was, after all, the period of Romanesque architecture that imitated Roman and Byzantine styles. There is justification in seeing similarities in the poses of the statues, but Begg muddies the waters by including other references which seem too obscure to prove credible, such as how the Egyptian ankh (not exclusively a symbol of Isis) "may account for some of the oddly shaped sceptres carried by Black Virgins who, like Isis, often favour the colour green".[10] The latter statement appears just as confounding as the former, and the reader is left wanting for evidence. In addition, Begg connects Saint Sara with Isis due to her epithet 'The Egyptian',[11] despite this being a most-likely misnomer derived from her being patroness of gypsies, who in the Middle Ages were thought to have come from Egypt.

Begg is careful to preface many of his statements with caveats such as 'probably' or 'no doubt', leaving the reader to make their own conclusions, but without the aid of supporting evidence. He does admit that the intentions of the original sculptors are unknown and unprovable, but suggests that the Church's silence on them must mean there is some secret.[12] This popular conspiracist approach has been much entwined with how the phenomenon of the Black Madonna has developed over the last half-century.

We are taken on a journey with Begg through the features of various goddesses and female monsters, most of whom have little or no link to Black Madonnas. As a Jungian analyst, Begg is obviously interested in how themes and archetypes can be woven through both neighbouring and distant cultures, but this ultimately appears to be a case of reaching a conclusion before looking for the evidence. This approach is quite common in literature on the Black Madonna and the continuation of pagan practices, and studies that cross-reference Black Madonna locations with the sites of earlier pagan temples do not appear to have compared the

---

[10] Begg 1996: 62
[11] Begg 1996: 15
[12] Begg 1996: 130

sample with those at dedications to White Virgins or indeed other saints. Because of our rich mythological past, it is easy to make connections between disparate societies because of linguistic similarities and to see every goddess who is occasionally depicted as black as a potential precursor.

Begg spends the most time discussing the worship of a Graeco-Roman Universal Great Mother with her sacrificial consort in the first centuries of the first millennium CE, dominated by the cults of Isis, Artemis and Cybele who had assimilated many other goddesses and were all known in Gaul.[13] There is evidence of Artemis being worshipped at Marseilles, Cybele at Lyon, and Isis in Paris. These goddesses' cults rivalled the emerging Christian one across Europe, but a turning point occurred with the declaration of Mary as *Theotokos* (Mother of God) at Ephesus in 431 CE,[14] which Begg says was a response to their rival cultic power.[15] Much is made of the fact that this happened at Ephesus, the city where Artemis' cult flourished one thousand years earlier, though it is quite likely that the Temple of Artemis was already in ruins by the 5th century. Begg traces the French Black Madonnas back to the Ephesian Artemis who was brought to Gaul in 600 BCE by the Phocaeans at Massalia (Marseille). There was certainly a preponderance of Artemis worship in the south of France but, peculiarly, Begg asserts that Metz Cathedral, in north-eastern France, was also built on a Temple of Diana (Artemis' Roman counterpart).[16] I found no reference to this elsewhere, apart from those who had quoted Begg.

References about churches on former goddess sites can be misleading, such as when he talks about Cybele – "The city of Cybele in France is without doubt Lyons, where her huge temple (86 by 53 metres) has been supplanted by the great basilica of Notre Dame de Fourvière (the old forum) and the oratory of the Black Virgins".[17] However he fails to mention that the basilica itself only dates from 1872-84 and the adjoining chapel from 1170. These are not straightforward cases of Christianity muscling in and

---

[13] Begg 1996: 17
[14] Begg 1996: 19
[15] Begg 1996: 93
[16] Begg 1996: 56
[17] Begg 1996: 58

converting living temples, which is the impression the reader might take away and use as a basis for their own narrative.

In discussing the etymology of Paris, Begg acknowledges the place of the Gaulish Parisii tribe who settled the area (although he gives them legendary origin and says their name derives from the Greek for 'frankness') but prefers the largely rejected alternative of 'Par Isis'. Worship of Isis would have come with the Romans; evidence has her veneration reaching as far as Britain; but Begg's assertion that her temple's remains lie beneath the Parisian church of St. Germain-des-Prés is a matter of medieval conjecture rather than archaeological proof. Similarly, he states that a statue of Isis stood in the church until the 1500s,[18] a piece of information gleaned from a 16th-century footnote about a statue that the author 'took to be Isis', hardly a firm evidential basis.

Begg quotes Black Virgin veneration as stemming from the Merovingian period, with Mauriac at 507, and the finding of other Black Virgins at Montserrat, Einsiedeln and Chartres throughout the 9th century.[19] The difficulty with this is that the findings he is talking about are all legendary accounts, written at these sites after the 12th-century carvings were made in order to strengthen their cults. He does however admit that the 1100s was a time when potent legends sprang up such as the Grail, unmentioned before that century, and that collectively there was a yearning for something lost needing to be found.[20] We see this in the stories of Black Madonnas bringing wisdom and blessings of a lost age after being unearthed following centuries in hiding from the 'enemy', at that time the Saracens. We see this yearning for a lost age recurring in the 20th and 21st century, marked by the increased interest in the Black Madonna; only now the enemy appears to be the patriarchal forces of the Catholic Church which have deprived humanity of the equality of the sexes. Begg, agrees, making the Jungian-inspired observation that "The return of the Black Virgin to the forefront of collective consciousness has coincided with the profound psychological need to reconcile sexuality and religion".[21] However, he says that she has always been a freedom fighter against the

---

[18] Begg 1996: 64
[19] Begg 1996: 20-1
[20] Begg 1996: 23-4
[21] Begg 1996: 28

patriarchy. I would argue that this notion is an early-modern overlay where the Black Madonna's image has figured in the struggles of oppressed peoples.

The Cult of the Black Virgin has undoubtedly been instrumental in sparking interest in the Black Madonna – it was certainly one of my own starting points – and invaluable for its gazetteer for those who wish to seek out the Black Virgin sites of Europe. However, its reliance on pseudo-etymologies, coincidences, and the theories concerning the Priory of Sion that run through it, plus its lack of referencing, makes it impossible to view as a factual authority on the subject. A more transparent and whole-hearted archetypal analysis of the figures concerned, a technique of which Begg is obviously fond, might have presented a less confusing picture to Black Madonna enthusiasts who are still quoting his text ad infinitum.

MOSS AND HANI - QUESTIONING ORIGINS

The response that Leonard Moss received from a clergy member as to why the Madonna was black, - "She is black because she is black"[22], instigated his study of the phenomenon. Moss rejects the idea that Mary was 'negroid', believing that she would have been Semitic. Like many others, Moss looks to the biblical *Song of Songs* (discussed in Chapter 2 of this book) for explanation of the meaning of blackness. After giving it consideration, Moss decides "*Nigra sum sed formosa*, which means "I am black but beautiful" may go a long way in fighting racism, but it tells us little about the colour of Mary".[23] I would say that the line has done the exact opposite, considering the warping of its translation from "I am Black *and* Beautiful", to something that implies blackness and beauty are normally oppositional states of being.[24] The line fed into the racism of the early-modern age and continues to do so. Although Moss rejects that race is an explanation for all Black Madonnas it does figure into his classification system.

Moss and Cappannari's hypothesis, that caused the famed

---

[22] Moss and Cappannari 1983: 53
[23] Moss and Cappannari 1983: 54
[24] See Lowe 2012 for a full discussion.

walkout of the clergy, states that the Black Madonna can be classified into three groupings: those that purposely match the colouring of the Indigenous population, such as the Madonnas of the Americas, those which have been found to have darkened over time through pigment oxidation or smoke damage, and those that have no apparent explanation.[25] For this final category, Moss considers possible artistic licence by medieval artists:

> *"Authorities on medieval art have demonstrated the influence of classical mythology on the paintings of the Middle Ages. It is entirely possible that some medieval painters borrowed from classical themes, dropped the original forms and related them to the Virgin Mary".[26]*

Whilst I think this explanation holds merit, Moss, however, imagines Church patrons giving little artistic control,[27] and rejects his own theory, saying that many of the images seem to pre-date the Middle Ages and are more likely to result from direct cultural contact. Moss' hypothesis is thus:

> *"The Black Madonnas are Christian borrowings from earlier pagan art forms that depicted Ceres, Demeter Melaina, Diana, Isis, Cybele, Artemis or Rhea as black, the colour characteristic of goddesses of the earth's fertility.'[28]*

Moss finds that the 30 images remaining in his third category are positioned around former Roman legion stations, including Montserrat, Einsiedeln, Chartres, Le Puy, and Tindari.[29] Tindari is amongst a host of Black Madonna sites in Sicily and Southern Italy. Moss discusses the culture of the region as being later to Christianise, and more prone to hanging onto old deities and ceremonies, therefore more likely to feature direct influence. The example given by Moss is intriguing in that, right up until the 19th century, a statue of Ceres and her daughter Proserpina were a substitute for the Virgin and Child at Enna, a former seat of Ceres' worship. If correct, this is a prime example of blurring between goddess to Madonna, although Moss does however note that in

---

[25] Moss and Cappannari 1983: 55-6
[26] Moss and Cappannari 1983: 65
[27] Moss and Cappannari 1983: 56
[28] Moss and Cappannari 1983: 65
[29] Moss and Cappannari 1983:57-8

this case, the statue is not black.[30]

Moss ascribes to the Jungian school of thought that black equals fertility of the earth, death, and fear of darkness. He believes syncretism and transmission occurred naturally with the coming of Christianity: "The adoption of new beliefs is facilitated when they can be equated in some fashion with older, more compatible experiences"[31] and quotes Salliens in saying that worship of the dark earth mother was universal.

Other authors have approached the topic of the Black Madonna from a Jungian standpoint, such as Jean Hani. His *La Vierge Noire et la Mystère Marial*, published in 1995, was made available in English in 2007 as *The Black Virgin: A Marian Mystery*. In his introduction, Hani mentions Durand Lefebvre and Salliens and says that they are written from a historical and archaeological point of view. He refers to their findings as conclusive: "Once the historical foundations of the origin and development of the Black Virgins had been firmly established, the question of their meaning and role can only be answered by appealing to religious, and secondarily to traditional, sciences".[32] I would hardly say that the history and origins of the Black Madonna were 'firmly established', but the focus of Hani's attention is these "traditional sciences of sacred geography and alchemy" for which his sources are Huynen and *Vierges Noires, la Reponse Vient de la Terre* by J. Bovin, (1988).

We have looked at how Begg and Moss have explored links to earlier goddesses. Hani relates the Black Madonna to Isis, Artemis, and Cybele in much the same way as Begg, picking out associations.[33] Hani is, however, fairly reserved in citing black goddesses, saying that, like depictions of Mary, they are only black sometimes: "probably to emphasize certain of her aspects or attributes".[34] Begg, on the other hand, overloads his text with insubstantial remarks, such as how "both Artemis and Black Madonnas tend to make their homes in trees",[35] giving the example

---

[30] Moss and Cappannari 1983: 61
[31] Moss and Cappannari 1983: 67
[32] Hani 2007: 2
[33] He does specify that he is speaking of Gallo-Roman Isis, another form of Magna Mater, as opposed to earlier Egyptian Isis. Hani 2007: 63
[34] Hani 2007: 8
[35] Begg 1996: 54

of Artemis Orthia and the Black Virgin of Bourg. Not only are these disparate examples, which is not made clear in the text, but it is also not a consistent trait of either figure.

In discussing Cybele, Hani says Salliens counts 47 towns where Mary succeeded Cybele[36] and backs this up with synchronicities, such as, how at Montserrat she has a crenellated crown and pine cone like Cybele, and the Feast of the Annunciation mirrors Cybele's date, 25 March. There are few who doubt that festivals and temples were purposefully overwritten and Christianised; but for statuary there is little evidence of direct transference.

Moss, on the other hand, states that he believes Artemis to be the prime progenitor for Black Madonnas rather than Cybele: "Now if the French Black Madonnas were former Cybeles, we ought to find them scattered more or less evenly all over France, since Cybele was worshipped by all Gaul. But such is not the case. Their distribution points to a Greek origin"[37] – namely the tin trade route of the Greeks who took their Ephesian Artemis with them wherever they travelled.

Unlike Begg, Hani distinguishes the origin stories that are pure legend, but says that the Madonnas being given these stories of miraculous discovery is an indication of their importance.[38] Hani is reasonable in his observations on origin theories, believing it unlikely that there is truth in the Black Madonnas being goddess statues mistaken for Mary and brought back from the Crusades, and stating that although Isis and Horus statues could have been mistaken for Madonna and Child, it was rare that they were black.[39] He quotes Delattre in his *Le Culte de la Sainte Vierge en Afrique* as saying the only way to distinguish early Isis and Mary statues is to look at the accompanying assemblages.[40] If statues were removed to France from their original context, their use would be a case of mistaken identity rather than syncretism.

Where Begg is less inclined to state primary sources, Hani more frequently uses them to back up his narrative. He quotes Pliny the

---

[36] Hani 2007: 18
[37] Moss and Cappannari 1983: 68
[38] Hani 2007: 15
[39] Hani 2007: 14
[40] Hani 2007: 17

Elder telling us that the original Artemis of Ephesus was ebony, and Pausanias that Laconia's Artemis was also ebony, whilst the temple of Phocis' was black marble.[41] A Middle Kingdom (third millennium BCE) Egyptian text states that Isis was born in the form of a black and red woman. In Apulieus' *The Golden Ass* she wears a black mantle over a red tunic. *The Core Cosmu* tells us Isis' grandfather honoured her with perfect blackness. However, searching for stray extracts that describe a goddess as black is hardly conclusive proof for her influence on Black Madonna statuary, and Hani admits that Isis was far from often portrayed as black.[42]

Hani compares the Virgin Mary supplanting various goddesses across Europe with the later example of Our Lady of Guadalupe absorbing the cult of Tonantzin (see Chapter 4). However, this is not a direct analogy, since the conversion of the Nahua people happened relatively overnight in comparison. We may be seeing reverse influence at work again here – because syncretism happened in the Americas it is assumed the same happened in Europe, which did not have the same 'frontier' dynamic as the Columbian settlements.[43] Hani does acknowledge that there is a huge gap between the polytheist period and the rise of the cult of the Black Virgin in the 12th century but approaches the question of why by blaming Church iconoclasm. I would argue this is only part of the reason; iconoclasm having had less of an effect on the Western Church in the intervening centuries than on the Eastern. Hani believes that statues, whether goddess or Mary, were hidden, only re-emerging when it was safer to do so during Charlemagne's reign at the end of the 8th century, to go on and influence the later cult of the Virgin. This theory, however, rests on the discovery legends, first recorded centuries later, being true. Does Hani, then, regard them as fact rather than legend?

Hani believes Mary could have been worshipped alongside goddesses by polytheists for a time, in a similar way to how some modern Hindus worship her.[44] In my opinion, these goddesses did not 'sneak in under the radar' of early Christianity. If anything, I

---

[41] Hani 2007: 18
[42] Hani 2007: 20
[43] Oleszkiewicz-Peralba 2007: 81
[44] Hani 2007: 16

think it was a semi or subconscious choice on the part of the Romans; a continuation of their penchant for assimilation and conflation of goddess qualities into whatever was the most prominent figure of the time. I agree with Hani when he says that the differences between polytheism and monotheism are more a matter of language than fundamentals. For example, the gods (with a lower-case g) of polytheism could be substituted for the saints and angels of Christianity with relative ease.[45] Christianity for the Romans was less a major change of world view and more an adjusting of focus. They took the qualities of these three popular goddesses (and possibly others) and expressed them in the Virgin Mary.

Whereas I would agree that it was very likely that there was syncretism occurring and influence from the dominant goddesses on the formation of the cult of Mary in the early centuries of the Christian era, I disagree that the statuary in question, carved in the 12th century, is directly inspired by them. As much time passed between the beginning of the Marian cult and its revival in the 12th century as has passed between the 12th century and now. As such, we should treat them as distinct time periods, with people who may have had very different world views. Other than potentially looking to classical themes for artistic inspiration, I do not think the medieval sculptors were actively encoding goddess worship into their creations.

HANI, ALCHEMY AND JUNG

One of the two main foci of Hani's book is his belief that the monastic orders who promoted Virgin cults were keepers of secret knowledge inherited from druidic Celts, and used alchemy, astrology, and the like to interpret her: "It was the intellectual elite that favoured the introduction of the cult of the Black Virgin, for they knew very well its lofty spiritual significance stemmed from the Celtic tradition".[46] He says that these 'sages' were 'reactivating' (presumably non-Christian) cults. He quotes Huynen: "The Black Virgin is a theological and symbolical construct that was

---

[45] Hani 2007: 67
[46] Hani 2007: 33

simultaneously introduced everywhere, because it conveyed a philosophical thinking and conception of Mary common to all the contemporary monasteries".[47]

I find this theory particularly far-fetched. Not only that, but it is one that relies on only these (White, male) intellectuals understanding her significance. Hani says of the cult: "people did not invent it, but received it". Hani's theory turns an organic, vernacular cult into an elitist one. The same can be said of those casting male-dominated secret societies like the Knights Templar and Freemasons as guardians of supposed 'secret knowledge' of the Black Madonna. Why should Mother devotion have not arisen from the 'common' people? It is from them that we learn all of her nicknames – La Moreneta, La Negrita, Mamma Schiavona (Slave Mama). The development of Marian devotion has been particularly vernacular as opposed to being driven by doctrine, however shadowy and secretive.

In his third chapter, Hani talks about God being both masculine and feminine and about people not understanding this. He applies Hindu terminology, explaining Mary in terms of *Maya* and *Shakti*. He considers her an avatar of Universal Substance and also relates her to the *Materia Prima* of alchemy, to the Shekinah of Judaism, and to the Wisdom of the Bible. These are some worthy philosophical thoughts, but not within the scope of this book to fully explore. Hani is particularly concerned with the alchemical allegory, which he links to the Hermetic Secret Doctrine that was said to have been handed down via the goddess Isis.

For Hani, the culmination of the Marian Mystery was the proclamation by an apparition of the Virgin Mary herself at Lourdes that she was the Immaculate Conception.[48] By telling us that she is the Immaculate Conception, he believes that she is confirming she is *Materia Prima*, for only unmanifest potential could bring forth Christ, the Light of the World, out of darkness. For this reason, he says that the Black Virgin is the symbol of *Materia Prima*. The main problem with this argument is that if this was such a crucial point and the intended emphasis, why was the apparition of the Immaculate Conception not a Black Virgin herself? I am surely

---

[47] Huynen in Hani 2007: 33
[48] Hani 2007: 5

not the first to question this.

Hani states that to identify the Black Madonna as the dark potent earth of *Materia Prima* is not a materialist reduction of the Virgin to coarse matter, but the whole allegory nonetheless reduces her to a vehicle or vessel for the true product.[49] The black is something to be dissolved or burned away, associated with the alchemist's sin and ego. For me, this is very dubious ground. Whilst the alchemical interpretation may be noble in motivation, its implications are that black equals the most base state, and is oppositional to the end goal of lightness and purity. Associating this with a figure that, like it or not, since the early-modern era has been discussed in terms of being racially Black is not a positive step.

Hani says alchemical signs are present in Black Virgin churches such as Chartres, though this claim is quite hollow, as he admits that they also proliferate elsewhere. He nevertheless goes on to interpret Guingamp using this system; mostly what he thinks is encoded in the colours of the Virgin's gowns in depictions there.[50] Although Hani concedes that not all Black Madonna churches share these alchemical symbols, he says they were all built using sacred geometry, and quotes Louis Charpentier, who wrote an extensive theory on the construction of Chartres[51] (see Chapter 1). Hani raises the question of why Christian churches were built on pagan sites and answers using Charpentier's line of reasoning. According to him, the builders of these churches were in possession of the same knowledge as the druids of centuries before concerning the telluric energies of certain sites.[52] Once again, 20th-century writers mystify the period with ideas about a shadowy male elite, and once again, the preservation and transmission of 'secret knowledge' appears to be the most valuable factor to them.

Hani says that praying to the Black Madonna is like the alchemical process; it effects change. Although he clarifies that, saying this power is limited to only black statues of the Virgin would be ridiculous, "the black image, perhaps because of its

---

[49] Hani 2007: 112
[50] Hani 2007: 117
[51] Hani 2007: 121
[52] Hani 2007: 122

fascination, was better adapted to provoke in the soul of the faithful a shock calculated to bring about a conversion".[53] This seems to suggest that for all his talk of the inherent specialness of the Black Virgin, it is only her Othered appearance that makes her effective; the exotic effect of a dark divinity amongst White Europeans. This insight is particularly astute, since modern White European audiences' reactions to the Black Madonna are arguably based in racial stereotypes inherent in our society, which I will discuss further in the concluding chapter.

In his final chapter, Hani also takes a Jungian approach, veering away from the Black Virgin to talk about the animus and anima, Jungian terms for an inner masculine and feminine, and the uniting of the Divine Androgyne within oneself. Although he correctly differentiates male and female from masculine and feminine, his argument does seem to imply that men are only born with masculine qualities and females with feminine.[54] He puts forward the Jungian model that suggests that heterosexual intercourse and marriage are the keys to spiritual completeness, using biblical quotes to support it. This model has been adequately criticised elsewhere so I do not plan to go into critical depth here other than to say that this heterosexist view, so widely considered 'normal', is modern and Western in its construction, and certainly not found throughout all world spirituality.

The chapter appears to suggest that women exist to aid men's spiritual evolution: "Now in this process towards reintegration, the role of woman is primordial. She helps man to understand himself, to realize his being, to 'become what he is'. Woman's charism, says P. Evdokimov, is 'to give birth to the man hidden in the heart'. And, also in this connection, we can say that woman is always 'mother', that maternity envisaged in its widest sense, is her fundamental characteristic".[55]

In this whole demeaning theory, Woman is reduced to 'Adam's helper', the passage on the creation of Eve being one that Hani also quotes. She is reduced to her biological function, which Hani inherently ties to the Divine Feminine. The belief that there are

---

[53] Hani 2007: 127
[54] Hani 2007: 140
[55] Hani 2007: 149

only two sexes and that they are in oppositional duality is a social construct; one that Western society is only starting to overcome. It is not universal. One only has to look at Native American or other Indigenous belief systems to see a different outlook on gender.

Dualist thinking that says wholeness can only be achieved through union with someone of the opposite sex should not be relevant to the Black Madonna. Reduction of Woman to vessel or channel for the birth of the Male is what our long history of sexism is built on. Neither should analysis be based on primitivism, in which the Jungian musings of those such as Hani and Begg are steeped. The 19th-century idea of primitivism, which saw Black Africans as being 'closer to nature', was doubled with a European longing to 'get back in touch with our primitive roots', which Jungians saw personified in these statues of a Black woman.[56] Her association with fertility can also be attributed to 19th-century over-sexualised notions about Black women.[57] This fertile 'Earth Mother' interpretation is one that has also been picked up by Goddess Feminism.

DIFFERING FEMINIST PERSPECTIVES ON THE DARK MOTHER

Feminist scholarship of the Black Madonna bases most of its analysis around their succession from the goddesses of antiquity. The Goddess Feminism of the 1970s-80s is a revival of 19th-century ideas about a prehistoric matriarchal society that were being conceived around the time when the fight for womens' rights was beginning. This was built on by Jungian psychology of the early 20th century, with those such as Erich Neumann, who speaks about the Matriarchal preceding the Patriarchal, but does so in terms of psychic development, not linear history. Rejected by some, for its sexism in essentially reducing woman to a vessel, and for some of its even more questionable aspects, Jungian analysis has nevertheless been adopted where it serves the greater narrative formed by Goddess Feminists of the 1980s.

China Galland, a popular author amongst Goddess Feminists,

---

[56] Knight 2011: 123
[57] Knight 2011: 124

encounters Jungian interpretation in her first meeting with a Black Madonna, the Virgin of Einsiedeln, Switzerland. Her *Longing for Darkness* (1990) is a personal quest into dark deities that mirror an inner feeling of seeking darkness in the form of ancient wisdom, beginning with Tara and progressing to the Black Madonna. She is influenced by the work of Jungian analyst Fred Gustafson, whose book *The Black Madonna* (1990) explains the legend of the Black Madonna of Einsiedeln in archetypal and alchemical terms.[58] Galland, herself a recovering alcoholic, relates the process to battling addiction and begins to be able to verbalise her longing for a positive, transformative darkness, like that of the tale.[59] She uses these new tools of Jungian analysis and alchemical allegory to work out her own thoughts on the Black Madonna, which, although their intention is positive, are based in primitivist associations: "Whilst she is trying to revalue darkness and to counter racism, unfortunately her inclusion of the "darkness" of the ethnicity of people of colour in this list with other images of darkness serves to reinforce stereotypes and to separate white people as categorically different from people of colour".[60]

Other authors such as Lucia Chiavola Birnbaum make the focus solely and explicitly racial. To Birnbaum, the Black Madonna is racially Black because she, and her ancestors Isis et al. all stem from a prehistoric, unnamed dark mother goddess from Africa. Witnessing her first Black Madonna procession, Birnbaum had what she describes as "an overwhelming bodily memory of the ancient African dark mother",[61] leading her to research their link. Alessandra Belloni echoes Birnbaums' sentiments in *Healing Journeys with the Black Madonna* (2019), and she recognises the need for the Black Madonna in the modern day. When she says "In this

---

[58] Briefly, the legend says that the hermit Saint Meinrad retreated to the *Finsterwald* (dark forest) in 835 CE with little more than the statue of the Virgin to furnish his cell. On his entry to the forest he saved two fledgling ravens from two preying hawks. During his time there he is beset by demonic apparitions. Years later, after Meinrad was murdered by thieves, the ravens alerted the nearby town to his death and identified the murderers, bringing them to justice. Gustafson interprets the Finsterwald, as well as the Black Madonna in it, as the unconscious and the dark feminine. The demons are Meinrad's shadow side whereas saving the ravens is said to represent a victory for the emerging unconscious. Gustafson also relates them to the Raven principle of alchemy and sees the story as alchemical metaphor. See Gustafson 1990, Chapter 1.

[59] Galland 1990: 151-2

[60] Knight 2011: 132

[61] Birnbaum 2001: xxvii

time of world turmoil and paradigm shifts, I feel there is a great need to acknowledge that God is a woman and She is black"[62] she does not see the emergence of what I would call the modern Black Madonna as a reaction to current social climate, as I would argue, but rather as a continuation of pre-Christian Earth Mother worship.

Birnbaum explains that her research is highly influenced by the work of 1960s archaeologist Emmanuel Anati and 1980s archaeologist Marija Gimbutas. Gimbutas, especially, has been championed by the modern Goddess Movement and her findings presented as credible proof of an early matrifocal society, although in academic circles her work has been heavily criticised for presenting a hypothesis and then skewing the evidence in its favour. Discussion around this subject is very sensitive and highly politicised. Birnbaum equates criticism of Gimbutas with "hostile male backlash" against Feminism, just as she assumes that those who questioned a prehistoric Great Mother to be doing so from a place of institutionalised racism and unacceptance of humanity's African origins.[63] Despite Birnbaum's assertion that rejection of the narrative comes from 'male scientists' (whom she repeatedly speaks of in the collective), criticism of matriarchal theory has also come from other feminist authors. Female archaeologist Ruth Tringham has accused Gimbutas of ignoring evidence to fit her thesis.[64] Lotte Motz, in her *The Faces of the Goddess* argues that all goddesses are not expressions of one female divinity, nor are they all inherently mothers. Rosemary Radford Ruether, also a feminist scholar, has been criticised by Goddess theologians for not embracing Gimbutas' theory and for continuing to concentrate on Christian sources.[65]

Gimbutas' narrative centres around a peaceful golden age without war or violence, where men and women worshipped the Goddess and lived in harmony with nature until patriarchal nomads from the Russian steppes swept in and conquered without mercy in waves between 4400 and 3000 BCE.[66] Ruether says that

---

[62] Belloni 2019: 23
[63] Birnbaum 2001: xxviii-xxix
[64] Ruether 2005: 27
[65] Ruether 2005: 4
[66] Ruether 2005: 21

the mythic narrative within which Gimbutas presents her evidence "is so symbolically compelling that it has become a kind of dogma for many people involved in this Goddess quest. Disputing its details is treated as treasonous heresy directed against female hopes, perpetrated by heartless academics".[67]

As Ruether points out, this narrative is a powerful modern identity myth for those who oppose the patriarchy's hold on society. "By imagining a time – indeed the primaeval time – before this culture of violence and domination, one can also imagine a time after it, a day when Euro-Americans can reclaim their original and more authentic mothering, peaceful, ecologically sustainable cultural selves."[68] Whilst empowering, the evidence it is based on is unsound. In Gimbutas' view, a large assemblage of female figurines equals a female-dominated culture, though, as Ruether points out using the examples of modern Hinduism and Medieval Christianity, this is not always the case.[69] Other symbols are drawn in to support Gimbutas' hypothesis, certain animals such as bears which she genders as female,[70] triangles which become the pubic V, and the colour black representing the fertile (feminine) earth. As attractive as this symbolic language is, it is only a modern guess at a prehistoric worldview that we are never going to fully understand. Male symbolism is explained away – Neolithic horned bull heads become female wombs with fallopian tubes. Other phallic symbolism is minimized, and Gimbutas contradicts herself by stating that there was no understanding of the male's part in procreation whilst also stating that snakes and phalluses represent the 'stimulating principle' directed towards the Goddess.[71] All evidence is made to point to the reverence of maternity.

Motz, on the other hand, concluded from the later world goddesses that she examined:

> "1. They are of varied origin and have not descended from a single being.
> 2. They derive their significance from the phenomenon that they rule

---

[67] Ruether 2005: 21
[68] Ruether 2005: 22
[69] Ruether 2005: 23
[70] Motz, alternatively explains the bear figurines as reverence of the awesome powers of nature and associated with the hunt rather than a denotation of human maternity. Motz 1997: 12
[71] Ruether 2005: 26

or represent — the earth, the sun, the tribal group — and not from
motherhood.
3. They bear the stamp of their social and religious environment.
4. Not the birth giver but the birth helper is of great importance.
Those conclusions do not point to the existence of a sovereign,
primaeval mother who gave birth to all.'[72]

Motz finds more goddesses that are warlike or virginal in the middle Eastern and Greek pantheons, with the prime exception of Demeter, the sorrowing mother of Persephone, whose protective maternal aspect is nevertheless a reaction against the patriarchal forces of its time rather than of earlier origin.[73]

One of the main foci of Gimbutas' work, and something that Birnbaum focuses on to further her African Mother Goddess theory, is the class of prehistoric figurines known as 'Venus figures'. For Birnbaum, that these are anything other than "figurines of the dark mother"[74] is unthinkable. Feminist readings often disregard any alternate interpretations of these large busted female figurines, even when they are not deposited in an obviously religious context. The name, 'Venus' is an unhelpful distortion before we even begin to look at their context. The term 'Venus', ascribed in the 19th/early 20th-century by prehistorians because of the idea that these figures express prehistoric beauty standards, connotes that they are goddesses, despite having no link to the Roman Venus. Continuing to call them this has helped to perpetuate the misidentification.

Because of their shape, they are consistently interpreted as pregnant mother goddesses, but both Motz and Ruether suggests that those found near grain bins and ovens could have celebrated abundance of food in their depiction of large bellies.[75] Motz accuses the archaeologist Mellaart, whose findings at Çatal Hüyük provided the basis of Gimbutas' interpretation, of altering the proportions of figures in his drawings "so that a maternal rather than erotic being is presented".[76] Another theory, put forward by LeRoy McDermott, argues that the figures may represent self-

---

[72] Motz 1997: 3
[73] Motz 1997: 13
[74] Birnbaum 2001: 8
[75] Ruether 2005: 35
[76] Motz 1997: 21

portraits from the point of view of the artist, without mirrors or ways to regard themselves, accounting for the seemingly disproportional tapering of the limbs. McDermott believes the frequent focus on large breasts or potentially pregnant bellies could well be an artistic response to these women noticing changes in their biology with maturation and pregnancy.[77] Although there are potential holes in his theory, whilst making it he also considers the suggestions of others, such as that they were for hunting and fertility magic, or by men as an early form of pornography. He views the latter as a modern Western projection, and equally so the desire to regard them as goddesses.[78] The difference with Goddess literature is that other explanations are rarely considered.

Preconceptions seem to also figure in Birnbaum's thoughts on Black Virgins. In *Black Madonnas,* (1993) she talks about the legend of the Black Madonna of Chiaramonte Gulfi in Sicily. We find out in her *Dark Mother* (2001) that on finally visiting the site, "I was dismayed to find that the Madonna, whom I had read was black, had been sculpted of undarkable white carrara marble."[79] She decides that this 15th/16th-century white marble must have been a replacement for a darker original. I found no references elsewhere to a Black Madonna of Chiaramonte Gulfi, other than in Begg's second edition of *The Cult of the Black Virgin,* released in 1996, where he includes it in the addenda to the gazetteer.[80] His only quoted source is Birnbaum. This appears to be another case of interpreting the evidence only in a way that benefits one's narrative.

Birnbaum talks about "black Madonnas on the white continent of Europe"[81] reminding us that, for her, the Black Madonna has always been about ethnicity. She dips into the *Song of Songs* association and says that Mary could have realistically been Ethiopian. As with the other authors, she mentions that classical writers have described Isis, Cybele et al. as black, but fails to mention how infrequently this occurs.[82] In relating the path of Palaeolithic migrants from Africa walking into Europe to the

---

77 McDermott 1996: 227
78 McDermott 1996: 233-4
79 Birnbaum 2001: 100
80 Begg 1996: 273
81 Birnbaum 2001: 126
82 Birnbaum 2001: 136

distribution of sites of later Black Madonna cults, Birnbaum, even more so than the other authors we have looked at, does not seem to take into consideration the immense span of time between these two cultures. She advocates the study of Romani culture's relationship with its Black Madonna, Sara la Kali, but not for its own merit. She sees them as an isolated throwback of prehistoric matriarchal culture (as she says they have matrilineal marriage practices) which we may learn from. On the contrary, Roma women appear to have as many, if not more, patriarchal struggles than non-Roma.[83]

CONCLUSION

The style of writing in the popular realm is inherently different from the academic approach to Black Madonnas. For Birnbaum, Begg, Starbird, and others, linguistic connotations such as anagrams, words spelled backwards or words that sound like modern English words are mentioned despite being of seemingly little consequence; for example, when Birnbaum speaks about the archaeologist Anati "whose name recalls the Canaanite goddess Anat",[84] or the goddess Ma'at "whose name connotes mother"[85] (despite this not being the actual meaning of her name). These little references, dropped into the text, help to build a picture that will be pleasing to their target audience, yet muddle the historic evidence with the fable. I pondered how easy it would be in the age of the internet to create false legends, however well-intentioned, which spread and within a few repetitions become fact. In my early research I noted references to the Madonna being black because she is burned, either from the sun or from the sin of others. The Virgin statue of the medieval Glastonbury Abbey was reported to have miraculously survived the fire that destroyed the Old Church in 1184, and continued to perform miracles hence. I looked for any references that the statue, rarely depicted except on a medieval seal, might have ever been referred to as a Black Madonna and found none. But how easy would it be to infer this because of the

---

[83] blog.romarchive.eu/breaking-the-silence-romani-womens-experience-in-the-romani-civil-rights-movement/ (accessed 03/06/2020)
[84] Birnbaum 2001: xxxiv
[85] Birnbaum 2001: 19

circumstances, adding to it supporting 'evidence' that there was a side chapel at the abbey dedicated to Our Lady of Loretto, an Italian Black Madonna. No doubt if I made the speculative leap, I would soon see this repeated elsewhere as fact: Glastonbury had a Black Madonna. I will look out for such references following this book's publication!

I would argue that the above authors and others are not historians but myth-makers in their approach and ultimate goal. They weave an intriguing story that captivates their audience. However, when they explore mythic landscapes of the Black Madonna and the Goddess they are compelled to include historic 'proofs' to bolster their legitimacy. That a mode of worship can be relatively new and still be authentic is anathema to them in a modality where continuity equals worth.

It does not matter if modern devotions to the Black Madonna are a reconstruction of beliefs. We can see from the Caribbean diasporic religions of earlier chapters that this can be successful. The comparison is not perfect – Western audiences wanting to connect with an ancient form of the Sacred Feminine are doing so from a position of privilege rather than necessity, unlike the Africans brought to the Americas as slaves. Whereas the latter were separated from their origins by physical distance, the former are separated by time, and for both there is a void of information in between.

Much of the literature on the Black Madonna is fixated on finding ancient origins and proving continuity from those times. Whilst presenting as a counterculture reaction to the patriarchal systems of Church and State, this approach actually reinforces the materialist structure of antiquarianism and old-school archaeology. This 'Authorised Heritage Discourse' favours the ancient and monumental, placing importance on the object (in this case the statue or icon) and not on the intangible parts of the culture to which they belong. Movement towards honouring and preserving elements such as song, dance, and ritual has been made worldwide in 2003 when UNESCO drafted the Convention for the Safeguarding of Intangible Cultural Heritage (ICH). Studies of vernacular religion – worship as it is practised by ordinary people rather than as it is described in dogma, sits within the same framework as ICH.[86]

As mentioned earlier, there is a similarity between attitudes today and the attitudes of the 12th century that we glean from the romance literature of the lost Grail – the lost Feminine in some eyes – that harked back to a more chivalric time. Similarly, the formation of legends of the unearthed Black Madonna in that century mirror our modern desire to discover and reveal lost wisdom, which has led to the wealth of titles on the shelves of booksellers, not only on the Sacred Feminine of the Bible but the hidden wisdom of multiple cultures. The desire of the Feminist Goddess movement to recover a 'golden age of matriarchy' is in some ways also comparable to the African diasporic concept of 'Ginen' and the Aztec concept of 'Aztlan', both idealised mythologised concepts of the Motherland that are only partly based on a physical location. We see this concept played out in depictions of 'Avalon' in Glastonbury, England, such as in the feminist fiction of Marion Zimmer Bradley who imagines an egalitarian society with priestesses serving a Mother Goddess.

The desires of both eras seem to reflect a need to feel religious ownership. Here and now it is the desire to reclaim the Goddess; in the 12th century it was the need to reclaim Jerusalem from Islamic rule. Goddess feminists may not be waging a physical crusade against the Vatican but are nevertheless typified by a feeling of resistance and yearning. And the Black Madonna, in both centuries, proves to be the perfect emblem of resistance. Lest we forget, the history of the modern Black Madonna is not just the history of devotion but the struggles against slavery and Empire – so often left out of our elementary education. The Black Madonna is the emblem of social struggle as much as of Mother devotion. At Montserrat in the Middle Ages, the Virgin came to be thought of as a champion of Christianity, going into battle against Muslim troops during the reconquest of Spain and converting the 'infidels' through her dark visage.[87] Today the Black Madonna is a freedom fighter in countless forms – on the banners of revolutionaries, feminists and Indigenes still struggling against White male

---

[86] Alessandra Belloni's work straddles these two approaches in her conservation of the songs and dances of living traditions whilst referring to continuity from antiquity.
[87] Foster 2016a: 23

domination. I hope that in discussing the trials of these Indigenous and diasporic peoples, I have shone a light on what I consider to be the Black Madonna's most vital role.

CHAPTER 10

Conclusion – Why do People Need the Black Madonna?

INTRODUCTION

Although, for some non-Christians, the Black Madonna is still viewed with suspicion as an aspect of a religion in which they would rather not have any part, others relish the chance to reclaim this Black mother figure from the hands of the Church and reinterpret her as they see fit according to their own belief system. For some this is using her image to represent a Lwa or Orisha. For others, she stands for a powerful ancient goddess such as Isis, pulled forward into the here and now. Others view her archetypally; an expression of the darkness of the unconscious mind or the Divine Feminine within everyone. Some make pilgrimages to Black Madonna sites and pray or interact in whichever way they see fit. Some create rituals at home or in their community using the Black Madonna, whilst others create art to spread her image and message to the world. She is most actively harnessed when she adorns the banners of revolutionaries and peaceful protestors, or when her righteous anger is expressed through response to yet another case of racist oppression.

ART AND EXPRESSION

The Black Madonna has made several appearances in fiction, sometimes in the mainstream. One book that proved to be an early inspiration for myself is *The Secret Life of Bees* (2001), by Sue Monk Kidd. The bestselling book, and subsequent movie, follows 14-year-old Lily on a quest to discover details about the mother who may or may not have left her before her death. In the company of her housekeeper Rosaleen, Lily runs away from her abusive father; her only clue being a Black Madonna from a honey label with a town's name on the back. Lily is led to the house of the bee-keeping Boatwright sisters who take both Lily and Rosaleen in. The sisters keep a Black Madonna from a ship's prow in their house, in whose presence they hold a weekly matriarchal Church meeting. Lily's search for a mother figure is embodied in the Madonna and her keepers, who help her to learn about her birth mother and grow into womanhood.

Set against a backdrop of 1960s racism, the book won both praise and criticism for its portrayal of prejudice. In her review, Carrisa Smith says that for all its good intentions, the book is unintentionally racist in making the central character a White girl.[1] In Sue Monk Kidd's defence, she too was a teenage White girl growing up in the southern United States at that time. It makes sense for her to write from that perspective with all of the naivety of the teenager that she was, rather than try to write empathetically about a Black woman's experience. Smith accuses Monk Kidd of portraying the Boatwright sisters as two-dimensional stereotypes who are only there to serve Lily's story rather than being well-rounded characters in their own right. Although Smith has valid concerns about accurate depictions of African-Americans in fiction, I believe the archetypal nature of the sisters is an intentional signpost to aspects of the Madonna. June Boatwright is the emotionally distant activist whilst her sister May is the Mary who sorrows for all of the woes of the world, the Mater Dolorosa. August Boatwright personifies the mothering and wise Madonna whose presence overarches the others as matriarch of the household. All of these qualities make up the Black Madonna, and Lily learns from each of them. They are anchored in the spiritual symbol in their living room, Our Lady of Chains. The Madonna of the book provided part of the inspiration for the painting on the cover of this book.

As an artist myself who has depicted many Black Madonnas, I find it difficult, when asked, to answer why I began, and the fascination is something that requires further personal

---

[1] christandpopculture.com/the-secret-life-of-bees/

investigation. The icon in Chapter 5 inspired by the Polish Black Madonna and associated with Ezili Danto was my first, and remains one of my most popular images with my customers. I was living at the time in a household that had Vodou altars, and although neither Catholic or Vodouisante myself, I found the culture a rich inspiration for artistic expression with its colourful chromolithographs of saints and intricate veves. I was soon receiving commissions from Vodouisante friends to paint their favourite Lwa. Although my work has always been multicultural, my recent set of paintings depicting Celtic saints and goddesses are obviously very White European. I welcomed painting the Black goddesses and Black Madonnas of this book as a way of reminding myself and my audience that divinity is reflected in as many colours as there are shades of the human race, and they have proven hugely popular. Although it is only a semi-conscious decision on my part to make at least half of my body of work ethnically non-White, I hope that it is a good use of my White privilege in opening more people's eyes to divinity as female and Black. It is certainly not my intention to overshadow the work of artists of colour who are greatly deserving of recognition, and I would recommend readers look up the rich heritage of Black art in the cultures that are included in this book.

Some artists, such as renowned musician Alessandra Belloni connect with the Black Madonna through traditional music and dance. This Italian-American percussionist specialises in the Tarantella, an Italian folk rhythm accompanied by tambourines, that is bound up with local devotions to the Black Madonna. As with much of world dance, the Tarantella is therapeutic and cathartic and is used by Belloni in healing ceremonies, particularly for women. Her own spiritual journey led her to write and perform the folk opera *The Voyage of the Black Madonna* in 1990 and to later write about her life experiences in *Healing Journeys with the Black Madonna*. I attended the book launch in 2019 where Belloni performed and taught the audience some of the chants mentioned in her book, introducing us to a Black Madonna tradition that is

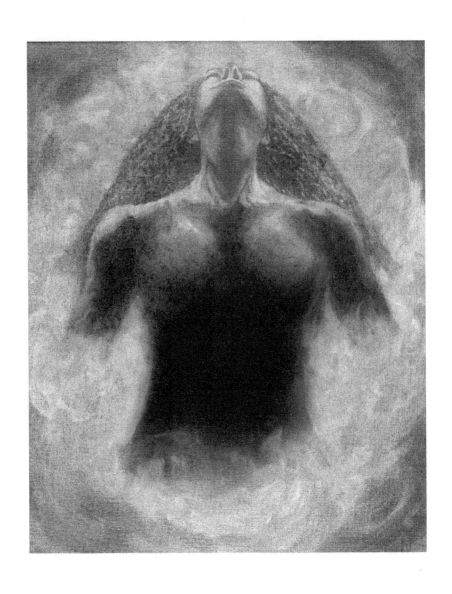

Above: *'Black Goddess Rising'. An intuited piece not based upon any goddess or Black Madonna in particular but who captures the essence of the strength and direction that the Divine Feminine takes into a new era.*

living and thriving in Southern Italy to this day.

Belloni and many others act as guides on Black Madonna tours in Europe, and host workshops to connect with the Dark Mother. In September 2015, I hosted a Black Madonna workshop myself in Glastonbury, UK, with a friend, Katie Player. Katie is active in the local Goddess community and particularly specialises in Sacred Drama workshops and the mysteries of ancient goddess cults. We dreamed together about creating future Black Madonna tours ourselves, following in the footsteps of Katie's friend, the late Lydia Ruyle, and used the workshop as a test for interest in the Black Madonna and potential uptake on such a tour. For me personally, the workshop was a good place to help arrange and order the mass of research I had begun to gather on the subject, which would eventually evolve into this book. The tag lines we used for the workshop's advertisement were:

"DISCOVER the Black Goddess in Her many forms

CREATE your own sacred image

MOVE with Her in ritual dance

HONOUR Her in divine celebration"

Being the researcher and artist, I led on the first two sections, beginning with a morning session that discussed the history and legends of the Black Madonnas that I had researched thus far. We then progressed to a collage-making exercise where the participants were able to create their own devotional image from a mixture of Black Madonna photographs coupled with sacred symbols that have sometimes been associated with her. Later, Katie led a section on expressive movement, set to particular pieces of music that had relevance to the Black Madonna, including a Polish Marian hymn and a Vodou song to Ezili Danto. Finally, Katie led participants on a guided visualisation to meet the Black Madonna, and afterwards, if they wished, discuss what they experienced.

When asked what had attracted them to the workshop, attendees reported that they were interested in finding out about goddesses related to the image of the Black Madonna, or had visited one years before and wanted to reconnect and learn more about her. One attendee said that it was the first workshop she had found on the Black Madonna in Glastonbury and that she gained a lot from it: "dreams, and an abiding devotion to the dark mother". It was obvious from the positive reactions to the day's activities that there is a place for working with the Black Madonna amongst modern Western spiritual communities.

PILGRIMAGE

Although church attendance reportedly continues to fall, the act of pilgrimage is becoming more popular than ever, including both 'official' and emerging pilgrimages.[1] The latter kind – personal acts of devotion, 'feeling the energy' of a place, and any behaviour unsanctioned by the Church falls into the category of what is termed 'vernacular religion' which is a term introduced by Leonard Primiano as an alternative to talking about folk religion: "religion as it is lived: as human beings encounter, understand, interpret and practice it".[2] The important distinction is that here, vernacular does not mean that it is unorthodox or people 'doing religion wrong'. Sepp explains that vernacular religion is the lived religious experience of everyone, giving equal importance to hierarchical High (ecclesiastical, dogmatic) religion and Low (simple, folk) religion, despite the value-loaded titles[3].

The performance of vernacular religion can be seen in the actions of the hybrid 'spiritual tourists' who are likely to regard themselves as "spiritual, not religious", like the 'energy pilgrims' of Anna Fedele's Magdalene study. It can also be seen in more defined community activities such as the various pilgrimages we have encountered in this book. These countercultural, self-organised and self-led devotions function on the margins of the orthodoxy, often outweighing the Church-prescribed alternatives. These Black Madonna devotions have developed independently, yet under an umbrella of similarity. One similarity between the Hindu pilgrimage to La Divina Pastora in Trinidad and the Gypsy pilgrimage to Saint Sara in France (besides both potentially representing a reinvention of the goddess Kali) is that they operate adjacent to an official Catholic holiday, which arguably they both

---

[1] www.nytimes.com/2014/12/21/sunday-review/the-new-allure-of-sacred-pilgrimages.html
[2] Primiano 1995: 44 in Sepp 2014: 28
[3] Sepp 2014: 28

outweigh. Like the tradition of taking Saint Sara's statue out into the sea, the Black Madonnas of Cuba and Brazil are floated in their local bays in a symbolic cleansing for all in attendance. As with the patronesses of Cuba and Brazil, saint pilgrimages in Haiti often have a dual purpose of also honouring the ancestral spirits of Africa, an action far beyond the power of the Church to control or stop. Often these occur in natural beauty spots, appropriated to become church sites.

In 1843, an earthquake in Haiti created the waterfall of Sodo (Saut d'Eau), at a spot near where a Marian apparition had occurred two years earlier. It became an immediate shrine to the Vodou rainbow serpent Danballah Wedo, likely due to the rainbows that formed in the waterfall's mists.[4] Its popularity as a pilgrimage site for the Virgin Mary was compounded by a further apparition in 1849, leaving an image on a palm leaf. The president decreed that a church to Our Lady of Mount Carmel be erected there, which became a focal point for an annual pilgrimage. We may of course see this as an attempt to crowd out the Vodou devotions to the Lwa Danballah, although its more likely to have been about the president's own political aims. However, knowing the dual practices of many Haitian people, it is unsurprising to see that the Vodou devotions continued hand in hand with the Catholic pilgrimage, celebrating Danballah and his wife, Aiyeda Wedo, other water spirits – the Simbis, and Ezili Danto in her form of the Virgin of Mount Carmel. A Catholic priest attempted to halt these 'superstitions' by cutting down the miraculous palm, but devotion simply moved to a different palm. After this second palm was felled, and the offending priest suffered a stroke and died, it is said that the Church turned a blind eye to Vodou devotions at Saut-d'Eau.[5] In 1964, the pilgrimage again became a target, this time of the president, when François 'Papa Doc' Duvalier banned university students from attending, since he recognised the motivating power of religion in the formation of resistance to his dictatorial rule.[6] The enactment of vernacular religion is most prevalent in places where there has been, or continues to be,

---

[4] Rey 2005: 168
[5] Rey 2017: wrldrels.org/2017/10/24/saut-deau/
[6] Rey 2017: wrldrels.org/2017/10/24/saut-deau/

oppression. And wherever that is, you will more often than not find a Black Madonna.

CONFLICT AND OPPRESSION

We have seen several cases within this book where the Black Madonna has become an emblem against slavery and dictatorial regimes but many more exist. Some of these lesser-known cases are highlighted by China Galland in *Longing for Darkness* (1990). She visited the *Virgen de San Juan del Valle* on the Texan border with Mexico at a time in the 1980s when those fleeing civil wars in Central America faced indefinite detainment in the Rio Grande Valley upon seeking asylum.[7] One of the most striking moments is when she comes across the icon of *Madre de los Desaparecidos* – Mother of the Disappeared. This painting, by iconographer Robert Lentz, depicts the sorrow for the lost dissidents, 'disappeared' at the hands of the Chilean regime. The white handprint, dripping paint, was the mark of El Salvador's death squad. This mark on a house meant the inhabitants were a target.[8] The Madonna mourns the appearance of the hand in solidarity with her faithful.

Galland observes how the political and spiritual intersect, and there is no greater example than with Our Lady of Częstochowa. The icon on wood resides in the monastery of Jasna Góra in Częstochowa, Poland. Its legendary origin attributes it to the brush of St. Luke, but the current version is thought to be 14th century at the earliest. We encountered this icon in Chapter 5, and how replicas ended up on the frontlines of the Haitian Revolution. To fill in the detail of how she became the defender of the Poles, we first find that she is credited with victory over Swedish forces in 1655. The monastery was besieged by Swedish soldiers in their thousands, but against incredible odds, 350 soldiers and monks fought them off. The Virgin was crowned Queen of Poland for the defence that was believed to be her doing. In 1987, China Galland joined the annual pilgrimage to Częstochowa whilst Poland was under a frightening Communist regime. She was amongst hundreds of thousands of people walking from all over Poland to

---

[7] Galland 1990: 264
[8] Galland 1990: 273

see the Virgin, despite being ever-fearful of the State police forces. The State had more to fear from the pilgrimage, however. A movement in such numbers was too difficult to police, and members of the trade union and resistance movement Solidarity, outlawed by the government, were able to mingle into the crowd, carrying its banners. Solidarity's leader at the time and later president of Poland, Lech Wałęsa, was extremely devoted to Our Lady of Częstochowa and wore her face over his heart at all times. For him, the Madonna's position of non-violent resistance was the perfect parallel to his party.[9] And one that he would later be able to thank for their triumph over communism.

As both pilgrimages and public demonstrations grow in popularity, we can wonder if they will merge again in our lifetime, with a Black Madonna at their head, to bring about the end of fascist and corrupt governments.

PERSONAL CONCLUSIONS

I came to the conclusion during the course of this work that the enigma of the Black Madonna is an entirely modern/early-modern creation, but no less important for being so. Scholars of the Black Madonna coming from a more esoteric angle who search for ancient origins and proofs of her secret significance have skirted around the possibility that these were 'dark statues of the Virgin Mary' as opposed to 'statues of a dark Virgin Mary'. As we have seen, there appears little evidence that Black Madonnas were thought of as racially Black before Europeans embarked upon the slave trade and early-modern perceptions were marked by the inequalities that it produced.

I am persuaded by the theory that the colour was to deliberately denote antiquity and Eastern origin rather than race, and open to the idea that medieval artists imitated ancient goddess statues to produce this effect. There is no doubt that the Feminine has been revered in one form or another for millennia, and the statues of Isis and stories of various goddesses quoted as precursors to the Black Madonna have importance in how we relate to the archetype of the Black Madonna today. Despite this, I do not believe they are

---

[9] Galland 1990: 286, 291

conclusive evidence of an unbroken tradition of goddess worship or hints of secrets and mysteries kept hidden by the Church.

HOWEVER - and it is a big however - if the Black Madonna's significance has only been invented in the last few centuries, does that make it any less significant as a cultural phenomenon? Writing about her is mostly divided into two camps, those that would dive into the rabbit hole of esoteric theories, and those that remain firmly sceptical of there being any real enigma about these statues and icons. Yet the high academic viewpoint or 'authorised heritage discourse' does not allow for the fact that, whether or not based on factual evidence, acts of devotion and pilgrimage to Black Madonnas happen every day and that activity is very real. Academia would dismiss alternative narratives as worthless because they appear to have had their theories disproven. Nevertheless, this does not stop people worshipping. If we were discussing pilgrims of the 2nd century and had solid proof of them visiting grottos of the Black Madonna in their droves, it would likely be accepted as authentic and show her importance. This is because, in the development of 20th-century archaeology, authenticity has been bound up with what is ancient and material. The fact that the phenomenon of the popularity of Black Virgins (for the sake of them being Black Virgins) has only occurred over the past couple of centuries somehow makes it less worthy, delusional, misguided. Part of the difficulty is admittedly that modern pagans or alternative seekers tend to claim unbroken worship or lineage in much the same way as the medieval church fathers did with their foundation stories for their churches. This will always be a stumbling point in the discourse between Academia and alternative narratives, the rejection and acceptance of non-empirical evidence.

The 'truth', if that is what we are looking to find, is that for millions of people in the here and now, the Black Madonna represents something important, even vital at this time in the world's history. We have seen how colour-as-race came to be a preoccupation for humans from early-modern times, and how we have interpreted it in various ways, which has had a great bearing on how we observe these statues. We have seen how people choose to interpret the Black Madonna now, which I would argue is of no less value than how a medieval person would have thought about her. We must also remember that the recorded versions of what has been handed down through the centuries may not match the ideologies of the common people, and that medieval pilgrims may have taken away an altogether different experience from the 'authorised discourse' of the time, just as a visitor to churches and sacred sites today may do.

For many she is strength, a loving and caring mother to us all. For some she is the face of the eternal Goddess, merely morphed over time through various forms. To a significant proportion of the world she is a protector, a courageous champion of the oppressed and a symbol of freedom. And for others she is indeed 'just' a face of the Virgin Mary, but one that makes us stop and think about the vast variety of depictions of a 2000-year-old Middle Eastern woman.

LOOKING FORWARD – ISSUES OF RACE

For many people today, there is an inexorable need to view divinity as something other than White and Male, in other words, not in the image of those who have been the oppressors of history for so many centuries. What is the most obvious antithesis to this? Obviously, it is that God is a woman and that she is Black. Although this perspective is welcomed by many, we should stop and consider the social implications of portraying a Black woman in this way.

The Black Lives Matter protests of 2020 have brought to the fore much discourse on issues of race, including discussion on racial stereotypes including the 'Strong Black Woman'. Although we might think portraying a Black woman as a pillar of strength could only be a good thing, Black women have written about the stereotype's potential to harm. Roxanne Angela Donovan, Kara Manke and Marvarine Cole, amongst others, have written about this 'superwoman schema' and how it can be detrimental to Black women's mental health to feel that they have to be always striving to succeed; to not allow themselves to be sensitive and vulnerable like any other human being.[10]

---

[10] See examples at
www.greatergood.berkeley.edu/article/item/how_the_strong_black_woman_identit

The Black Madonna is a popular devotional construct amongst White Europeans and Americans, and modern discourse dictates that we should question our biases for opinions rooted in racial stereotyping. As Jennie S. Knight says: "challenging stereotypical images through critical reflection and education about the oppressive history of stereotypes can help people move toward a compassionate affirmation of shared humanity and divine presence".[11] We can certainly see the 'Strong Black Woman' stereotype, rooted in the fact that Black women constantly face adversity and prejudice in their everyday life rather than being able to simply exist. We also see shades of the 'Mammy' stereotype, which stems from the time when Black women in servitude were more active in raising the White children of the household than the children's own mothers. The Mammy is the stereotype of a large, motherly, asexual figure whom White people would look back on fondly in childish selfishness for what she could do for them rather than as a person in her own right.[12] The 'Dark Earth Mother' stereotype, to which much of the Jungian and Goddess Feminism analysis of the Black Madonna subscribes, comes from colonial ideas about Black Africans being closer to nature, more animalistic, and 'noble savages'.[13] We must confront whether our predilection for Black Madonnas is rooted in these stereotypes and, as Jennie S. Knight says, consider whether the historic worship of Black Madonnas served to justify colonialism rather than challenge European theft and subjugation at the time.[14]

Our final question for ourselves is "who does the Black Madonna serve?". We have seen how she has been interpreted by Black diasporic communities, and seen mestizo women's complicated relationship with a depiction of Mary that is both like them and an impossible aspirational model. But in modern Western society, who is she for? If White middle-class Americans and Europeans wish to venerate the Divine as a Black woman it is

y_both_helps_and_hurts,
www.researchgate.net/publication/280770795_Stress_and_Mental_Health_Moderati
ng_Role_of_the_Strong_Black_Woman_Stereotype and
www.theguardian.com/commentisfree/2018/jul/20/strong-black-woman-
stereotype-mental-health-depression-self-harm
[11] Knight 2011: 118
[12] Knight 2011: 133
[13] Knight 2011: 122
[14] Knight 2011: 122

essential that we question our own associations with the Black Madonna and what this means for our thoughts on, and behaviour toward, Black people. Not every Black woman wishes to be labelled a 'warrior'. Not every Black friend will want to connect with the divine in the same way. As a society just starting to face our history of colonialism and racism, we have a long way to go and a lot to learn, beginning with examining the attitudes of our past and listening to Black voices.

EPILOGUE – *LA CINTA*

A wise woman once told me in conversation about the idea of *La Cinta* – the concept of a common thread that connects seemingly unconnected cultures and time frames. It could be described as the undercurrent of the Goddess energy in the world, similar to the concept of the dragon lines that snake through the earth connecting sacred sites; *La Cinta* connects religious symbolism and expression of the Divine. What some might call coincidence, we can alternatively see as 'synchronous arisings' - almost like history repeating itself, but the repetition is of signs and symbols. The current is like an underground stream, just like the underground streams we find in close proximity to the grottos and crypts dedicated to the Mother, such at Notre Dame Sous Terre in Chartres. The places in which these commonalities arise are like wellsprings, gifting us with sacred knowledge. The word Cinta actually refers to the girdle traditionally worn around the waist of pregnant women in Mexico, and is the same cord that we see the Virgin of Guadalupe wearing in her image. *La Cinta* is also present in the snake symbolism that accompanies the Goddess worldwide, from Crete to the Bible, to India. Some Hindus wear a sacred thread composed of the strands of three goddesses, and one tantric form of the Goddess, Jagaddhatri, wears a snake as a sacred thread herself.[15]

Rather than painstakingly trying to trace and prove ancient origins for the image of the Black Madonna, and risk falling into a tangle of misinformation and conspiracies, why not take the available source material and create new devotions? As we have

---

[15] McDaniel 2004: 220

seen with the African outlook, authenticity does not have to equal unbroken tradition. Acknowledging that parts of Black Madonna worship today are not 'continuous' does not make them worthless. Noticing similarities between cultures that use imagery of the Feminine, the thread that has been named *La Cinta*, and working with them to weave new forms of worship in the African way that recognises that one and the other are *not* the same (for example the spirit and saint that share characteristics) may prove more rewarding.

In the African perspective: "Viewing African traditions and Catholicism [for example] as simply different forms of worship rather than fixed and discrete "religions" highlights the shortcomings of models of syncretism and opens the door to a religious orientation that embraces and often combines both traditions."[16] For the orisha priests that Ayodeji met (see chapter 6, De-Syncretisation), "religious distinctions such as Christian or Muslim did not constitute salient categories for conceptualizing or organizing religious action or affiliation. The attributes and cosmological position and function of a particular tradition were much more important."[17] It would be interesting to see this kind of syncretism in modern Black Madonna/Goddess worship without any false equivalence or need to figure out 'what came first'.

This kind of process is already in practice to some extent with those who wish to make more, or rather something different, of the Sacred Feminine in the context of Christianity than the limited amount available in the Church's official doctrine. Fedele's pilgrims on the Mary Magdalene trail were observed to practice forms of reinvention and transcultural borrowing in their rituals.[18] The latter does need some care in the context of appropriation, especially if the cultures borrowed from are a living tradition who may not appreciate the transformation of their modes of worship, especially when it is commodified. Yet, despite borrowing from it, the pilgrims still felt a resistance to the Church whose rituals they were (perhaps) unconsciously adapting. For those who have broken

---

[16] Ogunnaike 2020: 155
[17] Ogunnaike 2020: 160
[18] Fedele 2013: 11

from their traditional Catholic upbringings, it may be difficult to borrow from that culture in a positive and conscious way without feeling the need to do so as 'reclaiming ownership'. Reclamation is a driving force in the intentions of many of these Energy Pilgrims.[19] A number of this kind of visitor seek or wish to free sacred sites from those (usually the Catholic Church) who they see as having invaded and reappropriated it from an older, more authentic religion. This is usually attempted symbolically through ritual acts to affect the 'energy' of the location.

Using the holistic approach of *La Cinta* in interpreting the contents of this book we see common threads running through its fabric – the qualities of wisdom, protection, strength, activism, grieving, birthing, devouring, nurturing, and more. I would encourage the reader who wishes to work with the Black Madonna in a spiritual fashion to take note of these themes and any others that come to mind to create your own rich tapestry, free of false equivalence and free to flow in a usable, powerful way that respects the truly global phenomenon of the Black Madonna.

---

[19] Fedele's moniker for this kind of pilgrim, of the kind to see themselves as spiritual rather than religious, and who are primarily concerned with the energy of the places they visit. Fedele 2018: 116

Bibliography

Anderies, J. P. (2006). *The Virgin of Regla Diaspora of a Dark Madonna in The Spanish Colonies.* University of Denver

Anzaldúa, G. (1996). *"Coatlalopeuh:* She Who Has Dominion Over Serpents" in *Goddess of the Americas: Writings on the Virgin of Guadalupe.* Castillo, A. ed. Riverhead Books

Apueleius, Adlington, W. & Gaselee, S. (1922). *The Golden Ass.* London: William Heinemann

Ashe, G. (1988). *The Virgin.* (rev. ed.) Arkana

Baigent, M., Leigh, R. & Lincoln, H. (1982). *The Holy Blood and the Holy Grail* (2006 reissue). Arrow

Bakker, F. L. (2003). "The Mirror Image: How Hindus adapt themselves to the Creole Christian world of the Caribbean" Academia.edu (accessed 20/01/20)

Barnstone, W. & Meyer, M. W. (2005). *The Gnostic Bible.* Shambhala

Bartlett, R. (2001). "Medieval and Modern Concepts of Race and Ethnicity" in *Journal of Medieval and Early Modern Studies 31:1, Winter 2001.* Duke University Press

Beavis, M. A. (2012a). "The Deification of Mary Magdalene" in *Feminist Theology 21 (2)*

Beavis, M. A. (2012b). "The Cathar Mary Magdalene and the Sacred Feminine: Pop Culture Legend vs. Medieval Doctrine" in *The Journal of Religion and Popular Culture 24:3, Fall 2012*

Beavis, M. A. (2012c). "Reconsidering Mary of Bethany" in *The Catholic Biblical Quarterly 74, 2012.*

Beavis, M. A. (2013). "Who is Mary Magdalene?" in *Women in the Bible.* The Center for Christian Ethics at Baylor University

Begg, E. (1996). *The Cult of the Black Virgin* (rev. ed.). Arkana

Bellegarde-Smith, P. (2006) "Broken Mirrors: Mythos, Memories, and National History" in *Haitian Vodou.* Bellegarde-Smith, P. & Michel, C. eds. Indiana University Press

Bellegarde-Smith, P. & Michel, C. (2006). *Haitian Vodou.* Indiana University Press

Belloni, A. (2019). *Healing Journeys with the Black Madonna.* Bear and Company

Benard, E. & Moon, B. (Eds.). (2000). *Goddesses Who Rule.* Oxford University Press

Berger, P. (1988). *The Goddess Obscured: Transformation of the Grain Protectress from Goddess to Saint.* Robert Hale Ltd.

Bernard, A. (2011). "Vierges Noires: un Média Complexe et Singulier" in *Le Temps des Médias, Revue d'histoire n° 17 – Automne 2011*

Bhanoo, S. N. (2012). "Genomic Study Traces Roma to Northern India". *New York Times 11 December 2012.*

Birnbaum, L. C. (1993). *Black Madonnas: Feminism, Religion and Politics in Italy.* Boston, Northeastern University Press.

Birnbaum, L. C. (2001). *Dark Mother: African Origins and Godmother.* Authors Choice Press

Boodoo, G. (1993). "The "La Divina Pastora/Suparee Ke Mai" Devotions of Trinidad" in *International Review of Mission 1993*

Bordigoni, M. (2005). "Sara in Saintes-Maries-de-la-Mer. Metaphor of the gypsy presence in the 'world of Gadjé'" in *Gypsy Studies, National Federation of Solidarity Associations for Action with Gypsies and Gens du voyage, 2005, pp.12-34*

Braham, P. (2018). "Song of the Sirenas: Mermaids in Latin America and the Caribbean" in *Scaled for Success The Internationalisation of the Mermaid.* Hayward, P. ed. John Libbey Publishing ltd.

Bugslag, J. (2005). "Pilgrimage to Chartres: The Visual Evidence" in *Art and Architecture of Late Medieval Pilgrimage in Northern Europe and The British Isles: Texts.* Brill: Leiden, Boston

Burns, M. (2014). ""Hiding Beneath Mary's Skirt" Catholicism and Quest for Transethnic

Identities" Academia.edu (accessed 03/02/2020)

Caesar, Julius (1869). *De Bello Gallico* (W. A. McDevitte and W. S. Bohn, Trans.) New York, Harper and Brothers

Callahan, P. (1981). "The Tilma Under Infra-Red Radiation: An Infrared and Artistic Analysis of the Image of the Virgin Mary in the Basilica of Guadalupe" in *CARA Studies in Popular Devotion, vol. II, Guadalupe Studies, n° 3. Washington D.C.: Center for Applied Research in the Apostolate*

Capone, S. (2016). "Re-Africanisation in Afro-Brazilian Religions: Rethinking Religious Syncretism" in *The Brill Handbook of Contemporary Religions in Brazil.* Engler, S. & Schimdt, B. eds. Leiden: Brill

Carty, M. (2003). *The Vodou Religion.* Dorrance.

Clark, M. A. (2001). "¡No Hay Ningun Santo Aqui! (There Are No Saints Here!): Symbolic Language within Santeria" in *Journal of the American Academy of Religion, 2001*

Chandola, S. (2007). *Entranced by the Goddess: Folklore in north Indian religion.* Heart of Albion Press

Charpentier, L. (1972). *The Mysteries of Chartres Cathedral.* (Sir R. Fraser and J Jackson, Trans. London: Research Into Lost Knowledge Organisation

Chatterjee, D. (1995). "Harnessing Shakti: the Work of the Bengali Support Group" *Feminist Activism in the 1990s.* G. Griffin ed. 2005 London and Bristol: Taylor & Francis.

Christophe, M. A. (2006). "Rainbow Over Water: Haitian Art, Vodou Aestheticism, and Philosophy" in *Haitian Vodou.* Bellegarde-Smith, P. & Michel, C. eds. Indiana University Press

Cisneros, S. (1996). "Guadalupe the Sex Goddess" in *Goddess of the Americas: Writings on the Virgin of Guadalupe.* Castillo, A. ed. Riverhead Books

Coburn, T. B. (1991). *Encountering the Goddess.* Sri Satguru Publications

Connolly, D. (2005). "At the Center of the World: the Labyrinth Pavement of Chartres Cathedral" in *Art and Architecture of Late Medieval Pilgrimage in Northern Europe and The British Isles: Texts.* Brill: Leiden, Boston

Crosley, R. O. (2006). "Shadow-Matter Universes in Haitian and Dagara Ontologies" in *Haitian Vodou.* Bellegarde-Smith, P. & Michel, C. eds. Indiana University Press

d'Este, S. & Rankine, D. (2011). *The Cosmic Shekinah.* Avalonia

Delaporte, Y. (1965). *Les Trois Notre-Dame de la Catédrale de Chartres.* University of California

Dianteill, E. (2002). "Deterritorialization and Reterritorialization of the Orisha Religion in Africa and the New World (Nigeria, Cuba and the United States)" in *International Journal of Urban and Regional Research Volume 26.1 March 2002* (George, K. trans.) Blackwell

Dolan, P. T. "Catholic in the Morning, Voodoo by Night: An Analysis of Marie Laveau's Syncretistic Practice of Roman Catholicism and Voodoo" Academia.edu (accessed 03/02/2020)

Dold, P. (2003). "Kali the Terrific and Her Tests: The Sakta Devotionalism of the *Mahabhagavata Purana*" in *Encountering Kālī: In the Margins, at the Center, in the West* Fell McDermott, R. F. and Kripal, J. J. eds. University of California Press

Doniger, W. (1975). *Hindu Myths.* Penguin

Eichler-Levine, J. (2013). "Imagining Mary Magdalene: The Discourse of Hidden Wisdom in American Popular Culture" in *Postscripts: The Journal of Sacred Texts and Contemporary World 7.1.* Equinox

Elizondo, V. P. (1977). "Our Lady of Guadalupe as a Cultural Symbol: The Power of the Powerless" in *Liturgy and Cultural Religious Traditions.* Ed. Schmidt, H. & Power, D. Concilium 102. New York, Seabury

Fedele, A. (2009). "From Christian religion to feminist spirituality: Mary Magdalene pilgrimages to La Sainte-Baume, France" in *Culture and Religion, 10:3*

Fedele, A. (2013a). *Looking for Mary Magdalene: Alternative Pilgrimage and Ritual Creativity at Catholic Shrines in Contemporary France.* Oxford and New York: Oxford University Press

Fedele, A. (2013b). "'Black Madonna' versus 'White Madonna': Gendered power strategies in alternative pilgrimages to Marian shrines" in *Gender and Power in Contemporary Spirituality: Ethnographic Approaches.* Fedele A. and Kim Knibbe K. eds. New

York: Routledge

Fedele , A. (2018). "Translating Catholic Pilgrimage Sites into Energy Grammar: Contested Spiritual Practices in Chartres and Vézelay" in *Pilgrimage and Political Economy Translating the Sacred*. Eds. Coleman, S. & Eade, J. Berghahn Books

Foster, E. (2016a). "The Black Madonna of Montserrat: An Exception to Concepts of Dark Skin in Medieval and Early Modern Iberia?" in *Envisioning Others: Race, Color, and the Visual in Iberia and Latin America*. Ed. Patton, P. A. Brill, Boston

Foster, E. (2016b). "Out of Egypt: Inventing the Black Madonna of Le Puy in Image and Text" in *Studies in Iconography volume 37*. Medieval Institute Publications, Western Michigan University

Fraser, A. (1995). *The Gypsies*. Blackwell

Galland, C. (1990). *Longing For Darkness: Tara and the Black Madonna*. Penguin

Gebara, I. & Bingemar, M. C. (1989). *Mary Mother of God, Mother of the Poor* (P. Berryman, Trans.). Burns & Oates Ltd. (Original work published 1987)

Gledhill, S. (2012). "Afro-Brazilian Religions" in *Brazil Today: An Encyclopedia of Life in the Republic, vol. 1*. John J. Crocitti, ed. Santa Barbara: ABC-CLIO

Gonzalez-Crussi (1996). "The Anatomy of a Virgin" in *Goddess of the Americas: Writings on the Virgin of Guadalupe*. Castillo, A. ed. Riverhead Books

Graves, R. (1961). *The White Goddess* (rev. ed.). Faber

Gupta, R. K. (2003). "Kali Mayi: Myth and Reality in a Banaras Ghetto" in *Encountering Kālī: In the Margins, at the Center, in the West* Fell McDermott, R. F. and Kripal, J. J. eds. University of California Press

Hani, J. (2007). *The Black Virgin: A Marian Mystery* (R. Proctor, Trans.). Sophia Perennis. (Original work published 1995)

Harding, E. U. (1993). *Kali: The Black Goddess of Dakshineswar*. Nicolas Hayes Inc.

Hayes, A. L. (2010). "The Pilgrimage sites of St. Mary Magdalene in Provence: August 2009 and May 2010" in *Anglican and Episcopal History Vol. 79, No. 3 and No. 4*

Hixon, L. (1994). *Mother of the Universe: Visions of the Goddess and Tantric Hymns of Enlightenment*. Quest Books

Jackson, L. (2016). *Isis: The Eternal Goddess of Egypt and Rome*. Avalonia

Johnson, E. A. (1989). "Mary and the Female Face of God" in *Theological Studies 50*, no. 3

Kingsbury, K. & Chesnut, R. A. (2019a). "In Her Own Image: Slave Women and the Re-imagining of the Polish Black Madonna as Ezili Dantò, the Fierce Female Lwa of Haitian Vodou" in *International Journal of Latin American Religions*

Kingsbury, K. & Chesnut, R. A. (2019b). "Brazil's Black Supernatural Sister Queens: Our Lady of Aparecida and Oxum" in *Global Catholic Review*

Kinsley, D. (2003) "Kali" in *Encountering Kālī: In the Margins, at the Center, in the West*. Fell McDermott, R. F. and Kripal, J. J. eds. University of California Press

Kloß, S. (2016). "Manifesting Kali's Power: Guyanese Hinduism and the Revitalisation of the 'Madras Tradition'" in *Journal of Eastern Caribbean Studies Vol. 41, No. 1, April 2016*

Knight, J. S. (2011). *Feminist Mysticism and Images of God: A Practical Theology*. Chalice Press

Knott, K. (2012). "Hinduism in Britain" in *The South Asian Religious Diaspora in Britain, Canada, and the United States*. Coward, H. G., Hinnells, J. R. and Brady Williams, R. eds. Suny Press

Kripal, J. J. & McDermott, R. F. (2003). "Introducing Kali Studies" in *Encountering Kālī: In the Margins, at the Center, in the West* Fell McDermott, R. F. and Kripal, J. J. eds. University of California Press

Lasso de la Vega, L. (1649). *Nican Mopohua*. English Trans. By D. K. Jordan, pages.ucsd.edu/~dkjordan/nahuatl/nican/NicanMopohua.html Accessed 20/04/18

Lele, Ó. (2012). *Sacrificial Ceremonies of Santeria: A Complete Guide to the Rituals and Practices*. Destiny Books.

Lowe, K. (2012). "The Global Consequences of Mistranslation: The Adoption of the "Black but …" Formulation in Europe, 1440–1650" in *Religions*. MDPI

Mahabir, K. "Virgin Mary as Mother Kali: Christians Share a Church with Hindus in Trinidad and Tobago" Academia.edu (accessed 14/04/2020)

Markale, J. (2004). *Cathedral of the Black Madonna: The Druids and the Mysteries of Chartres* (J. Graham, Trans.). Inner Traditions. (Original work published 1988)

Martínez, R. (1996). "The Undocumented Virgin" in *Goddess of the Americas: Writings on the Virgin of Guadalupe*. Castillo, A. ed. Riverhead Books

Matthews, C. (2001). *Sophia: Goddess of Wisdom, Bride of God* (rev. ed.). Quest

McDaniel, J. (2004). *Offering Flowers, Feeding Skulls: Popular Goddess Worship in West Bengal.* Oxford University Press

McDermott, L. (1996). "Self-Representation in Upper Paleolithic Female Figurines" in *Current Anthropology Vol. 37, No. 2 (Apr., 1996), pp. 227-275*

McDermott, R. F. (2003). "Kali's New Frontiers: A Hindu Goddess on the Internet" in *Encountering Kāli: In the Margins, at the Center, in the West* Fell McDermott, R. F. and Kripal, J. J. eds. University of California Press

McNeal. K. E. (2002). "Miracle Mother" in *Caribbean Beat issue 54.*

McNeal, K. E. (2003). "Doing the Mother's Caribbean Work: On Shakti and Society in Contemporary Trinidad" in *Encountering Kāli: In the Margins, at the Center, in the West* Fell McDermott, R. F. and Kripal, J. J. eds. University of California Press

McNeal K. E. (2011). *Trance and Modernity in the Southern Caribbean: African and Hindu Popular Religions in Trinidad and Tobago.* University Press of Florida

McNeal, K. E. (2012). "Seeing the Eyes of God in Human Form: Iconography and Impersonation in African and Hindu Traditions of Trance Performance in the Southern Caribbean" in *Material Religion, volume 8, issue 4.*

McNeal, K. E. (2013a). "Shakti Puja in Trinidad" in *The Encyclopedia of Caribbean Religions.* University of Illinois Press

McNeal K. E. (2013b). "Hindu Healing Traditions in the Southern Caribbean: History, Sociology, Praxis" in *Caribbean Healing Traditions Implications for Health and Mental Health.* Sutherland, P. Moodley, R. & Chevannes, B. eds. Routledge 2014.

Michel, C., Bellegarde-Smith, P. & Racine-Toussaint M. (2006) "From the Horses' Mouths: Women's Words/Women's Worlds" in *Haitian Vodou.* Bellegarde-Smith, P. & Michel, C. eds. Indiana University Press

Monk Kidd, S. (2001). *The Secret Life of Bees.* Viking Penguin.

Montgomery. E. J. (2016). "Syncretism in Vodu and Orisha An Anthropological Analysis" in *Journal of Religion & Society Volume 18 (2016)*

Montilus, G. C. (2006). "Vodun and Social Transformation in the African Diasporic Experience: The Concept of Personhood in Haitian Vodun Religion" in *Haitian Vodou.* Bellegarde-Smith, P. & Michel, C. eds. Indiana University Press

Mookerjee, A. (1988). *Kali: The Feminine Force.* Destiny Books

Morrow Long, C. (2009). "Marie Laveau (1801-1881): A New Orleans Voudou Priestess" in *Louisiana Women.* Allured, J. and Gentry. J. eds. Athens: University of Georgia Press

Moss, L. & Cappannari, S. (1953). "The Black Madonna: An Example of Culture Borrowing." in *The Scientific Monthly 73* (1953): 319-24.

Moss, L. & Cappannari, S. (1983). "In Quest of the Black Virgin: She Is Black Because She Is Black." In *Mother Worship: Themes and Variations.* Ed. James. J. Preston. vols: Chapel Hill, University of North Carolina Press, 1983. 53-74

Motz, L. (1997). *The Faces of the Goddess.* Oxford University Press

Nabarz, P. (Ed.). (2013). *Anahita: Ancient Persian Goddess and Zoroastrian Yazata.* Avalonia

Neumann, E. (1963). *The Great Mother: An Analysis of the Archetype* (2nd ed., R. Manheim, Trans.). Routledge and Kegan Paul

Ogunnaike, A. (2020). "What's Really Behind the Mask: A Reexamination of Syncretism in Brazilian Candomblé" in *Journal of Africana Religions, Vol. 8, No. 1, 2020* The Pennsylvania State University

Oleszkiewicz-Peralba, M. (2007). *The Black Madonna in Latin America and Europe, Tradition and Transformation.* University of New Mexico Press.

Pérez, A. (2018). *Montserrat.* Geocolor.

Perez, E. (2010). "The Virgin in The Mirror: Reading Images of a Black Madonna Through the Lens of Afro-Cuban Women's Experiences" in *Journal of African American History 95 (Special Issue: "Explorations within the African Diaspora"), no. 2 (2010): 202-28*

Picknett, L. (2003). *Mary Magdalene: Christianity's Hidden Goddess.* Robinson

Rankine, D. & d'Este, S. (2005). *The Guises of the Morrigan.* Avalonia

Redgrove, P. (1989). *The Black Goddess and the Sixth Sense* (2nd ed.). Paladin

Rodriguez, J. (1994). *Our Lady of Guadalupe: Faith and Empowerment among Mexican American Women*. University of Texas Press

Rey, T. (2005). 'Toward an Ethnohistory of Haitian Pilgrimage' in *Journal de la société des américanistes 91-1, 2005*

Ruether, R. R. (2005). *Goddesses and the Divine Feminine*. University of California Press

Rypson, S. (2008). *Being Poloné in Haiti*. Warszawa

Sahagún. *Florentine Codex: Introduction and Indices*.

Schaup, S. (1997). *Sophia: Aspects of the Divine Feminine Past and Present*. Samuel Weiser, Inc.

Scheer, M. (2002). "From Majesty to Mystery: Change in the Meaning of Black Madonnas from the Sixteenth to Nineteenth Centuries" in *The American Historical Review Volume 107, Number 5*. The American Historical Association.

Schipflinger, T. (1998). *Sophia-Maria: A Holistic Vision of Creation* (J. Morgante, Trans.). Samuel Weiser, Inc.

Schmidt, B. (2008). "Oshún visits the Bronx – Possessed Women in the Cuban Orisha Religion" in *Diskus 9 (2008)*

Sepp, T (2014). "Pilgrimage and Pilgrim Hierarchies in Vernacular Discourse: Comparative Notes from the Camino de Santiago and Glastonbury" in *Journal of Ethnology and Folkloristics 8 (1)*.

Serra I Pérez, E. (2018). *Montserrat*. Geocolor

Sommer, D. (1994). "Who Can Tell? The Blanks in Villaverde" in *Mixing Race, Mixing Culture: Inter-American Literary Dialogues*. Monika Kaup, M. & Rosenthal D. eds. University of Texas Press, 15 Aug 2002

Starbird, M. (1993). *The Woman with the Alabaster Jar*. Bear and Company

Starbird. M. (1998). *The Goddess in the Gospels*. Bear and Company

St. Victor, O. (1988). *The Masked Madonna*. Sancta Sophia

Tann, Mambo C. (2012). *Haitian Vodou*. Llewellyn

Teish, L. (1985). *Jambalaya*. HarperCollins

Teish, L. (1996). "The Warrior queen: Encounters with a Latin Lady" in *Goddess of the Americas: Writings on the Virgin of Guadalupe*. Castillo, A. ed. Riverhead Books

Tsuji, T. (2008). "Mothers—Hyphenated Imaginations: The Feasts of Soparee Ke Mai and La Divina Pastora in Trinidad" in *Man in India: An International Journal of Anthropology, 88 (1-2), 2008*

Tsuji, T. (2009). ""They don't do culture": Mother Kali as a Matrix of National Culture in Trinidad" in *Wadabagei: A Journal of the Caribbean and Its Diasporas, 12 (3), 2009*.

Tsuji, T. (2016). *The Power of Mary in Trinidad. Inspiration and Seduction for the Colonial Construction of Religions* Academia.edu (accessed 16/04/2020)

Urban, H. B. (2003). ""India's Darkest Heart": Kali in the Colonial Imagination" in *Encountering Kāli: In the Margins, at the Center, in the West* Fell McDermott, R. F. and Kripal, J. J. eds. University of California Press

Valenzuela, L. (1996). "*Virgencita*, Give Us a Chance" in *Goddess of the Americas: Writings on the Virgin of Guadalupe*. Castillo, A. ed. Riverhead Books

Vilatte, S. (1996). "The devout black image of Notre-Dame "Puy-en-Velay" in *Belgian Review of Philology and History , Volume 74, 1*

Villaverde, C. (2005). *Cecilia Valdes*. Lane, H. trans. Fischer, S. ed. Oxford University Press

Warner, M. (1976). *Alone of All Her Sex* (1990 reissue). Picador

Warren, M. (2005). *The Truth Sings in Circles: The Trail of the Black Madonna*. Athena Press

Węgłowski, A. (2105). *Bardzo Polska Historia*. Znak

Whitmont, E. C. (1997) *Return of the Goddess*. Continuum

Widmalm, M. (2015). *God is Not Alone*. Avalonia

Wiley, E. (2005). "Romani Performance and Heritage Tourism: The Pilgrimage of the Gypsies at Les Saintes-Maries-de-la-Mer" in *TDR Vol. 49, no. 2 (Summer 2005)*

Wolkstein, D. & Kramer, S. N. (1983). *Inanna: Queen of Heaven and Earth*. Harper & Row

Young, G. M. (1999) *Goddess on the Cross*. Capall Bann

Index

OTHER BOOKS FROM AVALONIA

Celtic Saints of Western Britain by Nic Phillps

An exceptional exploration of the lives and deeds of many of the saints of Wales, Cornwall, Devon and Somerset. Included are better-known saints such as David, Nectan, Michael and Piran, as well as some of the more enigmatic figures, such as Cuby, Helen, Just and Morwenna..

ISBN: 978-1905297870

The Cunning Man's Handbook: The Practice of English Folk Magic 1550-1900

"The desire to understand magic in any specific cultural context is an intellectual puzzle not only for scholars but believers" – author Jim Baker

A comprehensive and challenging exploration of the practices and beliefs of Cunning Folk in Britain and America between 1550-1900, their heyday.

ISBN: 978-1905297689

Epona: Hidden Goddess of the Celts

P.D. Mackenzie Cook's unique study of Epona positions her in a broad cross-cultural context. The story he presents is at the same time historical, speculative, and deeply personal - at once a scholarly survey, intriguing detective story, and spiritual message to be taken to heart.

Dedicated to the hidden goddess in every woman, and to men who genuinely love them in all their depth and complexity.

ISBN: 978-1905297962

Thracian Magic: Past & Present

A phenomenal volume of work by the Bulgarian author Georgi Mishev, which opens up the treasure trove of folklore and magical practices of the Balkan Peninsula into the English language for the first time. The author examines the magical practices of modern day Bulgaria and the surrounding Balkan countries, tracing them to their roots in the ritual traditions of Thrace and the Mystery Cults of the ancient world.

ISBN 978-19052974

www.avaloniabooks.com

Lightning Source UK Ltd.
Milton Keynes UK
UKHW010626250321
380963UK00003B/112